Instruments of Change
Motivating and Financing Sustainable Development

Theodore Panayotou

UNEP
United Nations Environment Programme

Earthscan Publications Ltd, London

First published in the UK in 1998 by
Earthscan Publications Limited

Copyright © UNEP, 1998

Published for and on behalf of the United Nations Environment Programme.

The views expressed are those of the author and do not necessarily reflect those of the United Nations Environment Programme.

A catalogue record for this book is available from the British Library

ISBN: 1 85383 467 X

Typesetting and page design by PCS Mapping & DTP, Newcastle upon Tyne
Printed and bound by Biddles Ltd, Guildford and Kings Lynn
Cover design by Yvonne Booth
Cover photo © UNEP/Vesselin Voltchev/Topham

For a full list of publications please contact:

Earthscan Publications Limited
120 Pentonville Road
London N1 9JN
Tel: (0171) 278 0433
Fax: (0171) 278 1142
Email: earthinfo@earthscan.co.uk
http://www.earthscan.co.uk

Earthscan is an editorially independent subsidiary of Kogan Page Limited and publishes in association with WWF-UK and the International Institute for Environment and Development.

This book is printed on elemental chlorine free paper from sustainably managed forests.

Contents

Figures, Tables and Boxes

FIGURES

TABLES

BOXES

Acronyms and Abbreviations

BOD	biological oxygen demand
CDM	Clean Development Mechanism
CFCs	chlorofluourocarbons
COD	chemical oxygen demand
CPO	crude palm oil
CTO	Certifiable Tradable Offset
DGA	Director General of Water [Chile]
DOE	Department of Energy [USA]
EPA	Environmental Protection Agency [USA]
EPB	Environmental Protection Bureau
EU	European Union
FCCC	Framework Convention on Climate Change
FGB	Forest Guarantee Bond
GDP	gross domestic product
GEF	Global Environmental Facility
GHG	greenhouse gases
GNP	gross national product
HIID	Harvard Institute for International Development
IFC	International Finance Corporation
IFMA	Industrial Forest Management Agreement
NEF	national environmental fund
NFFO	Non-fossil Fuel Obligation [UK]
NGO	non-governmental organization
NIMO	Niagra Mohawk [US utility company]
NPV	net present value
NTFPs	non-timber forest products
ODA	official development assistance
OECD	Organization for Economic Cooperation and Development
PROPER	Programme for Pollution Control, Evaluation and Rating
SPM	suspended particulate matter
TDRs	transferable development rights
TEPs	tradable emission permits
TRI	Toxic Release Inventory [USA]
TVEs	townships and village enterprises [China]
UNCED	United Nations Conference on Environment and Development
UNCTAD	United Nations Conference on Trade and Development
UNDP	United Nations Development Programme
UNEP	United Nations Environment Programme
VOCs	volatile organic compounds
WBCSD	World Business Council on Sustainable Development

Foreword

Market-based 'instruments of change' offer policy makers major advantages over command-and-control regulations that have traditionally been used for environmental protection. Economic instruments can encourage behavioural change among comsumers and polluters of environmental resources, while also raising revenue for environmental protection efforts. The use of these instruments has clearly increased in recent years. A 1997 survey of OECD countries found some 320 applications of economic instruments for environmental protection – more than double the number of applications found in a similar survey eight years earlier.

Yet, economic instruments are not yet being widely used in developing countries and countries in transition. The limiting factors include the fact that the experience gained by developed countries in the use of these instruments is not easily transferable to developing nations or transitional economies. In many instances, developed countries have used these instruments to raise revenue rather than as incentives to change behaviour, so they do not offer appropriate models for other countries. Furthermore, the growing experience of developing countries themselves has not been well documented and is therefore not easily shared.

The book directly addresses these issues, by taking stock of the available economic instruments; analysing the experience of developed and developing countries; and suggesting how they might be better used in developing countries and transitional economies as agents of change towards sustainable development. As the author suggests, a good place to start is with the gradual introduction of selected economic instruments adapted to local conditions, to lend flexibility, financial support and increased efficiency to the existing regulatory regimes.

I see several such entry points for the effective introduction of economic instruments, particularly in the context of Multilateral Environmental Agreements. For example, the Kyoto Protocol on global warming, which specifies binding commitments for industrialized nations to reduce their emissions of greenhouse gases, offers an excellent opportunity to highlight how economic instruments – in this case tradable emissions permits as well as other economic instruments – can help realize the objectives of these agreements.

In UNEP, we have been actively engaged for some time in efforts to support the sharing of experiences, particularly by developing countries and countries in transition, in the use of economic instruments. I am convinced that this book provides an honest assessment of the uses and misuses of economic instruments, and balanced views on how their application can be improved.

Dr Klaus Töpfer
Executive Director
United Nations Environment Programme

Acknowledgements

I benefited from the assistance of many people in preparing this study; not all can be mentioned here by name. I am particularly indebted to Hussein Abaza of the United Nations Environment Programme (UNEP) for his encouragement and support. I also benefited from discussions with several colleagues at the Harvard Institute for International Development (HIID), especially Jeffrey Vincent and Anil Markandya. Comments and suggestions for improvement from anonymous referees are also gratefully acknowledged. Above all, I wish to thank my research assistants, Colin Mahoney and Margaret Laude for their hard work and dedication to better documenting consecutive drafts. Ms Laude, in particular, drafted some of the cases and helped with researching several others. Julia Blocker expertly and patiently typed several drafts of the document and pleasantly accommodated frequent alterations. Of couse, I remain solely responsible for the view expressed and any errors committed.

Chapter 1

Introduction

Every nation aspires to sustainable development, but few know how to pursue it and even fewer are taking effective action to bring it about. Sustainable development involves change, indeed a sea of change in the behaviour of consumers and producers and in the allocation of resources among uses and over time. But what are the instruments of change? Can change be mandated by tough laws and strict enforcement? Can weak institutions and backlogged courts in developing countries enforce tough laws? Even if they can enforce them, can they afford them? Compliance to and enforcement of rigid rules and regulations is especially costly, and the upgrading of seriously deficient environmental infrastructure requires resources far beyond the fiscal and financial capacity of most cities and governments. It is understandable, then, that many policy makers are frustrated with their mandate to pursue sustainable development since they lack the necessary instruments to bring about change, especially as it concerns the protection of the environment and the conservation of natural resources along a path of rapid economic growth. Naturally, they turn to the experience of more advanced countries for transferable instruments, but this avenue offers more pitfalls than guidance on how to motivate and finance sustainable development in a cost-effective manner.

Environmental policy and management, as originated in developed countries, has tended to be divorced from economic policy and sustainable development. Having achieved high levels of economic development with unrestricted access to resources and unhindered by environmental concerns, developed countries have sought to protect their environment and ultimately their quality of life, from the side-effects of economic activity, primarily air and water pollution, hazardous waste, and more recently, global climate change. In that context, environmental management was seen as a necessary restriction or regulation of economic activity to contain environmental damage within acceptable bounds. Therefore, it appeared reasonable to set environmental policy independent of economic policy, as a set of quantity constraints on the level of pollutants and the depletion of resources such as emission standards and maximum allowable harvests. The cost of doing so was thought to be low relative to the high income levels already achieved in these countries.

The experience with standards-driven environmental policy in developed countries over the past decades suggests that the mandated environmental standards and technologies acted as a drag on economic growth and the costs have been far greater than expected, though still quite affordable given their high incomes.[1] This realization has induced developed countries to seek more efficient or at least more cost-effective means of achieving the same level of environmental protection through the use of economic or market-based instruments, but still their use is very limited and the context still one of environmental quality rather than sustainable development.

For developing countries and transitional economies, the divorce of environmental policy from economic policy and from efforts to achieve sustainable development is meaningless and potentially disastrous both economically and environmentally. Where standards of living are unacceptably low, where poverty is a major cause and consequence of environmental degradation, where natural resource exploitation is the engine of growth, and where formerly planned economies struggle to restructure and recover, imposing constraints on economic activity to protect the environment for its own sake rather than as an input in sustainable development has very limited appeal. Under these conditions, environmental policy cannot be divorced from economic policy and development strategy. Moreover, under conditions of (desired) rapid economic growth and massive structural change, mandated standards and technologies that allow no room for change, differential response and adjustment to rapidly changing circumstances are both very costly and difficult to enforce. Command-and-control regulations require generous use of resources such as capital, government revenue, management skills and administrative and enforcement capabilities, the very factors that are in scarce supply in developing and transitional economies.

The challenge for developing countries and transitional economies is to identify and adopt instruments that integrate environmental and economic policy; instruments that are parsimonious in their use of scarce development and management resources; instruments that allow differential response by economic units and adjust flexibly to changing circumstances; instruments that motivate behavioural change as well as generate financial resources to finance environmental infrastructure. The search for instruments of environmental management in developing countries and transitional economies is a search for instruments of sustainable development. Economic instruments such as user fees, impact levies, betterment charges, pollution taxes, tradable pollution permits, transferable development rights and payments for environmental services, among others, meet most of these conditions and are uniquely suited for the integration of environmental and economic policy and can be designed to advance sustainable development.

Economic instruments can motivate a change in behaviour by changing the incentive structure facing consumers and producers towards more environmentally sound and sustainable choices and actions; they can help minimize the cost of achieving any given level of environmental improvement and sustainability; and they can raise significant amounts of financial resources for environmental and other investments. At the same time, economic instruments can be misused if not properly selected and tailored to suit the problem at hand and to fit into the sociocultural context into which they are introduced.

Despite their many advantages in terms of both efficiency and sustainability, economic instruments are not widely used and their introduction faces many obstacles. First, the experience with economic instruments is very limited and much of it comes from developed countries. These countries have used them primarily as sources of government revenues rather than as incentives to alter behaviour, and not at all as instruments for the integration of economic and environmental policy or as vehicles of sustainable development. Given the very different conditions prevailing in developing countries, the developed country experience is not readily transferable; it does, however, contain useful lessons for both developing countries and transitional economies.

Second, developing countries themselves have been experimenting with economic instruments for some time and though this experience is more relevant, it is anecdotal and largely undocumented. It is also important to note that developing countries are a very heterogeneous group, both in terms of stage of economic and political development and in terms of ecological and geographic conditions. These differences limit the direct transfer of developing country experience (eg, from Southeast Asia to sub-Saharan Africa). Nevertheless, the fact that a dissimilar group of developing countries has been able to adopt and adapt economic instruments for environmental management to their local conditions bodes well for the introduction of these instruments elsewhere in the developing world. Furthermore, traditional societies have a wealth of incentive-based instruments for resource management, such as communal property rights and customary use rights, which provide a cultural basis and insights for the introduction of modern economic instruments.

Third, the slate for the introduction of economic instruments is far from clear. There are already in place command-and-control regulations dictating pollution and resource depletion standards and specific technologies. Their complete abandonment and replacement by economic instruments is out of the question for reasons that range from the costs of economic disruption to political economy considerations. The most promising entry points for economic instruments are in improving the efficiency and flexibility of existing regulations, in raising fiscal revenues for their better enforcement and in reconciling economic and environmental policy, all of which would help advance sustainable development. A good place to start is with the gradual introduction of selected economic instruments adapted to the local conditions, to lend flexibility, financial support and increased efficiency to the existing regulatory regimes. Fiscal reforms, industrial restructuring, trade liberalization and privatization, among others, are windows of opportunity for the introduction of efficiency and flexibility into environmental policy through economic instruments.

The financing advantage of economic instruments has long been recognized by environmental policy makers in both developed and developing countries where pollution charges or property taxes are more often levied as sources of revenue than as incentives for more environmentally sound behaviour. Hence, they tend to be set at a high enough level to generate the targeted expenditures (usually required to finance the enforcement and monitoring of command-and-control regulations), but not high enough to induce a change in behaviour.

Financing of sustainable development, however, must always be *incentive financing*, a concept that has at least two meanings. First, the financing instrument should not only be non-distortionary, but it should also aim to mitigate a market failure, internalize an externality and correct the incentive structure. Second, financing of environmental investments should be of catalytic, multiplier or leverage value to mobilize additional financial resources or induce further policy changes.

Sustainable development can indeed be defined operationally in terms of its financing. Development that does not pay its full costs (including environmental and social costs) along the way is socially non-optimal and non-sustainable. It is only by inextricably linking the provision of incremental environmental infrastructure, the conservation of resources and the protection of the environment to private (and public) investments and consumption activities that place additional demands on existing infrastructure, natural resources and the environment, that sustainable development will be attained and sustained. Economic instruments can help bridge the financing gap of sustainable development in three ways:

1   by motivating a behavioural change that reduces environmental changes and hence the magnitude of needed investments;
2   by generating revenues that can be used to finance these investments; and
3   by inducing, directly or indirectly a redeployment of a society's resources towards more environmentally sound and sustainable mix of activities.

Despite their many advantages and promise, economic instruments are not a panacea, but an important part of the toolkit of environmental policy along with regulations and public investments among others. Economic instruments help reduce the cost of delivering any given level of environmental improvement, but they do not make environmental policy altogether costless. While win–win policy solutions abound in the presence of policy distortions and inefficiencies that are commonplace, especially in developing and transitional economies, policy reforms, institutional changes and resource reallocation involve transition costs and trade-offs that are not trivial, and in some circumstances are considerable. Economic instruments help contain but do not eliminate these costs.

In summary, economic instruments, properly designed to fit the specific circumstances of developing and transitional economies, can be powerful instruments of change. They can both motivate a change of course away from unsustainable practices and generate the resources necessary to pave the road to sustainable development. The purpose of this book is to take stock of the available economic and related instruments; to analyse the experience of developed and developing countries with their use and misuse; and to explore ways in which they might be better designed and introduced in developing countries and transitional economies as agents of change towards sustainable development. Since both the theory and practice of economic instruments are rapidly evolving as a growing number of countries experiment with them, the purpose of the monograph is not to be exhaustive but indicative of the available options and of creative ways to adapt them to address specific problems.

Chapter 2
Full-cost Pricing and the Role of Economic Instruments

A combination of institutional, market and policy failures results in underpricing of scarce natural resources and environmental assets, which is then translated into underpricing of resource-based and environment-intensive goods and services. Institutional failures such as absence of secure property rights, market failures such as environmental externalities and policy failures such as distortionary subsidies, drive a wedge between the private and social costs of production and consumption activities. As a direct result producers and consumers of products and services do not receive correct signals about the true scarcity of resources they use up or the cost of environmental damage they cause. This leads to the socially wrong mix of economic output: overproduction and overconsumption of commodities that are resource-depleting and environment-polluting (price P_0 and output Q_0 in Figure 2.1), and underproduction and underconsumption of commodities that are resource-saving and environment-friendly. Thus, the emerging pattern of economic growth and the structure of the economy is one that undermines its own resource base, and is ultimately unsustainable, since relative scarcities are not respected.

Market failures such as environmental externalities (and public goods) leave important social costs (and benefits) outside the producers' and consumers' decision calculus. The lack of market prices for environmental services effectively sets the marginal environmental cost (that is, the cost to society from the diminution of these services by one unit) equal to zero from the individual producer's or consumer's perspective. This becomes one more source of underpricing of environmentally-damaging commodities and overpricing of environmentally-friendly commodities (movement from point A to point B in Figure 2.1). The latter is not only relatively more costly but also absolutely more costly because of the loss of resources and scale economies as resources shift from more sustainable to less sustainable activities.

Institutional failures such as open access and insecure tenure, reduce the user's benefits from the conservation of depletable resources and remove the marginal user (or depletion) cost from the decision-maker's calculus (movement from point B to point C in Figure 2.1). The cost of depletion to the user is effectively set equal to zero and unchanging regardless of scarcity even though the cost of depletion to

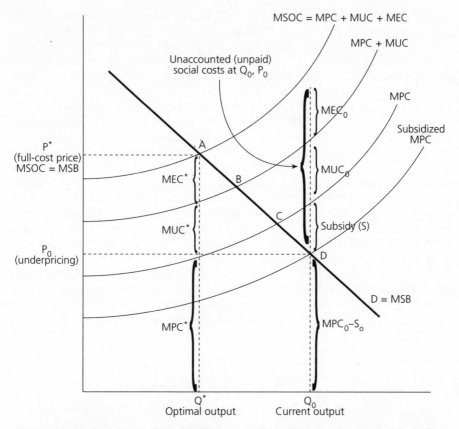

Note: Unaccounted social costs ($S + MUC_0 + MEC_0$) lead to underpricing (P_0) and overproduction (Q_0). Removal of subsidy, internalization of external and depletion costs results in full-cost pricing (P^*) and optimal production (Q^*). Economic instruments can serve as a device for internalizing unaccounted social costs and incorporating them into the supply price of the commodity. At point A, the optimal price P^* equals the marginal social opportunity cost (MSOC), which is equal to the marginal production cost (MPC) plus the marginal user cost (MUC) plus the marginal environmental cost (MEC). At the optimal equilibrium point A, resources freed by the reduction of the polluting output from Q_0 down to Q^* move to other products with lower social costs (eg resource-saving and environment-friendly goods). The MPC^* is internalized by the removal of distortionary subsidies. The MUC^* is internalized through secure property rights (assuming no discrepancy between private and social discount rates; if such discrepancy exists output taxes or tradable production quotas can be used for further correction). The MEC^* is internalized through taxes, charges, tradable permits or other economic instruments (optimal tax = optimal price of permit = MEC^*).

Figure 2.1 *Full-cost Pricing*

society is high and rising. As a result the resource is undervalued, and used excessively and inefficiently. Resource-based goods and services are thereby underpriced and overconsumed.

Policy failures such as input subsidies for producers, reduce marginal production costs (the cost of capital, labour, energy and materials) below their social opportunity costs, that is, the true cost of these factors of production to society, encouraging inefficient and excessive use of subsidized inputs (movement from point C to point D in Figure 2.1). Prominent among policy failures are energy and capital subsidies, industrial protection, depletion allowances and capital rationing. Energy subsidies are a 'tax' on energy efficiency and hence on energy-saving technologies. Capital subsidies are a 'tax' on labour employment, which, in an environment of abundant labour, leads to encroachment on natural resources such as forests and fisheries by unemployed or under-employed labour. Industrial protection limits external competitive pressures to improve efficiency and to adopt new technologies and products that are environmentally and economically more sustainable. Depletion allowances for new materials are a 'tax' on reuse and recycling, and hence on the development and transfer of recycling technologies. Interest rate ceilings and capital rationing deprive smallholder agriculture, rural industry and small business of the funds necessary for capital investment and technological innovation.

The results of these three sets of failure of a country's markets, institutions and policies are significant underpricing of resources and commodities with considerable social costs that result in overconsumption of these commodities and depletion of resources. The other side of the coin is that too few resources are allocated to socially beneficial activities such as education, health, environmental protection and conservation of resources for the future. Underpricing of resources is essentially a subsidy of unsustainable development and (hence) a tax on sustainable development.

FULL-COST PRICING

Full-cost pricing of resources, goods and services requires that all costs, present and future, internal (private) and external to the user that are incurred by society during production and consumption are incorporated and fully covered by the price of the good or service. It is immaterial whether these costs are actually paid out of pocket or simply incurred or imposed on others as environmental damages or diminished future availability. All real resources with alternative uses, current or future, used up in the production or consumption of a commodity must be reflected in its price in order to avoid resource overproduction and/or overconsumption, resource depletion and environmental degradation. In a market economy, relative prices are the only signals of relative values that drive resource allocation; underpricing some commodities and overpricing others conveys the wrong signals and perverse incentives and results in wasteful use of resources; in a world of scarcity, sustainable development is incompatible with economic waste. Full-cost pricing is a necessary, though not always sufficient, condition for sustainability. The latter calls for inter-generational equity in addition to efficient allocation between uses and over time. But, full-cost pricing goes a long way in motivating and financing sustainable development.

By full-cost pricing we mean the incorporation of all incremental (marginal) opportunity costs of production (and consumption) into the supply price of the commodity so that all related scarcities and sacrifices of society are reflected in the supply price facing the consumer or user who then determines whether and how much of the commodity to consume or use depending on one's preferences and income. The market demand price would then reflect valuation of the commodity by the marginal consumer who is willing to pay just the supply price (or marginal social opportunity cost).

$$P = MSOC$$

and

$$MSOC = MPC + MUC + MEC$$

and hence

$$P = MPC + MUC + MEC$$

is the full-cost pricing formula where P = market price; MSOC = marginal social opportunity cost; MPC = marginal production cost (the opportunity cost of labour, capital, energy and materials used up in production); MUC = marginal user cost (forgone future benefits due to current depletion); and MEC = marginal environmental cost (damages imposed by the activity on other individuals or activities and/or the natural environment).

Figure 2.1 depicts those various incremental costs as functions of output as well as the market demand (D) curve which reflects the marginal social benefit (MSB) from consuming the corresponding levels of output. As is seen in the figure, underpricing output at P_0 (by subsidizing production cost and ignoring depletion and environmental damage costs) results in excessive output Q_0 (leaving less of everything else). Full-cost pricing cuts output by half (in this case) down to Q^* whose costs are fully paid and hence is more likely to be sustainable. As we will see below, economic instruments are useful devices for bringing into the equation (internalizing) unaccounted social costs and operationalizing full-cost pricing (see legend to Figure 2.1 for more details).

It should be noted that externalities could also be positive as is the case with forest conservation or reforestation which protects downstream farms from flooding or soil conservation which protects dams from siltation. In this case, the market fails to account for all the social benefits of these activities; as a result, too little forest management, reforestation and soil conservation take place. Again, society is worse off as a result and both forests and farms are less sustainable than they would be if the full social benefits of these activities are accounted for and their generator is appropriately rewarded. Again, economic instruments serve as useful devices for internalizing these benefits to their producers through commensurate payments for services provided to society at large.

Full-cost pricing has many advantages. First, it provides the correct signal regarding relative scarcities and a strong incentive to economize and use resources efficiently, by presenting the user with the same cost that society faces. With full-cost pricing, many, if not most,[1] unsustainable production and consumption levels, patterns and practices will no longer be viable and resources would be freed to flow to more sustainable activities. From a fiscal perspective, full-cost pricing reduces the burden on the state budget from subsidies to producers and consumers and from deficits of public utilities that do not fully recover their costs. From a financial perspective, full-cost pricing reduces the need for additional capital to expand supply systems. In the case of utilities and public services facing increasing supply costs, (marginal) full-cost pricing results in financial surpluses that can be used to finance environmental improvements, to provide basic services to poor people at affordable rates, or to make up the revenue shortfall from the reduction of distortionary taxes. Furthermore, full-cost pricing conserves natural resources and reduces environmental damage thereby reducing the need for financial resources to undertake defensive or mitigatory expenditure.

For example, meeting growing energy demands by improving energy efficiency and conservation through full-cost pricing of energy, rather than by expanding supply eliminates the need for new power plants and hence the need for funds to finance scrubbers to reduce SO_2 or to plant trees to offset the additional CO_2 emissions. The savings in financial resources could be enormous, while the economy is guided closer to a sustainable development trajectory. Similarly, water pricing that improves efficient use and encourages conservation eliminates the need for construction of additional reservoirs, water treatment facilities and wastewater disposal plants to meet growing demand; financial resources necessary for mitigation of environmental impacts of dam construction are also saved. Of course there are cases where supply expansion becomes necessary, but postponement and a smaller scale conserve financial and environmental resources. In financial terms, postponement or reduced scale result in savings in interest payments; in environmental terms postponement result in savings due to improved information and knowledge about the resources at risk and the development of environmentally less harmful technologies and substitutes. It is true, full-cost pricing implies higher costs for producers and higher prices for consumers in the short-run, but the long-term benefits in terms of more sustainable economic growth outweigh these costs, although some cushioning of the impact on low-income groups might be necessary.

INTERNALIZING EXTERNAL COSTS THROUGH ECONOMIC INSTRUMENTS

Economic instruments such as removal of distortionary subsidies, secure property rights, pollution taxes, user charges, tradable emission permits and refundable deposits aim to correct market, policy and institutional failures, institute full-cost pricing and bring about a realignment of resource allocation with society's objectives and interests: a necessary condition for sustainable development. Economic instruments, when appropriately set, equal the unaccounted incremental opportunity costs and thereby bridge the gap between private and social costs created by market, institutional and policy failures (see Figure 2.1). As such, economic instruments are tools of internalization of omitted social costs in private decision making and restoration of efficient relative prices reflecting true scarcities and conveying correct market signals. Secure property rights do this indirectly by bringing depletion cost and (when broadly defined) environmental cost into the preview and economic calculus of the 'user' of the resource or environmental asset who now acts as 'owner.'

The importance of internalization of environmental costs in sustainable development and the critical role of economic instruments in bringing it about was duly recognized by the United Nations Conference on Environment and Development in Rio de Janeiro, June 1992. Principle 16 of the Rio Declaration states:

> *'National authorities should endeavor to promote the internalization of environmental costs and the use of economic instruments, taking into account the approach that the polluter should, in principle, bear the cost of pollution with due regard to public interest and without distorting international trade and investment'* (United Nations, 1992).

Economic instruments are ideally suited for reconciling environmental concerns with development needs and integrating environmental and economic policies by virtue of their

1   market correction quality,
2   efficiency or cost-minimization objective,
3   flexibility in accommodating heterogeneity, and
4   adjustability to changing circumstances.

Indeed, economic instruments can not only be used to reduce the apparent environment/development conflicts but, if properly designed and implemented, can actually make economic development a vehicle of environmental protection and vice versa. Economic instruments can be used to provide the kinds of signals concerning resource scarcity and environmental damage that induce efficient resource use and minimization of waste needed to make sustainable development possible. And while some economic instruments may be distributionally regressive, the resources freed by greater economic efficiency, and the revenues generated by these instruments can be more purposefully directed at addressing equity issues.

The key to the promise of economic instruments is their ability to harness the power of the market and the self-interest of the individual and to turn these presumed adversaries of sustainable development into powerful allies. This is done not by mandated or prescribed actions, but by changing the economic incentives facing producers and consumers; by taking full advantage of their self-interest and superior information at their disposal without requiring the disclosure of such information and without creating large and costly bureaucracies. Economic instruments in effect transfer from bureaucrats to the market the responsibility of identifying and exploiting new and additional low-cost sources of pollution control. Incentive-based systems provide the regulators with the capability to reach and control previously unregulated sources of environmental degradation. With tradable emissions permits, for example, dispersed, small-scale sources too costly to reach or in financial difficulty can be encouraged to control their pollution voluntarily. They can do so by selling their pollution reduction credits to higher-cost pollution abaters who in turn would find it in their own best interest to purchase them rather than control their own emissions to a higher level at a higher cost (Tietenberg, 1993). This is a major advantage for developing countries with large numbers of small-scale polluters and undeveloped regulatory systems.

EFFICIENCY, COST EFFECTIVENESS AND EQUITY

Another advantage of economic instruments of enormous importance to both domestic and international environmental policy (and ultimately to sustainable development) is the separation of the question of who controls pollution or practises conservation from the question of who pays for it. This makes possible the attainment of an equitable distribution of costs and benefits without sacrificing efficiency or cost effectiveness, another necessary condition for sustainable and optimal development.

Clearly, to minimize society's costs (ie, to be cost-effective), those who are able to do it at the lowest possible cost should carry out pollution control and resource conservation. To be efficient, no more pollution control should take place than is justified by the ensuing benefits (ie, pollution control should be carried out to the point where the incremental pollution control costs just equal the incremental benefits or additional damages avoided). To be equitable, the cost of pollution control should be paid by those for whom society has determined it is fair to do so. If the society's sense of fairness, as determined by the political process, accords the rights to a clean environment to the society at large, the users of the environment for the disposal of waste (polluters), whether producers or consumers, ought to pay the cost of pollution control and abatement. Indeed, in this case polluters are liable not only for the cost of pollution control to the socially optimal levels, but they are also liable for payment for the use of the assimilative capacity of the environment, a scarce, renewable, but depletable resource with alternative uses.

This 'polluter pays principle' is widely accepted by most countries as a fair distribution of pollution control costs. This principle is a statement about cost distribution or fairness, not about efficiency. It does not tell us who should control pollution or how to control pollution, only that the costs are to be paid by the polluters. Mistakenly, polluters are thought to be the producers of goods and services; however, consumers are indeed the ultimate polluters since, without demand, the polluting products would not be produced in the first place. In practice, the pollution control costs are shared between producers and consumers according to the elasticity of demand[2] for the polluting product in question.

Another misconception of conventional wisdom is that the private sector is the most important, if not the exclusive, source of pollution and environmental degradation while governments are viewed mainly in the role of environmental regulators. In reality, governments and state enterprises are themselves major sources of pollution and environmental degradation, either directly through public production, consumption and investment or indirectly through subsidization of polluting activities and other misguided policies.

How are the pollution control costs to be allocated among polluters? Fairness here requires that the costs be allocated in proportion to the damages caused by each polluter (which are considered proportional to emissions within the same airshed or watershed) and not according to their pollution control costs. A combination of efficiency and equity (with the polluter pays principle as the operative rule of fairness) dictates the following:

1   pollution within a given airshed or watershed is controlled up to the point where the marginal cost of control equals the marginal benefit;
2   those who have the lowest possible pollution control cost do most of the abating until the marginal abatement costs are equalized across all sources; and
3   the cost of pollution control is paid by those who generate the pollution in proportion to their emissions.

Initially, producers bear the cost of pollution abatement; ultimately, both producers and consumers do so, their relative shares depending on the elasticities of demand and supply.[3]

The polluter pays principle is not the only possible distributional rule. Different societies in different cases may allocate the rights to the use of the environment to the polluters, in which case the operative distributional rule is the 'beneficiary pays principle.' According to this principle, those who expect to benefit from pollution control or conservation are expected to pay the costs according to the benefits they expect to derive. This may sound unfair and regressive because the layman's perception of polluters is that of large, wealthy corporations and multinationals, while the affected parties are perceived to be poor and helpless.[4] However, there are many counter-examples of poor 'polluters' and wealthy affected parties (potential beneficiaries of pollution control).

Consider, for example, the case of upland shifting cultivators who deforest watersheds causing downstream flooding and sedimentation of irrigation and hydroelectric reservoirs that provide wealthy farmers, urban residents and industries with water and energy. In this case, clearly the beneficiary pays principle appears to be 'fair' and distributionally progressive. Again, it should be made clear that although we can generally characterize policies and instruments that favour the poor over the wealthy as distributionally positive or progressive, it is the particular society concerned that determines what is a 'fair' or 'just' distribution of costs and benefits.

Another example of the beneficiary pays application, which is also seen as fair and equitable, is the conservation of the so-called global commons. It is widely accepted that the cost of biodiversity conservation and control of greenhouse gases (GHG) ought to be borne by the developed countries, the major beneficiaries. Again, this does not imply that it is solely the developed countries that would actually conserve their biodiversity or control their greenhouse gas emissions. Efficiency requires that biodiversity conservation and CO_2 emission reductions and sinks take place where they can be achieved at the lowest possible cost, which may be in developing countries. Fairness or equity under the beneficiary pays principle requires that the cost of biodiversity conservation and CO_2 emissions be borne largely by developed countries. However, since the developing countries would also benefit, while the developed countries have historically been the main generators of GHG, this distribution of costs may be thought of as an application of the polluter pays principle.

It is also possible that the property rights to environmental assets (or to their services) are divided between polluters and affected parties (potential beneficiaries of pollution control). For example, polluters may be entitled to use the environment for the disposal of waste, free of charge, up to the socially optimal level of pollution. Beyond this level, polluters are subject to a pollution tax or charge, the implication being that the society at large owns the right to the environment beyond this level.

ECONOMIC INSTRUMENTS AS SOURCES OF REVENUES

Economic instruments can also raise large amounts of revenues that can be spent on public goods that improve environmental quality or used to reduce distortionary taxes such as income taxes, which diminish the incentive for work, or sales taxes which distort consumption decisions. Indeed there is more experience with economic instruments as sources of revenues than as incentives to change behaviour. In both developed and developing countries, economic instruments have largely been used to raise funds that can be directly spent to reduce the harmful side-effects of pollution. Paradoxically, the potential of economic instruments as revenue generators may lead to perverse behaviour, as the incentive and revenue functions are in direct conflict. Regulators collecting pollution fees and fines may have incentives to maintain pollution levels to fill their budgetary coffers. For example, the revenue maximizing behaviour of China's local Environmental Protection Bureaus (EPBs) is well documented (Panayotou, 1995a). The effectiveness of specific instruments as sources of public revenues will be discussed further in Chapter 5.

Chapter 3

Economic Instruments: Typology, Advantages, and Limitations

The set of economic instruments available for implementing an economic incentive approach to natural resource management and environmental protection spans a wide range of options and possibilities and the potential permutations and combinations are virtually limitless. *Any* instrument *that aims to induce a change in behaviour of economic agents by internalizing environmental or depletion cost through a change in the incentive structure that these* agents *face (rather than mandating a standard or a technology) qualifies as an economic instrument.* Different instruments have advantages over other instruments in some applications and circumstances, and severe limitations in others. The application and relative advantages and limitations of each type of instrument will be addressed in connection with particular sectors and sets of objectives and conditions in later chapters. In the present chapter we focus on:

1   a typology and brief description of the range of economic instruments that have been actually used or proposed;
2   their general applicability in different sectors; and
3   their major advantages and limitations.

The categories of economic instruments presented here represent a move along a continuum from a Coasian[1] world of minimal intervention by better defining property rights, through market creation and Pigouvian[2] measures, to the use of legal instruments such as liabilities and performance bounds. Figure 3.1 presents an indicative rather than exhaustive summary of economic instruments for environmental management, classified into seven broad categories:

1   property rights;
2   market creation;
3   fiscal instruments;
4   charge systems;
5   financial instruments;
6   liability systems;
7   performance bonds and deposit refund systems.

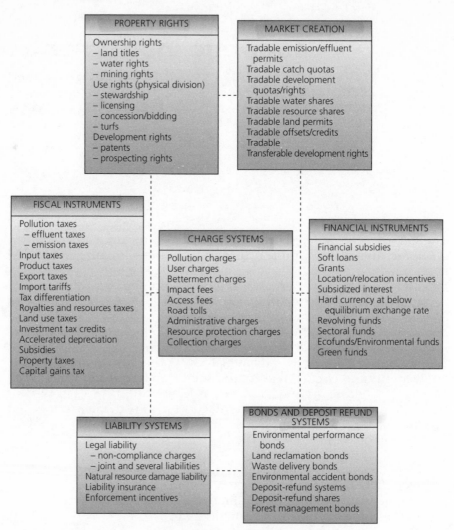

Note: Broken lines indicate affinity between different categories of instruments

Figure 3.1 *Economic Instruments for Environmental Protection and Natural Resource Management*

In Table 3.1 we present a matrix of these categories of economic instruments and their sectoral uses.[3] The sectors parallel those identified by Agenda 21. The table can be read across columns indicating the rich variety of incentive-based instruments for placing the particular sector on a sustainable path (and generating revenues to finance environmental investments). For example, biodiversity can be conserved to form part of the future productive capital through patents and prospecting rights, transferable development rights, charges for scientific tourism and natural resource liability. These instruments become more effective by removing barriers to conservation and perverse incentives such as land conversion subsidies and by introducing deforestation charges to internalize the social costs of habitat loss resulting from deforestation. Reading Table 3.1 down the columns and across the rows, it becomes evident that there are fundamental principles of incentive creation and revenue raising that can be applied to different sectors, thereby economizing on administrative and enforcement structures. For example, secure property rights are as essential for biodiversity conservation and protection of fragile ecosystems as they are for the protection of land, forest, and water resources.

Below we discuss each broad category of instruments and their constituent components, as outlined in Figure 3.1.

PROPERTY RIGHTS

This class of instruments is based on the recognition that excessive resource depletion and environmental degradation arises from misleading price signals which result from the absence (or thinness) of markets in resource and environmental assets. To the extent that the failure of markets to emerge is due to the lack of well-defined, secure, and transferable property rights over resources (as opposed to other reasons such as high transaction cost or failure to enforce contracts), establishment of secure property rights should lead to the emergence of markets and scarcity prices for the resource in question (assuming other barriers are absent). With exclusive and secure property rights, resource depletion is internal to the owners/users, whereas under open access it is external to the users. The consequence of this internalization is that a rational owner will not engage in resource extraction unless the price of the resource commodity covers not only the extraction cost but also the depletion or user cost, which is the forgone future benefit as a result of present use.

As shown in Figure 3.1, property rights are of three main types:

1　ownership rights, such as land titles and water rights;
2　use rights, such as licences with geographic designation, concession bidding, usufruct certificates and access rights (eg, to roads, parks, etc); and
3　development rights as distinct from both ownership rights and use rights.

Unattenuated, indefinite ownership is the purest form of property rights, while short-term use rights lie at the other extreme. For scarce resources with no significant externalities, unattenuated, private ownership rights are likely to result in the most efficient resource use and management (including long-term investment and conservation). This is only the case provided private property is consistent with the social norms and traditions of the society concerned; otherwise, the private property owners do not feel (fully) secure or high enforcement

Table 3.1 *Economic Instruments by Sector*

	Property Rights	Market Creation	Fiscal Instruments	Charge Systems	Financial Instruments	Liability Systems	Bonds & Deposit Refund Systems
Land & Soils	Land titles; Use rights	Tradable land permits	Property taxes; Land use taxes	Pollution charges	Soil Conservation Incentives (loans, etc)	Enforcement Incentives	Land reclamation bonds
Water Resources	Water rights	Water shares	Capital gains tax	Water pricing; Water protection charges	Green (blue) funds	–	Environmental accident bonds
Oceans & Seas	Turfs Licensing	Fishing rights; ITQs	Pollution taxes	–	–	–	Oil-spill bonds
Forests	Communal rights	Concession bidding	Taxes/royalties	User charges Access fees	Reforestation incentives (subsidies)	Natural resource damage liability	Reforestation bonds; Forest management bonds
Minerals	Mining rights	Tradable resource shares	Taxes/royalties	User charges	Sectoral funds	Liability insurance	Land reclamation bonds
Wildlife	Stewardship	–	–	Impact fees Access fees	Location/relocation incentives	Natural resource damage liability	–
Biodiversity	Patents; Prospecting rights	Transferable development rights	Product taxes Input taxes	Charges for scientific tourism	Ecofunds	Natural resource damage liability	–
Water Pollution	–	Tradable offsets/credit; Tradable effluent permits	Effluent taxes	Water treatment fees; Pollution charges	Low interest loans	Non-compliance charges	Waste delivery bonds; Environmental accident bonds

Air Pollution	–	Tradable emission permits	Emission taxes	Pollution charges; Betterment charges	Technology subsidies; Low interest loans	Non-compliance charges	Environmental accident bonds
Solid Waste	–	–	Property taxes	Collection – charges, Impact fees	Liability	Deposit-refund insurance	Deposit-refund systems; Waste delivery bonds
Hazardous Waste; (zero assimilative capacity)	–	–	Differential taxation; Product taxes	User charges; Collection charges	Waste delivery incentives	Joint & several liability; liability insurance	Deposit-refund systems Bonds
Toxic Chemicals	–	–	Differential taxation; Product taxes	User charges; Impact fees	–	Legal liability; Natural resource liability; Liability insurance	Deposit-refund systems
Human Settlements– land use– congestion	Land rights Buy-own-transfer (BOT) Arrangements	Tradable development quotas; Transferable development rights	Property taxes; Land use taxes	Betterment charge; Development charge; Land use charge; Road tolls	Location/ relocation incentives	–	Development completion bonds
Global Climate	–	Tradable CO$_2$ permits; Carbon offsets; Tradable emission entitlements; Tradable forest protection obligations	Carbon taxes; BTU tax	Pollution charges	CFC replacement incentives; Forest compacts	–	–

Note: List is representative, not exhaustive.

costs partially or fully offset the social gains from improved resource management.

Property rights need not be private – they can be communal or public (state) – but they need to be well defined, secure and transferable if they are to effectively internalize depletion costs. Where traditional, customary or communal rights exist, the best policy might be the recognition and strengthening of these rights rather than their supplantation with private property rights, especially if the latter is alien to the local culture.

Private property rights

Divergence between the private and social discount rates also creates a wedge between private and social objectives but it does not, by itself, 'invalidate' private ownership. As an economic instrument of efficient revenue allocation, this divergence can be bridged either by eliminating its source (economic and political uncertainty, high-interest rate policies, etc) or by introducing supplementary economic or regulatory instruments, for example maximum allowable cut in forestry, a tax on the rate of resource extraction or subsidies for soil conservation.

Assignment of property rights as an instrument for the internalization of external costs has several advantages:

1   It goes to the root of the problem: the absence or malfunctioning of markets due to undefined property rights.
2   It relies on the government to do what it does best, which is to create the institutional infrastructure and legal framework for the efficient functioning of markets; the government allocates property rights and the markets allocate resources.
3   Since the government allocates property rights only once, leaving future changes to the market, it has relatively low administrative costs and it minimizes distortionary interventions in the price system.
4   Property rights can be easily attenuated (restricted in certain ways) to internalize other external costs or to pursue other social objectives, through liens, easements and other restrictions of use and disposal.
5   Unlike taxes and charges, property rights adjust automatically to changing circumstances (ie, once established they meet the automaticity criterion from then on).
6   Regardless of how property rights are distributed, efficiency is ensured as long as the property rights are clear, exclusive, transferable and enforceable, and no other market failures are present.

The property rights approach to the internalization of external costs has a number of limitations, which, though important, do not outweigh the advantages in most circumstances, and could be remedied with additional instruments. One limitation is that the assignment of property rights is a politically contentious issue subject to rent seeking and corruption and can be used as an instrument to achieve political objectives (eg, reward political supporters). A second limitation is that the assignment (distribution) of property rights has momentous distributional implications. If granted free of charge, property right holders are given ownership to the entire present value of the infinite stream of rents flowing from the resource. If the rights are sold or auctioned, the issuing authority acquires the present value of rents which it can then expend or redistribute according to its own social, environmental, economic or other objectives.

The once-and-for-all distributional impact or property right assignment has a double-edged implication for social policy. On the one hand, it can be used as a means of improving wealth distribution; on the other hand, it creates strong pressures from politically powerful groups and organized interests who stake a claim to rights over natural resources in the public domain. While assignment of secure property rights to open access resources is certain to improve efficiency, management and conservation, it may also deprive the poor of access to common resources important for survival, unless they are the recipients of the property rights.

Property rights are particularly applicable to land and soils (land rights), water resources (water rights), minerals (mining rights) and other natural resources that can be parcelled out and enclosed, or their boundaries easily demarcated and defended, as the ability to exclude non-owners is critical to the effectiveness of property rights as an economic instrument. Property rights are less applicable to situations where the resource is mobile or fugacious (moves across boundaries, eg marine fisheries), or where significant externalities infringe on the content of the property rights, as when downstream land, water or a fishery resource are the receptors of upstream externalities (eg, damage from floods or water pollution resulting from upstream deforestation or runoff of agrochemicals). In both these cases – a fugacious resource or significant externalities – the security and exclusivity of the property right is compromised and the right might no longer act as an incentive for efficient use and management. At the limit, the behaviour of the 'owner' resembles that of an exploiter of open-access resources who maximizes short-term capture and minimizes long-term investment. This behaviour is also exhibited by farmers with only use rights or insecure land titles; they tend to 'mine' rather than farm the land.

Finally, property rights (at least in their conventional form) are not a suitable instrument for environmental management where the resource itself or its use generates significant externalities, for example, a forest in an upstream watershed. In this case, property rights to the forest within the watershed fail to internalize the environmental benefits of forest conservation (and environmental costs of forest harvest) to downstream activities. The result would be too little forest conservation and too much forest harvest from the society's point of view. If the externality were private, involving one or very few easily identified parties, the assignment of secure property rights to both upstream and downstream activities would be sufficient to produce an efficient allocation, through either: (a) bargaining between the parties involved, or (b) unitization, that is, one party would buy out the other and unify the upstream and downstream activity under a single management, thereby internalizing the externality.

In the case of a public (widespread) externality with many sources and receptors, the bargaining between the parties is constrained by high transaction costs (information, negotiation, policing, etc). Unitization, which can be effected either through assignment of property rights to the entire river basin or to a single owner, could result in monopoly control (another market failure) even if the distributional considerations could be addressed.

A consequence of the above limitations of property rights is their unsuitability for management of environmental resources such as air, water, atmosphere and the global climate. However, as we will see below, it is still possible to harness the advantages of property rights in the protection of the environment and management of fugacious resources[4] and avoid their limitations through innovative market creation such as tradable emission permits and tradable catch quotas.

Attenuation of property rights through regulation of use (eg, building-plot ratios) or restriction of certain types of development (zoning) often occurs to internalize externalities or public good aspects which are significant but not significant enough to 'invalidate' private property. Economic instruments such as differential land use taxes, development charges and impact fees can be used for the same purpose.

Communal property rights

When externalities or public good aspects are pervasive, as in the case of critical watersheds, forests with significant ecological functions, fisheries, wildlife and biodiversity, the necessary restrictions and regulations of private use could be so many and their enforcement so costly that collective forms of ownership are a more efficient means of internalizing environmental costs. If externalities are local (eg, local watershed, village forest, or local fishery), communal property rights combined with private use rights (regulated by the community) could internalize external costs with minimal management efficiency loss, especially when the community has a cohesive social organization and a tradition of collective resource management. It is important to stress here that the management responsibility for the communal resource (regulation of use, conservation, protection and investment in productivity enforcement and sustainability) lies with the collective owner, the community, and not the individual users. The community may exercise the management responsibility either directly through collective community institutions or internalize it to individual users through obligations, regulations, norms, taboos and various social sanctions (see Box 3.1).

Box 3.1 Communal Property Rights: the CAMPFIRE Programme in Zimbabwe

The Communal Area Management Programme for Indigenous Resources was initiated by the government of Zimbabwe to achieve better wildlife resource management. Local committees are encouraged to make their own decisions on the best management of natural and wildlife resources, given clear property and management rights. Initial programme funding was provided by the national government and international environmental NGOs and technical support is provided throughout the programme.

The most popular (and profitable) activity is managed safari hunting. Other activities include wildlife tourism and sales and marketing of natural products. The funds raised are invested back into the programmes or used to compensate farmers whose livestock is damaged or killed by managed wildlife. Because the community has a direct interest in the sustainable management of these resources and can earn a profit, this allocation of property rights produces the same management decisions we might see if the resource were owned by a single, private investor. The programme has the added advantage of supporting the traditional lifestyle of the community.

Source: Thomas et al (1997).

State property rights

Where externalities or public good aspects dominate (eg, major national watersheds, offshore fishery, biodiversity and unique environmental assets), the most efficient means of internalization is likely to be state ownership with regulated individual use rights through concession and licensing. In this case the management responsibility lies with the state and could be exercised either directly through state agencies or indirectly through regulations and incentives. In the case of global public goods such as forests and biodiversity, where national sovereignty precludes global community property rights, internalization is effected through global conventions and international transfer mechanisms, internationally tradable emission permits or transferable development rights (see below).

MARKET CREATION

Unlike the case with the management of natural resources, property rights in their conventional form are not an appropriate instrument for the protection of the environment. In the case of most natural resources, a great deal of the benefits and costs of resource use and conservation occurs on site and therefore can be made internal to the user through secure ownership of the site. Property rights effectively internalize depletion cost (scarcity value) and on-site environmental cost. Any external cost (off-site effects) or public-good aspects are internalized through supplementary instruments such as regulations and incentives. In the case of environmental pollution, however, individual property rights to the environmental media of air, water and atmosphere are neither feasible – exclusion is not technically possible – nor desirable; there is zero opportunity cost to allowing more people to enjoy clean air. Indeed environmental quality is a public good that is grossly under-supplied by free markets because it is not possible for private providers to recoup the cost of supply.

One solution is for the state to provide the desired level of environmental quality (like other public goods) and pay for it through general taxation. This can be effected through a combination of pollution control regulations, incentives and public investment in pollution abatement. An alternative (often a more cost-effective one, as we will see below) is to try and mimic the market, in fact, to create a market in environmental quality. This approach treats the environment as a scarce, yet non-market and unpriced resource, which is overused because it is free. As a result, a solution might be to create a market in which the right to use the environment as a waste sink (a sort of use right) is assigned, priced and traded. Assignment (ie definition and allocation of the right to use the environment) would ensure a total aggregate use to the desired level of environmental quality, and specify the content of individual rights (shares). Pricing, the consequence of scarcity (resulting from the issuance of fewer environmental-use rights than demanded), would ensure a more rational use of the environment, because the more it is used the more it costs; the more it costs, the less it is used.

Tradable emission permits

Tradable emission permits are a tool for market creation. An aggregate level of allowable emissions is set for each airshed or watershed and allocated among polluters either according to the level of output or current level of emissions.[5] Since the aggregate emissions quota is set at or below the current level of emissions, an artificial level of scarcity is created and permits acquire positive value (market price) (see Box 3.2).

Establishing a system of emission permits has relatively high management costs, requiring the following:

1   Proper definition of airshed (trading permits across airsheds would create hot spots), which in turn requires knowledge of the sources and of the movement of pollutants under the local atmospheric conditions.
2   Monitoring of ambient air quality in the airshed (or water quality in the watershed) and the monitoring of the relationship between emissions and ambient air quality.
3   Capacity to monitor or randomly inspect individual emission sources to ensure that the emissions limit specified in the permit is observed.

4   A system of approving and recording credits, offsets and trades
    among permit holders.

Depending on the type of pollutant and the content of the permit,
management requirements could be significantly reduced. For example,
in the case of a global pollutant such as CO_2, there is no need to define
the airshed since it makes no difference where in the world CO_2 is
emitted or controlled, though ability to monitor sources and sinks is
still required for a workable CO_2 permit trading system. In the case of
local pollutants, systems of self-reporting, auditing and random inspec-
tion with sanctions for violations may suffice to replace a formal
system of approving and recording credits, offsets and trades.
Incentives for self-enforcement and group policing can be introduced
to minimize monitoring and enforcement costs, making the entire
group bear some cost for individual transgressions.
    Tradable emission permits are nothing but tradable emission
quotas, a concept that has wide applicability beyond air and water
pollution and greenhouse gases. Consider the example of a mobile (or
fugacious) resource such as an offshore fishery suffering from overfishing. Property rights cannot be assigned but a total allowable catch or
aggregate catch quota can be set (at say the maximum sustainable
economic yield) and allocated to existing fishermen in some equitable
way (eg according to average historical catches). Potential entrants can
be accommodated by reserving quotas for them or through the
purchase of quotas from retiring fishermen. If trading is allowed, the
individual tradable quotas would gravitate towards the most efficient
fishermen, ensuring that the allowable total catch is caught at the
minimum possible cost. Thus, overfishing is eliminated, the fishing
resource is protected, economic efficiency is achieved (ie fishery rents
are maximized) and fishermen who choose to leave the fishery, making
all this possible, are fully compensated. New Zealand has used this
system to manage its marine fishery.[6]
    The major obstacles to the wider introduction of tradable permits
systems are the lack of inventory of emissions and sources and the
weakness of monitoring and enforcement of systems in many developing countries. It is reasonable, however, to expect further experiments
and a few actual trades taking place in coming years.

Tradable development quotas

Space limitations do not allow discussion of all the available instruments
in the category of market creation; two more examples should suffice. A
number of countries with substantial tourist industries are facing a serious
problem of expansion and haphazard development of their most popular
resorts. In fact, the more attractive a resort is the more likely it is to be
degraded by overdevelopment. Experience shows that zoning and building regulations have been ineffective in many parts of the world to
regulate development and to maintain the quality of the tourist product

Box 3.2 Developing Emissions Trading in Almaty, Kazakhstan

The city of Almaty in the Central Asian Republic of Kazakhstan endeavours to develop an area-wide emission trading bubble as a cost-effective means of achieving its air emission reduction goals. Almaty has a persistent air quality problem. The existing air quality control strategy which includes technology-based normatives and non-compliance charges has not been sufficiently effective to achieve the air quality goals. Furthermore, the industry is concerned about the inflexibility and unpredictability of frequently changing control requirements based on ambient monitoring. The existing system fails to take advantage of significant differentials in the marginal cost of emission control between industrial operations to minimize costs of achieving air quality goals. High compliance costs and financial difficulties result in both undercompliance and underpayment of fees and charges.

Under the contemplated 'cap-and-trade' programme, 1200 companies that operate with proper authorizations within the city limits will be allocated a five-year stream of emission allowances. The starting allocation for each facility will be based on a formula that takes into account its actual emissions in 1991 and 1994. To achieve the air quality goal of 7–10 per cent annual reduction from industrial sources in the city (Decree No. 68), the allocated emission allowances will be reduced by 7 per cent (of initial baseline) per year. The companies will be required to operate within their emission allowances or purchase additional permits from other companies to cover any excess emissions. Firms that succeed in reducing their emissions by more than 7 per cent a year would be allowed to bank the surplus allowances for future use (up to three years) or to sell them to other firms. The city expects increased compliance and significant cost savings from the trading programme since high-cost pollution abaters will no longer be forced to achieve the same reductions as low-cost abaters. They could, instead, buy surplus allowances from the latter at a significantly lower cost, thereby stretching their limited resources further. The aggregate emissions will be reduced by 7 per cent as the undercompliance of high-cost abaters. For hot spots, sales of credits would be encouraged, but purchases would be permitted only from within the site; or certain facilities would be required to buy credits at a higher ratio, such as 2 tons of allowances for each additional ton emitted.

A significant source of capital for financing emission reduction at those companies that have the opportunity (ie are low-cost abaters) but lack the capital, would come from new and expanding companies which could buy into the bubble. The need for new and expanding companies to buy in is not likely to be a major barrier to entry and growth since their allowance requirements per unit of output would be lower than existing facilities by virtue of their ability to choose more efficient and less polluting technology. Firms which are currently not complying because they lack the capital to install control equipment are, under the programme, given access to the capital of the air credit buyers in order to undertake investments and to create sellable assets. These assets, or surplus allowances, can result from process changes, retrofittings, rebuilding, input change or relocation.

The city plans to monitor industrial emissions on a regular basis, and to require that companies maintain accurate records of materials used and of resulting emissions and that they report them to the city on a regular basis. To ensure compliance, the certainty-equivalent consequences of non-compliance will be made more costly than the cost of compliance.

Participating companies will be charged fees to hold, bank and trade allowances. The revenues collected from these fees will be used to finance monitoring and enforcement, thereby ensuring the financial self-sufficiency and sustainability of the programme. As the programme is still in the design stage, it is not possible to predict if it will work as envisioned; yet the interest and commitment of the city and the national policy makers to effective financing of environmental improvements directly by the polluters is not in question. It provides an inspiring contrast to other, less ambitious, initiatives by environmentally more advanced countries.

Source: Margolis et al (1995).

(especially in coastal areas). Examples range from Southern Europe (eg, Spain) to Southeast Asia (eg, Thailand) to the Caribbean (eg, Barbados). Some countries (eg, Cyprus) were forced to introduce moratoriums on all hotel and other tourism-related development for several years. The moratoriums were later swept by an avalanche of accumulated applications, pressures for hotel development and a rush to build mostly poor quality establishments from fear that the moratorium might be reintroduced. This is an example of a command-and-control intervention that has clearly backfired, causing the rate of construction to accelerate and its quality to decline, further downgrading the island's tourist product.

Policy makers are searching for instruments that will help them control and guide the pace of new development in tourist centres in desirable areas and directions and to upgrade existing establishments, thereby improving environmental conditions and the quality of their tourist product. Tradable development quotas are such an instrument. The relevant authorities can set a maximum allowable development (or construction) quota, measured in, say, cubic metres of available space (or number of rooms) for each year, in each area or zone, consistent with their objectives to limit development and improve quality. The aggregate quota in each area can then be allocated according to some equitable (widely accepted) formula. Possible alternatives include auctioning to the highest bidder with the revenues going towards the upgrading of public places in the town (eg, developing parks, improving roads, cleaning beaches and reducing air and noise pollution).

An alternative allocation is by proportion of land-ownership in the tourist zone. Under this arrangement each recipient of a quota has the choice of using it in his/her own land, selling it to others or simply banking it for future sale or use. The quotas thus gravitate to those with the most profitable development plans and projects. Development quotas and development rights can be made tradable across zones, but the terms of trade must be specified by the issuing authorities to prevent 'hot spots' of overdevelopment.

Tradable water shares

Another example of market creation is tradable water shares. This is similar to water rights but distinct in that the resource is indivisible in its physical dimension but divisible in its use (analogous to the environment).

Tradable water shares work as follows. The irrigation authority issues percentage shares to the water stored in the system during each season to farmers and other water users in the command area of a water system. Each shareholder knows his/her entitlement by multiplying the total amount of water in the system as announced by the water authority each season, by his/her share. For example, if the total quantity of water announced is 100 million cubic metres, if there are 20,000 households in the command area, and if an egalitarian allocation formula is chosen, the individual farmer's share would be 0.00005 which equals 5000 m^3 (= 0.00005 x 100,000,000) for the season.

The farmer, or rather, the water holder, is free to dispose of this water share as he/she pleases: use it in his/her own field; sell it to another farmer; bank it for future use; or sell it back to the water authority at the prevailing market price for use elsewhere, for example to supply urban users.

The institution of tradable water shares does presume the ability to meter water and monitor use, but these requirements are not beyond the capability of most water authorities and irrigation departments. There are alternatives such as the allocation of shares to water user associations who in turn allocate them to their members using their own (informal) distribution and monitoring mechanisms.

Those who currently use large quantities of water, either because they are large landholders with free water access due to their proximity to the system or because they cultivate water-intensive crops, might raise objections. This issue again can be addressed by selecting a share allocation formula that takes these concerns into account through partial grandfathering of existing users. In principle, there is no inherent difficulty in allocating shares to people outside the command area of a system, and it is especially desirable to do so for people in the catchment (or watershed) area of the system. Fiscal instruments such as taxes, royalties or charges can be imposed on water shareholders to skim off part of the rents (or of the annual water share appreciation) to fund the maintenance of the system and the protection of the watershed.

FISCAL INSTRUMENTS

Fiscal instruments such as taxes and subsidies can be used to bridge the gap between private and social costs/benefits. For example, the prices of polluting products such as gasoline or pesticides do not incorporate the social costs of damage to people's health and other activities which arise from their use because these costs are external to the decision maker (producer or consumer). Hence, polluting inputs and final products are generally underpriced, both absolutely (in terms of social costs) and in relation to non-polluting or less polluting products. This results in overproduction and overconsumption which in turn result in environmental damage at a higher than socially optimal level (see Figure 3.2 Q_0–Q^*).

Environmental taxes

Environmental taxes can be used to effect full-cost pricing: to bridge the gap between private and social costs. To do this, the tax should be set exactly equal to the marginal environmental damage corresponding to the socially optimal level of pollution (see Figure 3.2). This tax, known as a Pigouvian tax, is the embodiment of full-cost pricing, adjusting the price of a good precisely by the amount of the reduction in social welfare (at the margin) caused by the externality associated with the good. The result is not a zero level of pollution externality but an optimal level given the equality of the marginal benefit from the reduction of pollution to its marginal cost, or alternatively, by the equality of the marginal damage cost to the marginal benefit from the production of the good, as shown in Figure 3.2.

Environmental taxes can be levied on: (a) the pollutant itself (ie on effluents, emissions or solid waste); or (b) on final products associated

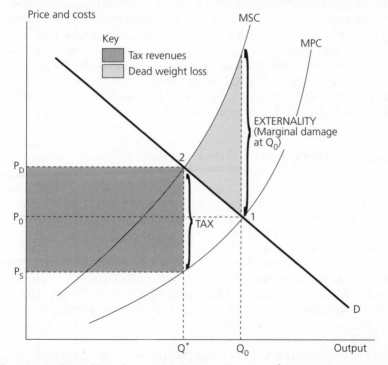

Note: The tax moves the equilibrium from 1 ⟹ 2; the output from Q_0 to Q^* (optimal); the price received by the producers, P_S goes down; the price paid by the consumer, P_D goes up. Deadweight loss is reduced to zero. (*Note that whether the tax is levied on the consumer or producer leads to the same result).

Figure 3.2 *Pigouvian tax*

with environmental externalities. Product taxes will be discussed in more detail below and in Chapter 4.

Despite their great potential, both as incentives for improved environmental behaviour and as generators of revenues for financing sustainable development, environmental taxes have not expanded as rapidly and as widely as it was hoped because of the political cost of higher taxes and concerns about their effect on competitiveness and distribution. While these concerns can be overcome with better design, better marketing and gradual implementation, wider adoption will continue to be rather slow, but accelerated somewhat because of the snowballing effect of an increasing number of successful introductions (see Box 3.3).

Emission and effluent taxes

Emission and effluent taxes are Pigouvian environmental taxes. They are imposed directly on the pollutant and are set at rates equal to the incremental damage from an additional unit of pollutant at the optimum pollution level (see Figure 3.3). Emission and effluent taxes are theoretically correct but face a number of practical difficulties. First, to set the correct tax we need estimates of the marginal benefit and marginal cost curves to determine the optimum pollution level. These can be very difficult to determine. Second, a low tax does not provide much of an incentive for environmentally sound behaviour, yet higher tax rates require complex tax structures and administrative mechanisms. And third, taxes based on actual discharges involve significantly higher administration and enforcement costs than taxes on products.

Taxes on inputs and final products

Taxes on inputs and final products whose production or consumption are associated with pollution externalities, though indirect and hence less efficient, have the advantage of relying on the administrative procedures of the existing tax systems. No monitoring of the sources and levels of emissions or effluents is needed and product taxes can be easily collected from producers at the time of exchange (sale, export, import). Examples include taxes on fuels, on industrial chemicals and on pesticides. Environmental taxes on final products are particularly suited to the control of consumption-related pollution, because consumers are made aware, through higher prices, of the environmental consequences of their choices (see Box 3.4).

An environmental tax on final products can be adjusted to ensure international competitiveness; exports can be exempted, since the products are not domestically consumed and inputs can be made subject to an equal environmental duty.

Box 3.3 Deforestation Tax in Brazil

One innovative instrument to address environmental and resource problems under local conditions is the 'deforestation tax' for unsustainable forest uses. This tax is used instead of mandating compliance with the reforestation requirement of Agenda 21 (four trees per cubic metre of wood extracted). This instrument represents a compromise between minimizing enforcement costs (in the case of small operators) and creating an incentive to reduce deforestation. This embryonic system of credits, offsets and (indirect) trades has both efficiency and equity benefits which were explicitly recognized and, in fact, motivated the instrument. Its major characteristics are:

- it avoids the prohibitively high costs of monitoring small reforestation projects;
- it takes advantage of economies of scale in reforestation by using the collected funds for large-scale reforestation projects; and
- it gives small scale forest users a lower cost alternative to direct reforestation.

As this system currently stands, it suffers from loopholes and low reforestation rates. The system can be refined and strengthened by increasing the charge and by allowing trading of reforestation obligations between small and large-scale forest users.

Source: Panayotou (1995a).

Differential tax structure

In the case of raw materials and intermediate products, a uniform environmental tax may result in distortions and perverse incentives if some inputs or uses result in greater environmental damage than others. To remedy this problem a differential tax structure is often introduced: materials with higher levels of externality are charged higher tax rates, while environmentally friendly products have their regular tax rate reduced (see Box 3.5).

The great advantage of a tax differentiation system is high administrative efficiency because it is integrated into the existing tax system and requires little additional collection and enforcement effort. As such, it is especially relevant to developing countries with low monitoring and enforcement capabilities.

Differential taxation of products and services (differential VAT) according to their environmental externalities has been used with some success in Western Europe and it holds even greater promise in developing countries undergoing their formative years of industrial development. This is discussed further in Chapter 8. A major limitation of a differential VAT in which tax rates vary with the products' pollution coefficients (or environmental damages) is its complexity and cost of administration, while a simpler tax rate structure might be too blunt an instrument for internalizing environmental costs.

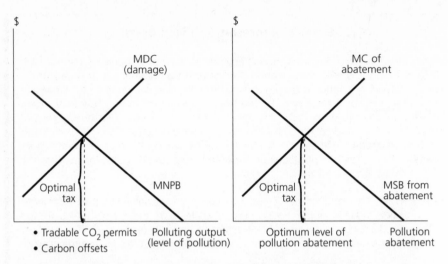

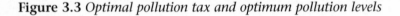

Note: MDC, marginal damage cost; MNPB, marginal net private benefit from production of economic output; MC, marginal cost (of pollution abatement); MSB, marginal social benefit (from pollution abatement).

Figure 3.3 *Optimal pollution tax and optimum pollution levels*

Subsidies

Fiscal instruments include not only taxes but also subsidies that aim to encourage less polluting behaviour. Instead of taxing the polluters to reduce pollution to the optimum level, polluters can be subsidized to reduce pollution. The optimal environmental subsidy is also equal to the marginal environmental damage at the level of the optimal tax (refer again to Figure 3.2). The outcome in terms of environmental improvement and static economic efficiency (resources expended for the improvement are minimized) is exactly the same except for differences in the transaction cost between collecting taxes and paying subsidies.

There is, however, one dynamic difference that favours taxes. In the long run, subsidies tend to induce new entrants into the industry (or the expansion of existing producers) which results in both an increase in pollution and an increase in the cost of the subsidy. Distributionally, the burden of environmental taxes falls on the producer and consumer of the polluting products while that of the subsidies falls on the taxpayers. In this connection, subsidies violate the widely accepted polluter pays principle of distributing pollution control costs (see Panayotou, 1998 for evidence from China). The one exception is Pigouvian subsidies which internalize positive environmental externalities such as the public good aspects (environmental services) of reforestation or soil conservation. The optimal subsidy equals the marginal environmental benefit where the marginal social benefit equals its marginal social cost (see Figure 3.4).

Box 3.4 The British Fossil Fuel Levy and Non-fossil Fuel Obligation

In an effort to shift electricity consumption away from fossil fuels and towards renewable energy, the British government introduced the Fossil Fuel Levy and the Non-fossil Fuel Obligation (NFFO). The Fossil Fuel Levy is charged on every electricity bill and the revenues are used to finance the NFFO. Therefore, the levy is a double subsidy for renewable energy. In 1996, the levy raised £94 million (or US$145 million) from fossil fuel users and was channelled to the development of renewable energy. This is the equivalent to an almost US$300 million 'price wedge' between fossil and non-fossil fuels. Furthermore, as of April 1998, the energy market will open to full competition and energy users will have the opportunity to choose their source of energy; if prices are comparable (and the levy-NFFO system helps renewables to compete), many users are expected to opt for more sustainable energy sources such as wind power and geothermal energy (Sykes, 1997). This case demonstrates that with the right instruments in place, deregulation and market liberalization can help promote more sustainable consumption patterns.

Source: Sykes (1997).

Cross subsidies and 'feebate' schemes

A hybrid of tax differentiation and subsidy is cross subsidization of environmentally benign activities from tax revenues on environmentally harmful activities. Examples include taxes on deforestation subsidizing reforestation (see also differential land use tax below) and taxes on fossil fuels subsidizing renewable energy development (see Box 3.6). The idea here is the simultaneous internalization of negative and positive externalities through charges in relative prices and self-financing transfers.

Investment tax incentives

Governments wanting to abide by the polluter pays principle and, perhaps more importantly, facing growing budget deficits, do not usually favour environmental subsidies, yet most governments are rather generous with investment tax incentives. The most common of such instruments are investment tax credits and accelerated depreciation for pollution control equipment and waste treatment facilities. While their impact on the budget is no different than that of subsidies, and while they equally violate the polluter pays principle, investment tax incentives are popular with governments for two reasons. First, their costs are hidden from public scrutiny and hence are an expedient way to provide hidden subsidies, and second, they give the appearance of promoting environmental protection without reducing competitiveness. Of course, the latter is not assured since the installation of the mandated (and subsidized) pollution abatement facilities does not

---

Box 3.5 The German Differential Petrol and Vehicle Tax

As part of its efforts to reduce vehicle emissions and promote the use of unleaded petrol and catalytic converters, the German federal government implemented in 1985 a tax differential of DM 0.04 per litre (subsequently raised to DM 0.10 per litre) in favour of unleaded petrol to change consumer behaviour. The differential tax was very successful: today, unleaded petrol accounts for 90 per cent of all petrol purchases in Germany. [Differential excise taxes have been used by virtually all western European countries to promote the use of unleaded petrol.]

At the same time, the German government introduced tax differentials for low or reduced emission vehicles and gave new cars with catalytic converters a tax holiday amounting to DM 3000 per car (subsequently lowered to DM 1100). This was done in a revenue-neutral way, in the sense that high taxes on high emission vehicles compensated for low taxes on low emission vehicles and the tax holiday for catalytic converter-equipped cars. The government also offered a car tax rebate as an incentive to equip older cars with catalytic converters making the system a 'feebate' scheme with both fee and rebate elements.

Source: Federal Ministry of the Environment (1993).

---

guarantee their efficient functioning. Indeed, many mandated water treatment facilities are often found to be in unserviceable condition to avoid operating and maintenance costs (see Panayotou, 1998 for some evidence from China).

Tax incentives for environmental investments, in the form of both tax credits and accelerated depreciation are practised in Canada, France, Korea and Taiwan, among others, while both Japan and Germany provide for depreciation and the Netherlands provides tax credits for environmental protection investments (Jenkins and Lamech, 1992).[7]

Transferable reforestation tax credit

An interesting tax credit incentive that operates in Costa Rica is known as the transferable reforestation tax credit. Landowners who choose to keep their land under forestry (or plant native species) receive a tax credit (ie they can deduct part of the costs from their taxes). This scheme benefits in particular, big, wealthy landholders who pay a significant amount of tax. To enable small landholders to share in the benefit of the scheme, the government introduced a transferable tax credit system; smallholders who keep their land under forestry earn tax credit that they can sell to wealthy taxpayers to offset their high taxes. The annual nature of both the credit and the investment (maintenance of land under forest) makes this tax credit scheme more effective than those discussed earlier. Yet a differential land use tax could have achieved the same result more directly.

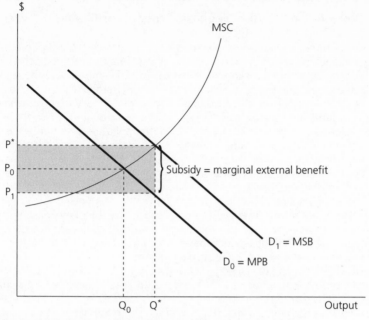

MSC, marginal social cost; MSB, marginal social benefit; MPB, marginal private benefit; shaded area, subsidy costs (to the government) or subsidy revenues for the industry.

Note: The pre-subsidy demand and supply clear at P_0Q_0, and the post-subsidy equilibrium is at P^*Q^*.

Figure 3.4 *Pigouvian subsidy*

Differential land use tax

A differential land use tax has been operating in some states in Germany for several years. Land uses are classified in a number of categories ranging from most environmentally beneficial (eg natural forest) to most environmentally destructive (eg industrial site). A charge is imposed when a landowner changes land use from a higher to a lower class. The more steps involved in environmental downgrading the greater the charge (charge multiplied by the number of steps). For example, the charge for downgrading from forestry to an industrial site is far greater than from agricultural to residential use. The effect of this differential land use tax is to internalize the environmental costs of forest conversion and land use change. A similar system has been proposed for Thailand that involves a system of land use taxes and subsidies depending on the corresponding externalities (Panayotou, 1991).

Industrial relocation incentives

A number of countries use tax credits and subsidies as industrial relocation incentives to induce polluting industries to move out of urban

Box 3.6 The Swedish 'Feebate' Scheme for Cleaner Power

A classic 'feebate' scheme has operated in Sweden since 1992 in the form of the nitrogen oxide charge and rebate. Combustion plants producing electricity and heat are charged $4.80 per kilogram of nitrogen oxide emitted and the revenues are rebated to the plants in proportion to their energy production. It is, therefore, not a tax but a revenue-neutral incentive for environmentally friendly behaviour. Plants that produce more energy per unit of emissions benefit, while those who are inefficient and highly polluting lose. Thus, the polluters underwrite the more efficient and cleaner plants. Power plants range from those making a payment ($1.2 million) to those receiving a net income ($1.7 million). Several elements are attractive about this system: (a) the charge has only an environmental purpose (it is not a tax) which makes it more acceptable to the industry; and (b) because plants are given an incentive to reduce pollution rather than being forced to do so by regulation, the most efficient response is chosen by the plants based on their own individual abatement cost circumstances (marginal abatement functions).

Differential taxation of products based on environmental impacts is beginning to be practised in developing countries. For example, Thailand used a differential tax between leaded and unleaded petrol in the early 1990s to encourage a shift to unleaded petrol and reduced health effects of lead emissions, especially in Bangkok. Cross-subsidization of environmentally friendly activities from taxes on environmentally harmful ones has been practised in Indonesia by requiring logging companies to pay a reforestation fee unless they reforest areas they cleared. Unfortunately, the reforestation fee was set at a level much below the cost of reforestation, thereby resulting in too much cutting and too little replanting.

Source: Swedish Ministry of the Environment (1991).

centres where the impact of pollution is high (due to exposure of large population, limited ventilation, overburdened assimilative capacity, etc) to less populated areas or industrial zones. Such credits and subsidies are justified by the high cost of relocation, the freeing of high-value land for more productive uses (eg, residential or commercial) and economies of scale in pollution control which come from consolidating similar industries within industrial estates. Turkey, for example, offers a 40 per cent tax deduction on investment during the two years of industrial estate construction. Small and medium size tanneries receive a 7 per cent rebate on investment.

Fiscal policy reform

Environmental taxes, if properly structured, can become a major thrust of fiscal policy reform. Conventional taxation throughout the world taxes work, income, savings, investment and value added and leaves untaxed (even subsidizes) leisure and consumption, resource depletion and pollution.

A reform of the fiscal system that would reduce conventional taxes and replace them with environmental taxes, so as to leave the total tax burden unchanged, would bring the economy closer to sustainable development by stimulating economic growth and resource conservation and discouraging resource depletion and environmental pollution. This is clear to see since the existing fiscal system of taxing social benefits introduces market distortion, while a reformed system that taxes social costs would remove market distortions and mitigate market failures. Fiscal reform that is by design revenue neutral would not generate additional state funds but it would save government expenditures on environmental regulation and pollution abatement and, in the long run, increase the tax base and hence tax revenues without increasing the tax burden. There is a rather heated debate as to whether a revenue neutral environmental tax would result in a double dividend: better environment and larger GDP. There is an agreement, however, that broad-based environmental taxes with incidence on low marginal tax inputs that replace revenue obtained from taxes with marginal tax rates are likely to result in zero or negative costs (benefit) to the economy.

While an overnight shift from 'taxes on value' to 'taxes on vice' is unlikely and potentially disruptive, a gradual shift towards environmental taxes would be a move in the right direction.[8] For example, income taxes could be reduced and the lost tax revenues replaced by product taxes on gasoline, chemicals and other polluting products. Of course, it would be more efficient to tax pollutants (SO_2, CO_2) directly rather than polluting products (fossil fuels), but tax setting and collecting would be more complex and costly, especially in developing countries with limited administrative and technical capability. It may also be true that product taxes tend to be regressive, but so are most conventional taxes; care must be taken in the design of such taxes so that the overall tax burden is progressive rather than regressive. Furthermore, the revenues from environmental taxes can be expanded in ways that mitigate or totally offset any adverse distributional impacts of these taxes.

CHARGE SYSTEMS

Environment charges are rarely distinguished from environmental taxes and are often used interchangeably, creating an unnecessary source of confusion and often a source of friction between ministries of finance and environmental agencies. In this study we distinguish between charge systems and fiscal instruments. Charges are defined as payments for use of resources, infrastructure and services and are akin to market prices for private goods. One way of thinking of charges is as 'prices' for public goods or publicly provided private goods. They differ from market prices for private goods because they are not market determined but are administratively set by a government agency, a public utility or other types of regulated natural monopoly. This contrasts them with taxes, which are not payments for 'services' but a means for raising fiscal revenue. Pigouvian taxes, however, may be thought of as a charge for the use of the environment's assimilative capacity (a natural resource or public good) and hence, analogous to a user charge.

A second difference between charges and taxes is that taxes are connected to the budget, forming part of the general government revenues, while charges are extra-budgetary, aiming to recover cost for a specific public investment or more appropriately, to finance the long-term marginal cost of supply. More importantly, charges are used as instruments of demand management and when set optimally (equal to the long-term marginal supply cost) they may or may not recover supply cost. When the long-term marginal supply cost is falling, 'optimal' user charges result in a deficit; when it is rising, they result in a surplus (see Figure 3.4). The deficit is usually met by a subsidy from the general budget, while the surplus either goes to the budget or more often is prevented through regulation of the tariffs charged by a public utility.

Due to this connection with the general budget and the propensity to supply utilities (eg, water, electricity), public services and use of infrastructure at zero or nominal cost, charges are perceived more as taxes than as prices. Yet, because there is a correspondence between use and payment, user charges are still seen as a means of partial cost recovery rather than as a source of general revenue. If anything, finance ministries might welcome a severance of the link between deficit generating utilities and the general budget. We may divide charge systems into three groups.

Pollution charges

The first group may be called pollution charges and it includes emission charges, effluent charges, solid waste charges, noise pollution charges, and product charges. When set at optimum levels (equal to the marginal damage cost), pollution charges are identical to Pigouvian taxes. Pollution charges are widely used in Europe, especially as revenue sources (see Box 3.7).

User fees

The second group of charges may be called direct or 'active' user charges and it includes utility charges (eg, for water, electricity, etc), road tolls and access fees (to parks, beaches, etc). These fees or charges are analogous but not identical to prices for private goods. Road tolls, for example, may be thought of as congestion prices not as prices for gaining access to roads. If there is no congestion, restricting access to roads through road pricing reduces social welfare because there is an unused opportunity to make someone better off without making anyone worse off, known as a 'Pareto improvement'.

Box 3.7 Pollution Charges in Russia

Pollution charges were introduced in the Russian Federation in 1991 since traditional command-and-control regulations throughout the economy were failing miserably. As in many formerly command economies, the charge is based on levels of pollution exceeding those allowed by industry-allocated pollution permits. The charge is based on the estimated average cost of implementing programmes to reduce emissions. The resulting amount calculated is then adjusted to reflect regional conditions, using a 'coefficient of ecological conditions'.

As in other countries in the region, funds collected from these charges are transferred to a national and several regional environmental funds. As part of the decentralization process, only a small portion of these funds are allocated to the state coffers, with the lion's share accruing to the regional environmental funds. While it is difficult to assess the success of the charges owing to the high level of evasion, there were almost $4 million in expenditures from the Federal Environmental Fund in 1994 alone. This is a mere drop in the ocean compared to the massive environmental problems facing the region and several improvements have been recommended:

1   simplification of the process and lowering of constraints placed on enterprises;
2   change from measurement based on a materials balance approach to more direct measurements of effluents and emissions;
3   more accurate and complete record-keeping; and
4   better monitoring and enforcement.

Source: Kozeltsev and Markandya (1997).

Betterment charges

The third group of charges may be called indirect or 'passive' user charges and they include betterment charges and impact fees. Betterment charges are usually imposed on private property that benefits from public investments. For example, private property values may increase manifoldly as a result of new roads, parks and environmental clean ups. While property taxes capture some of the windfall appreciation, betterment charges may also be imposed to collect revenues for financing the relevant public investment or for partial cost recovery. This is an application of the beneficiary pays principle and could be a major source of financing.

Impact fees

Impact fees are charges that aim to internalize the external cost of private investments (construction, tourism, or industrial development) on the landscape or the ambient environment. For example, a charge may be imposed per cubic metre of built-up space. The incentive effect here is stronger than with betterment charges, especially as it applies to new construction. As such, impact fees may be classified as 'visual pollution charges' and included in the first group. Generally impact fees are applied in cases of greater environmental impact, and may, in a sense, be thought of as the reverse of betterment charges.

FINANCIAL INSTRUMENTS

Financial instruments have many similarities with subsidy and tax incentive systems and share many of their limitations as well. Financial instruments are distinguished from fiscal instruments because they are often extra-budgetary and financed from foreign aid, external borrowing, debt for nature swaps and the like. Since funds are fungible and loans must be serviced and repaid somehow, the implications of financial subsidies are not very different from those more closely connected with the government budget. Often the motivation behind the creation of special funds for environmental protection or resource conservation is to avoid the scrutiny of the budgetary process. Yet, the propensity of many finance ministries to under-spend on resource conservation and environmental protection and to overspend on distortionary subsidies to environmentally destructive activities provides ample justification for earmarked environmental funds.

Environmental funds

When environmental funds are financed through environmental charges or external borrowing, they often become a source of friction with finance ministries that tend to regard them as soft funds, crowding out other higher-return private and public investments. Indeed, the principles of public finance dictate that such funds should not be earmarked if there is no direct relationship between what is bought and what is received, especially if the rate is based on ability to pay (ie taxes). In these cases, the revenues raised should go to the treasury to be reallocated across all consumers in the form of public goods such as roads, hospitals or schools. However, spending distortions such as subsidies and the fact that people's willingness to vote for new taxes and fees may depend on earmarking, may justify some form of earmarking.

Financial instruments such as revolving funds, green funds, relocation incentives and subsidized interest or soft loans for projects with significant positive externalities such as reforestation, may be justified as:

1   second-best responses to distorted or inefficient capital markets;
2   vehicles for internalizing positive externalities;
3   environmentally minded investors' willingness to pay for socially responsible investments; or
4   instruments for mobilizing additional financial resources for conservation, environmental protection and sustainable development.

While the instrumental value of financial incentives in a second-best world cannot be denied, the first-best policy is the correction of capital market imperfections, efficient budgetary allocations and full-cost pricing. Financial subsidies, soft loans, subsidized interest rates and foreign exchange or special funds are too blunt as instruments for the efficient internalization of external social costs.

LIABILITY SYSTEMS

Legal liability

This class of instruments aims to induce socially responsible behaviour by establishing legal liability for:

1   natural resource damage,
2   environmental damage,
3   property damage,
4   damage to human health or loss of life,
5   non-compliance to environmental laws and regulations, and
6   non-payment of due taxes, fees or charges.

The difference between liability systems and other instruments (except for enforcement incentives and non-compliance charges) is that the threat of legal action to recover damages is the economic instrument that internalizes the external cost in the first instance. Unlike taxes and charges that are set at the level of marginal damage cost to alter the relative probability of environmentally harmful products and activities, and unlike environmental bonds and deposit-refund systems which internalize ex ante, the environmental risk liability systems assess and recover damages ex post.

Liability insurance

Liability insurance has emerged as an instrument for pooling and sharing liability risks among liable parties. Liability systems are not recommended for developing countries with poorly developed legal systems, or with cultures that very rarely use courts to resolve disputes or award damages (although 'liability systems' are not unknown to traditional societies, where the tribal chief or the elders settle disputes and award damages). One particular type of liability system practised in the USA, the joint and several liability for hazardous waste sites, is particularly litigation-intensive and cost-ineffective. Legal fees rather than cleaning costs account for the bulk of the costs of the so-called Superfund for cleaning hazardous waste sites in the USA. This system is clearly unsuitable for developing countries, but even transitional economies with an inherited large number of contaminated sites would

Box 3.8 Performance Guarantee Bonds for Forest Management in the Philippines

In its efforts to halt deforestation and promote sustainable forest management, the Department of Environment and Natural Resources of the Philippines introduced a new type of forest lease agreement, known as Industrial Forest Management Agreement (IFMA). Under the agreement, private concessionaires are assigned responsibility for management of not only production forests but also protection forests and industrial plantations in deforested land, all within a single unit.

IFMAs are awarded not to the highest price bidder, but to the concessionaire who is prepared to post the highest performance guarantee bond to secure that all obligations under the lease would be discharged. A floor price of US$3.6 per cubic metre and a minimum value of $217 per hectare was also stipulated. The Forest Guarantee Bond (FGB) is in effect a refundable deposit with the government and has the following positive features:

1   It employs competitive bidding to allocate harvesting rights.
2   It encourages responsible long-term management by the concessionaire, who is rewarded with return of the bond with interest.
3   The concessionaire accumulates equity through improvements which can be realized through sale of rights.
4   It provides a means of penalizing the concessionaire in case of violation of the terms of the agreement and financial resources to effect remedy.
5   It provides a market signal of whether forest management is profitable in the particular area (low or no bond bids indicate unprofitability of management without government subsidy).

The form of FGB was left unspecified and most IFMA holders opted to post a surety bond obtained from a bonding company in exchange for a collateral and annual premium payments, rather than a cash bond deposited in one interest-bearing escrow account. While the system did not work as fully as envisioned, it has demonstrated the scope of innovative market-based instruments to internalize the benefits (costs) of good (bad) management in the form of capital costs. The system also aimed to some extent at subsidizing forest protection and reforestation from current revenue realized from timber. A drawback has been that the bond was not accompanied by a waiver of forest charges on timber contracted and was seen as an added burden rather than as an alternative to changes. [In a somewhat similar system, Chile requires forest concessionaires to acquire insurance policies to cover potential environmental damage.]

Source: Ruzicka and Speechly (1994).

do well to avoid burdening their privatization efforts and nascent markets with joint and several liabilities.[9]

PERFORMANCE BONDS AND DEPOSIT-REFUND SYSTEMS

Environmental performance bonds and deposit-refund systems are economic instruments that aim to shift responsibility for controlling pollution, monitoring and enforcement to individual producers and consumers who are charged in advance for the potential damage. Often the state is saddled with huge bills for cleaning up oil spills and contaminated land, for collection and treatment of hazardous waste, for reclamation of abandoned land after mining, for reforestation after logging and for man-made 'natural' disasters. In fact, a large portion of public environmental expenditures around the world is for restoration of degraded environments, which could be prevented or paid for by the polluters or beneficiaries of a cleaned environment. The government can reduce its share of the clean up and restoration bill (and, in fact, the overall size of the bill) by instituting, for example, deposit-refund systems, environmental bonds, bank guarantees for compliance with environmental rules and presumptive charges based on engineering or statistical output-waste coefficients, with refunds for improved efficiency.

Environmental bonds

Environmental bonds, for instance, ensure that:

1   resource extracting companies and potential polluters take adequate measures to minimize the environmental damage caused by their activities;
2   they effect clean up and restoration of residual damage in the most cost-effective manner; and
3   adequate funds are available for the clean up of waste and restoration of damaged environments by anyone who fails to comply. Environmental bonds need not be a constraint on economic activity, as they can be invested in interest-bearing accounts or replaced by bank guarantees. In developing countries environmental bonds can be made to work more effectively if they are guaranteed by a third, neutral party, are activity- and relative scope-specific, and bonds' rates are set carefully to reflect inflation and currency fluctuations (see Box 3.8).

Deposit-refund systems

Deposit-refund systems are applicable to a wide range of products and by-products from beverage containers and packaging of car batteries and vehicle hulks, to plastics and hazardous materials. In the absence of such deposit-refund systems, the government must expend scarce public revenues for their collection or leave such waste uncollected to litter water bodies and soils, thereby damaging public health and wildlife and

Box 3.9 Voluntary Agreements in Germany, the United States, Canada and India

Since the 1970s, various sectors of the German industry issued more than 70 self-commitments to reduce pollution, including greenhouse gases. For example, in March 1995, 15 industry associations in Germany voluntarily declared that they were prepared to reduce their CO_2 emissions by up to 20 per cent below 1987 levels by the year 2005. A year later, the Federation of German Industry issued an over-arching declaration committing its members to reduce CO_2 emissions by 20 per cent compared to 1990 levels. The government followed with a political declaration committing itself to refrain from additional regulatory measures on global warming prevention to allow the private initiative of the German industry to take effect. The government even went to the extent of promising either an exemption from any EU-wide carbon tax for those sectors of industry involved in the voluntary commitment, or a full credit for the CO_2 reductions achieved. In Europe, there are more than 300 voluntary environmental agreements.

In the United States, the government exempts private land owners from further requirements under the Endangered Species Act if they take approved voluntary measures to protect wildlife. As many as 225 Habitat Conservation Plans are now in existence under this programme. Critics call for the posting of bonds or other security in case additional conservation measures become necessary.

In 1991, the Federal Office of Pollution Prevention in Canada implemented a voluntary pledge programme called Accelerated Reduction/Elimination of Toxics (ARET). Under the programme, 278 private and public firms voluntarily pledged by the year 2000 to reduce their emissions of 30 persistent, bioaccumulative and toxic substances by 90 per cent and another 87 substances by 50 per cent. By 1995, emissions were reduced by 10,300 tons, including a 50 per cent reduction of high priority chemicals.

In a similar effort, the government of India has launched a campaign to encourage the industry (especially small and medium scale firms) to organize itself in Waste Minimization Circles. Each Circle brings together representatives of industries related either by process, product or location, to exchange information on waste reduction approaches and experiences. With leadership from within the group and technical assistance from a resource person from universities or technical institutions, each group meets periodically to discuss action-oriented ways to minimize waste.

Sources: http://www.ec.ca/aret/e12e1zchle.html; OECD (1995b).

harming the country's tourist potential and investment climate.[10] A great advantage of deposit-refund systems for developing countries is the inducement of a labour-intensive activity (waste collection) in an environment of low-cost, abundant, and underemployed labour.

Induced self-regulation

Induced self-regulation may be more efficient and cost-effective than direct government regulation because industries know best how to control their own waste. Self-enforcement is induced by reputational concerns and a desire to be accepted by other members of the association and by the community. The cost of policing and monitoring is significantly reduced and assumed directly by the source. The funds needed for environmental clean up and enforcement of environmental regulations are reduced and generated from within the industry in a manner that alters behaviour and the way of doing business (see Box 3.9).

An alternative approach is the establishment of Industrial Environmental Funds through presumptive charges on industries according to expected waste generation and use of such funds for environmental clean ups carried out by the private sector on a competitive basis. Combined with environmental auditing by accredited auditors and rebates (or surcharges) for better than (or worse than) average performance, such funds can serve both as incentive systems and as financing vehicles of sustainable development. For details on such a fund for Thailand, see Panayotou (1993a).

Chapter 4:
Creating Incentives for Sustainable Development

As noted earlier, economic instruments serve the dual function of creating incentives and of raising revenues for sustainable development. The relative significance of these functions varies depending on the type of instrument, the rate at which it is set and the elasticity of the demand for the commodity concerned. In this chapter we focus on the incentive effect of economic instruments and in the next chapter on their financing effect.

According to Stavins and Whitehead (1996), 'Market-based instruments are regulations that encourage behaviour through price signals rather than through explicit instructions on pollution control levels or methods'. This is literally true of taxes and charges and even tradable polluting permits but is only implicitly so of other instruments such as property rights and environmental bonds.

It is accurate to say that economic (in the sense of non-command) instruments encourage a change in behaviour through a change in the incentive structure, effected in a variety of ways from property rights, through price signals to legal liabilities and even official procurement policy (see Box 4.1). In what follows we examine how the various instruments we introduced in the previous chapter change the incentive structure phasing economic agents from those that promote environmental degradation to those that promote responsible management.

PROPERTY RIGHTS

With secure property rights, the price of resource commodities such as minerals, oil and timber reflects the resource depletion cost and provides the 'right' signals for efficient use and conservation in line with changing relative resource scarcities. This result is based on three assumptions:

1   that the resource markets that emerge following the assignment of secure property rights are competitive;
2   that there is no divergence between the private and the social rate of discount; and
3   that there are no significant externalities (such as negative environ-

---

Box 4.1 The US Green Procurement Policy

Since 1992, the Office of Federal Procurement Policy of the US Office of Management and Budget (OMB) and the Federal Energy Management Program (FEMP) of the US Department of Energy have been co-sponsoring the Federal Procurement Challenge. The Challenge helps federal agencies to comply with the Energy Policy Act of 1992 and Executive Order 12902, which directs all federal agencies to buy products that are among the 25 per cent most efficient in terms of energy and water use, or at least 10 per cent more efficient than DOE's national efficiency standards. Twenty-two federal agencies accounting for 95 per cent of federal purchasing are participating in the Challenge. The FEMP publishes energy efficiency recommendations for meeting the Executive Order and provides technical support for meeting the goals of the Challenge. The direct objectives of the Federal Procurement Challenge are to: (a) save taxpayers' money; (b) conserve energy, water and other natural resources; and (c) reduce federal emissions, including greenhouse gases, by the federal government. But more important than the direct benefits of the Challenge are the indirect effects that it levers: it helps support and expand the market for 'best-practice' energy-efficient, resource saving products; it lowers the cost of environmentally friendly products by providing scale economies and a large and reliable market; it provides leadership for state and city governments as well as corporate and other institutional purchasers to give preference to environmentally sound products and services in their purchases.

Source: US Department of Energy, Federal Energy Management Program (FEMP), The Federal Procurement Challenge,
http://www.eren.doe.gov/femp/procurement/challenge.html

---

mental impacts) from resource extraction that have not been internalized through the established property rights.

If these conditions are not met, secure property rights alone do not suffice to create the right incentives for socially optimal resource allocation: more specifically, non-competitive markets lead to a distorted time path of resource use; higher private discount rates lead to faster resource depletion than is socially optimal;[1] and unaccounted, negative environmental externalities have a similar effect. Hence, additional instruments are necessary to promote competition or regulate monopolies, to induce a longer time horizon and to internalize off-site effects.

While the policy maker has a large toolkit of economic and regulatory instruments (taxes, charges, subsidies and the like) to choose from to complement the assignment of property rights, the assignment of secure, exclusive and transferable property rights goes a long way in correcting the incentive structure and altering the behaviour of resource users to a form that more closely conforms to socially responsible behaviour.

One example of assignment of property rights is the granting of rights of use of a resource. User rights by themselves do not ensure efficient use and sustainability. For example, a user that conserves or invests in the resource assumes all the costs yet can capture only a small part of the benefits; the rest accrue to other users, who have an incentive to free ride. Even for resources with minimal externalities, (eg, cropland), use rights that are limited in duration and non-transferable (eg, usufruct or stewardship certificates) discourage conservation and investment by: (a) short-time horizon or uncertainty of tenure; and (b) the inability to recoup the costs and liquidate any equity value accumulated through investment in the resource such as land improvement, soil conservation and forest regeneration. Classic examples are logging firms with short-term forest concessions, shifting cultivators and farmers with short-term tenure. This problem can be partially addressed through longer contract duration, renewability and transferability of concession and use rights. At the limit, indefinite, freely transferable, comprehensive and exclusive use rights are equivalent to full ownership rights and have the same conservation incentive effects.

In situations where assignment of private rights is technically not possible or socially unacceptable, recognition of traditional command property rights and their protection against outside pressures may be a more efficient, equitable and sustainable arrangement than formal use rights (eg, licensing) or other attempts at apportionment. A key consideration is the existence in the community of a social organization for joint management and enforcement of norms of access and use.

MARKET CREATION

Tradable emission permits

Trading of pollution rights (or permits) would ensure that the assimilative capacity of the environment, a scarce resource, is put to its best possible use and that a given level of emissions reduction is achieved at the least cost. Over time, economic growth and the need for expansion of economic activity would induce industries to become increasingly more efficient in the use of the environment, to further reduce waste per unit of output and to develop new non-polluting technologies and products as well as more efficient pollution abatement methods, to make room for expansion with the limited number of pollution permits.

Industrial producers with a deficit of permits or with expansion plans must secure emission permits by reducing emissions from existing plants. Alternatively, they may purchase permits from other polluters who are either able to reduce emissions at a lower cost than them or who find it more profitable to sell their permits than use them themselves. Thereby, the desired reduction of emissions (and hence the desired level of ambient environmental quality) is attained at the minimum possible cost to society. At the same time, a strong incentive is provided for continued efforts to improve efficiency and to develop cleaner technologies.

Even if the aggregate quota of permits is set at the current level of emissions, the expansion of economic activity creates a scarcity of permits with all the desired incentives described above. Furthermore, government and non-government environmental organizations have always the option to purchase and retire pollution permits in order to speed up improvement in environmental quality. In the USA, for example, the Environmental Defense Fund (EDF), Department of Energy (DOE), Arizona Public Service and Niagra Mohawk (NiMo), a New York utility, participate in one such programme. They 'exchange SO_2 emissions allowances issued under the Clean Air Act's Acid Rain program for excess CO_2 emissions reductions that may be used to meet explicit commitments made to DOE to reduce greenhouse gas emissions' (Environmental Defense Fund, 1994). NiMo has agreed to then donate the CO_2 allowances to an environmental organization to be retired.

Whether the emission permits are issued free of charge, sold at a fixed price or auctioned to the highest bidder makes no difference from the point of view of economic efficiency. As long as they are fixed in number and freely tradable, the level of emissions reduction will be attained at the lowest possible cost to society. Distributionally, however, it matters a lot. Awarding pollution permits to polluters free of charge amounts to assigning property rights to them over the assimilative capacity of the environment, or at least a use right, up to the specified level described in the permit. Thus, the permit entitles the polluter to the present value of the stream of profits arising from free disposal of the allowable amount of emissions into the environment. If the permits are instead sold or auctioned, the state is the recipient of the revenues, which can then be passed on to the citizens either in the form of an increased supply of public goods or lower taxes.

Alternatively, emission permits could be allocated to the general public (say, one person/one permit) with the total number of permits fixed at the socially acceptable level of emissions. Polluters would then have to buy their permits from the general public, which has, under this allocation, the entitlement to the present value of benefits from the use of the assimilative capacity of the environment. In other words, the general public has the right to an unpolluted environment and should be compensated by the polluters for any reduction in environmental quality. This, unlike the allocations discussed earlier, is consistent with the polluter pays principle. Different combinations are also possible, for example 50 per cent to polluters and 50 per cent to the general public; or 30 per cent to current polluters, 20 per cent to future polluters, 20 per cent to the public, 20 per cent to the government (or the environmental protection agency) and 10 per cent to environmental NGOs.

Whatever the allocation, efficiency and environmental quality are not compromised, only the distributional implications are different. Therefore, those who criticize pollution permits as a right to pollute are correct only in the case where the polluters are given the permit for free. If the polluter has paid a market price for the permit, the criticism could only be that the 'price' of the permit is 'too low,' or the supply of permits is 'too large,' which is the equivalent to saying a higher level of environmental quality is desired.

Tradable development quotas

When choosing the number of tradable development quotas to be allowed, just as with emission permits, an aggregate level of development must be chosen. The resulting allocation of permits creates a market reflecting scarcity of space available for development. Since the quotas have a high and possibly rising scarcity value, they are used only for high-quality tourist development with more open spaces, green areas and environmentally sensitive landscaping that would allow charging higher prices.

Additional development quotas could be acquired by a developer through retirement of equal (or larger, eg, 1.5) existing built-up space in the same zone. This would act as a strong incentive for upgrading existing establishments, since no one else would be willing to incur the cost of demolition and new construction unless he/she planned to develop a higher quality, more profitable establishment. Moreover, owners of low-quality units can always sell their grandfathered development rights in the market for development quotas. The upgrading of existing units can also be accelerated by setting a less-than-one-to-one ratio of grandfathered development rights to development quotas or by introducing a graduated charge on built-up space (old and new), which would also vary by quality of establishment (two to three classes of quality).

Tradable water shares

Tradable water shares are another example of market creation to induce efficient resource allocation and create incentives to conserve the resource. Consider surface irrigation systems in developing countries. Farmers receive irrigation water free of charge. The result is overuse by those with easy access, with consequent waterlogging and salinization of soils while lands further afield or downstream suffer from shortage and water stress. The consequence is that the value of the marginal product of water in much of the irrigated agriculture is near zero or even negative, as waterlogged farmland becomes less productive, while other users (cities, industry, farmers with inadequate and unreliable supplies) are willing to pay a high price for additional water quantity. The value of the marginal product to the urban and industrial user is several times higher than that of farmers with easy and often free access to irrigation systems.

Calls for irrigation water pricing have been rejected by both farmers and governments as regressive and unfair since farmers are often among the lowest income groups. However, tradable water shares can address all the equity concerns of policy makers and at the same time improve the efficiency of water use by directing it to its higher value use. In fact, this instrument can improve income distribution by assigning property rights (water shares) to an increasingly scarce resource to smallholders and the landless and by providing them with a new market opportunity. At the same time water resource conservation is influenced as higher prices encourage more efficient use of the resource and the environment is spared of new dams and pipelines. Economic efficiency is increased as the price of water is equated to the marginal cost of its provision and the aggregate benefits from this scarce resource are being maximized. All these are necessary conditions for sustainable development.

To recap, the following outcomes are certain to result as we move from unowned and unpriced water to tradable water shares:

1   The water share holders will use their water share as they judge best for themselves, and they will be significantly better off as a result.
2   Water scarcities in previous deficit areas will fall and the effective price that users pay, for example to private vendors, will be reduced.
3   Water will flow to the higher value use much in the same way as it flows downhill by gravity.
4   Water will be used efficiently by both rural and urban users and conserved as a valuable commodity.
5   Supply expansion will become unnecessary or be postponed for several years, saving the environment from the impacts of new dam and/or pipeline construction.

Despite the many benefits of such an arrangement, there are different technical and institutional problems to resolve. Water share allocation requires the ability to control, monitor and meter water flows and water use. This may be technically difficult and costly, especially when it involves many small farmers scattered throughout the countryside. Transaction costs can be reduced significantly, however, by allocating bulk water shares to water user associations for further allocating to their members.

FISCAL INSTRUMENTS

Pollution taxes

Taxes on pollutants, known also as pollution charges, are applied directly to the offending substances thereby providing the maximum incentive and flexibility for the polluter to reduce pollution. As a result, pollution charges are more efficient than indirect taxes on inputs or final products. The latter does not provide an incentive to limit the pollutant itself, only to use less of the input or produce (consume) less of the final product. For example, taxes on products or inputs do not provide incentives for the development and installation of pollution abatement technologies. Only when the pollution-product coefficient is fixed are pollution charges and polluting product taxes equivalent. Depending on the elasticities of supply and demand, part or all of the pollution charge will be reflected in the price of the final product; a strong incentive for the consumer to switch to less expensive substitutes (which are also less polluting if these prices reflect negative environmental externalities) and for the polluter to switch to products that are less harmful to the environment.

Emission and effluent taxes can be structured in such a way as to provide a progressive incentive for pollution control. For example, in Germany, polluters who more than meet the set effluent standards are charged a lower rate while those who violate the standards pay a higher rate than the charge set for those who meet emissions standards. Care should be taken in the design of emission and effluent taxes so as not to create perverse incentives. Effluent taxes set as a percentage of pollutant in total effluent, for example, provide incentives to 'water down' effluents while having no effect on the reduction of total pollution emitted.

Taxes on inputs and final products

The taxes on inputs and final products induce a reduction in the use of environmentally harmful products and proportional reduction in the production of pollutants but they do not necessarily provide an incentive for pollution abatement. Their ability to act as an incentive for pollution reduction depends on their level being high enough and the demand for the product elastic enough to discourage the consumption and thus production of the product. Hence, taxes on inputs and final products tend to be less efficient than taxes on emissions or effluents but may save significantly in terms of monitoring, policing and enforcement costs (see Box 4.2).

Differential tax structure

The purpose of a differential tax structure as described in the previous chapter, is to induce a switching from polluting products to environmentally friendly substitutes. If no such substitutes exist, differential taxation becomes a distortion. Since tax differentiation has by definition an incentive purpose, the differential tax is often calculated to be revenue neutral. An example is provided by the differential taxation of leaded and unleaded gasoline practised in Thailand to induce switching to a cleaner fuel.[2]

Investment tax incentives

The investment tax incentive subsidizes overall investment and thereby induces an increase rather than a decrease in the level of pollution; there is no incentive to actually reduce pollution (only to install the equipment). Investment tax incentives are generally a source of distor-

---

Box 4.2 Sulphur Taxes in Sweden

In Sweden the tax on the sulphur content of fuels is a good example of living within your administrative means. While the 'best' instrument for reducing sulphur emissions is an emissions tax or tradable emissions permits, both of these approaches are complex to administer; economic instruments like these may be efficient, but they do not substantially reduce the requirement for monitoring and enforcement of the policy. The alternative implemented in Sweden in 1990 is a hybrid: a substantial tax is levied on the sulphur content of fuels (over $4 per kg of sulphur), but this is rebated for large emitters who can prove how much sulphur emission they have abated (through flue gas desulphurization, for instance). For large emitters, therefore, the effect of the sulphur tax is precisely the same as an emissions tax; for everybody else the tax on the sulphur content of fuels provides incentives to switch to low-sulphur fuels and to reduce energy use overall.

This tax on fuels is relatively simple to implement because it can be levied at the wholesale level. To date, administrative costs have been less than 1 per cent of revenue. For any country that has an excise regime for fuels, the sulphur content tax would be a straightforward addition to the existing administrative apparatus.

The Swedish sulphur tax has been extremely effective. The national target for sulphur emissions was met several years ahead of schedule, and the revenue from the tax was actually lower than projected, as a result of the extensive fuel switching and emission reductions that followed introduction of the tax.

Source: World Bank (1997a).

---

tion with hidden but large costs that should be avoided as much as direct subsidies.

Industrial relocation incentives

As a temporary incentive for relocation, the tax credit has some merit. But, just as investment tax incentives can be counter-productive to the long-term pollution reduction objective, if maintained for a long time, industrial relocation tax credits will become a subsidy for polluting industries, increasing pollution and draining the government budget.

Fiscal policy reform

The implied reduced incentives for work, savings, investment and conservation that are inherent in current tax policies and the increased incentives for leisure, consumption, resource depletion and environmental degradation result in less growth and more environmental degradation than would be the case were incentives the reverse. It has been argued that under certain conditions, the move from current tax policies to an environmental tax system would reap a 'double dividend': environmental improvement from reduced production and consumption of polluting products while reducing the disincentive for work and saving in the current tax system. This turns out to be true only under certain conditions that involve the reduction of high marginal tax rates on certain factors of production (eg, capital) and the replacement of the lost revenue by broad-based environmental taxes (eg, energy taxes) whose incidence falls on factors of production with low marginal tax rates. For a more comprehensive discussion of this issue, see Goulder (1995).

CHARGE SYSTEMS

The primary objective of pollution charges ought to be the change in the incentive structure facing the users of scarce resources so as to induce a realignment of their behaviour with social interests. In this spirit, user charges are instruments for reducing wasteful use, managing demand and inducing conservation and secondarily, are instruments for recovering cost or financing supply expansion.[3] Similarly, pollution charges are instruments for internalizing external costs and encouraging pollution control and secondarily, are a means for raising revenues to finance environmental investments (see Box 4.3). By the same theory, it is possible to design a system of charges that is revenue neutral (ie it raises no revenues), yet accomplishes the desired level of pollution reduction. Impact fees, when optimally set, can have significant incentive effect on the environmental soundness and the sustainability of investment projects as well as providing the needed resources for public infrastructure necessary to serve new developments without resulting in crowding and congestion.

Betterment charges can have an incentive effect too, but this is more limited and indirect than that of the user charges or impact fees. If set sufficiently high, betterment charges may reduce the incentive for private landowners to lobby government officials to influence the location, type and level of public infrastructure and services in order to benefit their property.

LIABILITY SYSTEMS

In a sense, all economic instruments have as an ultimate enforcement incentive the threat of legal action and the use of the state's coercive powers, for example if effluent taxes are not paid or an adequate number of emission permits to cover emissions are not purchased. Administrative and ultimately legal measures are provided to ensure compliance and these systems do have the effect of preventive incentives as long as the expected (certainty equivalent) damage payments exceed the benefits from non-compliance. The frequency with which liability cases are brought to the courts, and the magnitude of damages awarded, influence ex ante behaviour of potentially liable parties.

While there is some justified concern about moral hazard since the

---

Box 4.3 Pollution Charges in the Czech Republic

After the transition from a command economy in the early 1990s, the Czech Republic, like its neighbours, rewrote its environmental legislation. In the new legislation, the Czech Republic attempted to incorporate some of the environmental lessons of other industrialized countries, including less reliance on command-and-control standards. Among the economic instruments the Czech Republic experimented with were the following environmental charges:

- air pollution charges;
- water pollution charges;
- solid-waste disposal charges;
- charges for the off-take of water from waterways;
- charges for the withdrawal of underground water;
- levies for the sequestration of agricultural land from the agricultural domain; and
- charges for the mining of minerals.

However, like its neighbours to the West, the Czech Republic has set the charges at too low a rate to act as incentives to actively reduce pollution. In addition, the rates have been eroded by inflation. Nevertheless, the charges raised large amounts of monies for the State Environmental Fund. Air pollution charges alone raised about $120,000 in 1994.

Source: Stepanek (1997).

---

insured can be confident they are 'covered' for damages, the incentive effect of liability systems is not significantly dampened as long as the liability insurance premium varies with individual behaviour or performance. For example, vehicle accident insurance may vary with the individual's driving habits and/or past accident record; the knowledge that insurance rates will increase after a reported violation create incentives to avoid violations. Environmental damage liability insurance requires a system of monitoring and reporting of violations as well as enforcement. Where potential damages are very large relative to the ability of the individual agent to pay a certain minimum level of damages, liability insurance is mandated by law.

ENVIRONMENTAL BONDS AND DEPOSIT-REFUND SYSTEMS

Environmental performance bonds act as incentives for environmentally responsible behaviour only where the size of the bond exceeds the expected benefits from non-compliance and consequent forfeiture of the bond. They are easier to administer than pollution charges or impact fees but they do not have the same efficiency properties since the level of the bond is not incremental and not equated to marginal

---

Box 4.4 Deposit-refund systems in Korea

Korea uses an extensive waste disposal deposit-refund system which covers food, beverages, liquor bottles and containers, batteries, tyres, lubricating oil, electric home appliances (and any other item that generates toxic waste), bulky or heavy commodities that require treatment, non-degradable materials and harmful household commodities that should not be mixed with the general waste stream (Shin, 1994). The manufacturer is required to deposit a certain amount for each unit sold, refundable upon collection and treatment.

While the system can be improved by more careful selection of the items included, by increasing the deposit fee and by not restricting reimbursement to the original depositor, its potential for developing countries is enormous and largely unexploited. A great advantage of deposit-refund systems for developing countries is the inducement of a labour-intensive activity (waste collection) in an environment of low-cost, abundant and underemployed labour with significant economic, environmental and distributional benefits.

Source: Panayotou (1995a).

---

environmental damage; if set too low, a bond can be totally ineffective as an incentive. However, it is possible to structure the rebate of environmental bonds in such a way as to provide incentives for responsible behaviour at the margin.

As with environmental bonds, deposit-refund systems shift the responsibility for controlling environmental degradation to the producers and consumers of polluting products, who are thereby induced to return the by-products of their production and consumption for recycling or treatment and safe disposal or otherwise to finance their collection and return by others (see Box 4.4).

INDUCED SELF-REGULATION AND SUASIVE INSTRUMENTS

There are many other ways in which governments can induce the private sector to assume responsibility for waste minimization. For example, industrial associations for specific types of industries (eg, agrochemicals, sugar mills, palm oil mills, electroplating plants, etc) or for specific locations (eg, around a lake, on a river, on a segment of coast or in an industrial estate) can be given the choice of attaining a certain ambient level of water or air quality on their own or be directly regulated by a government regulatory agency. Experience in Germany with industries operating on the Ruhr river, in Thailand with sugar mills, and a variety of factories in Japan, suggest that a well-identified community of polluters will choose self-regulation and self-enforcement if they are convinced that they cannot otherwise evade environmental regulations. The government need only monitor ambient quality and impose charges on the association for non-compliance, or wave the 'threat' of direct regulation. This approach may not work in all situations but it will work in a sufficient number of cases to achieve a substantial reduction in the level of public funding necessary to promote sustainable industrial development.

Voluntary or suasive instruments also attempt a less heavy-handed, more collaborative approach to environmental management. There is growing evidence[4] that informal regulation such as internal management practices and external community pressures are just as important, and in some cases more important than formal regulation. There are many possible measures of firm-level environmental management (or respon-siveness) ranging from the formulation of environmental plans and the performance of environmental audits, through location decisions and environment investments in pollution control and abatement. Informal regulations can minimize the costs of monitoring and enforcement as well as empower those directly affected by the regulations.[5]

A new approach to self-regulation that gained considerable interest and momentum in recent years is the so-called 'informational regula-tion' which encourages the production of information about pollution generation both as a source of incentive for behavioural change and as a benchmark for subsequent regulation. The best known example is the US Toxic Release Inventory (TRI) which requires the industry to report the amounts of toxic materials they put into the environment. While this system has led to a reduction in the amount of toxics released, there is a debate over why this happened. One hypothesis is that the TRI gave firms a benchmark to compare their performance to that of other firms. A developing country example is provided by Indonesia's rating of the environmental performance of firms via a colour scheme and the public release of this information to induce a behavioural change. The release of information makes it possible for communities and markets to react to the environmental performance of firms and thereby creates reputa-tional and financial incentives to behave in a socially more responsible manner by controlling waste and investing in pollution abatement (see Afsah et al, 1995). Similar schemes are currently operating in a number of developing countries. Indonesia's PROPER (see Chapter 10) and the Philippines' 'Ecowatch' grade firms based on their environmental performance and publish the ratings.

Another informational scheme is ecolabelling, by which the indus-try voluntarily establishes reporting requirements to inform consumers of products' relative 'greenness'. In this way, the consumer registers demand for more environmentally-friendly goods by purchasing products that have been awarded ecolabels (see Box 4.5).

Indeed, there are several mechanisms for developing a culture of environmental compliance as indicated in Table 4.1. One such mecha-nism is the reaction of capital markets to the announcement of environmental events involving publicly traded companies. Dasgupta et al (1997) have found that capital markets in Argentina, Chile, Mexico and the Philippines 'have penalized firms suffering from adverse environmental events and rewarded firms with positive

Table 4.1 *Mechanisms for Developing a Culture of Industrial Environmental Compliance*

Mechanism	Requirements	Impact
Pollution inventories	Industry and government monitoring and dissemination of data on ambient environment and pollution loads;	Provides stakeholders with a basic environmental information base to understand pollution problems better and to make informed decisions
Information on enterprise performance	Industry monitoring pollution loads; communications strategy for disseminating information	Collection and dissemination of environmental information can result in (a) an informed constituency which can effectively demand improvement from firms with poor performance and (b) open discussions with communities which can reduce mistrust
Cleaner production techniques	Government: regulation & real natural resource pricing. Industry: commitment from management	Improvements in industrial processes and management reduce the volume of pollution generated; increase production efficiencies and cut overall operating costs.
Environmental management systems	International trade and market pressures; commitment from management	Ensures that impacts of industry facilities are managed by process of continuous environmental improvements that are regularly monitored, measured and reported
Supplier chain impacts	International trade and market pressures; larger firms concerned with reputation and quality of products	Large firms work with smaller ones to provide advice and mentoring on developing environmental management systems and improving overall environmental performance
Negotiated agreements and government-industry partnerships	Flexible government structures; political stability; trust between government and industry; persuasion and social pressures	Creates mechanism for consensus building among major stakeholders to commit to achieving clearly defined environmental goals

Source: World Bank (1997b).

environmental news'. They also found evidence that firms respond by improving their environmental performance. For example, Chilgener of Chile suffered a loss of 5 per cent of its market share after it released a cloud of toxic air pollution over Santiago in April 1992; in September 1992 the company announced an investment of $115 million to control air pollution (Dasgupta et al, 1997).

Box 4.5 The Nordic Ecolabelling Scheme and Other Emerging Schemes

In 1989 the Nordic countries (Finland, Iceland, Norway and Sweden) introduced the Nordic Ecolabelling scheme, the first harmonized voluntary multinational ecolabelling programme. The objectives of the scheme are to guide consumers in choosing the least environmentally harmful products, to encourage the development of environmentally friendly products and to tap market forces to reinforce the effect of environmental legislation. The Coordinating Body for Eco-Labelling oversees the Nordic White Swan Environmental Labelling scheme by setting general guidelines. The scheme is operated by the national boards in each member country, which establishes specific criteria and award labels. The criteria are based on life cycle analysis of products, including consumption of natural resources and energy and generation of air and water emissions and solid waste. Internationally standardized test methods are applied and reporting of testing procedures and data is required. The Nordic Ecolabelling scheme parallels the EU Eco-Label scheme.

Several developing countries, including China, Korea, Peru and Cost Rica, are beginning to introduce ecolabelling schemes. Following the Rio Summit, the Chinese government introduced the 'Ten Points for Environment and Development', which designates the development of environmentally friendly products as one of the country's priorities. In 1993, the National Environmental Protection Agency (NEPA) announced the establishment of the National Environmental Labelling Programme, and in 1994, the establishment of the China Committee for Environmental Labelling to administer the Programme, select product categories, set criteria, and approve certifications.

Sources: Yang (1996).

Chapter 5

Raising Revenues for Sustainable Development

FINANCING NEEDS

The financial needs of individual countries and of the global economy for pursuing sustainable development depend critically on what is assumed about national and international policies. Without phasing out the distortions of market and policy failures, sustainable development would be an uphill struggle. What is needed is reversal of the flow not a march at a different pace in the wrong direction.

Keeping this in mind, we may classify financing needs into: (a) private vs. public; and (b) internal vs. external. The private sector needs funds to comply with regulations, to pay pollution charges, to undertake environmental investments, to retrofit or relocate existing plants and equipment, to redesign products and to invest in technological innovation. This is not to say that these apparent funding needs of the private sector are all new and additional. An increasing number of industrial firms, particularly in Organization for Economic Cooperation and Development (OECD) countries (eg, 3M, Dupont, Dow Chemicals, Volvo, Bayer) report that as a result of environmental regulations, they have uncovered within the firm a large number of environmental projects that generate surplus financial resources (profits) that can be used to undertake further environmental investments within the firm. For example, in the United States, 3M reports that over a ten year period more than 1000 such projects were identified and implemented, generating profits of over US$1 billion. For an economic analysis of these win–win opportunities, see Panayotou and Zinnes (1993).

The public sector's financial needs for environmental management and sustainable development are varied and far-reaching. Financial resources are needed for combating poverty and improving health, for halting deforestation and controlling desertification, for reducing population pressures and protecting fragile ecosystems, for rehabilitating deforested watersheds and promoting sustainable agriculture, for providing clean water and sanitation, and for addressing urban congestion and air pollution problems, to mention only a few. Clearly, no developing country has the resources to address all these problems directly, not even to stabilize environmental degradation at current levels. Nor are there prospects that adequate resources can be transferred from external sources to address these problems through direct public sector investment. Therefore, public sector expenditures are by necessity limited to interventions that have catalytic or demonstration value and that lever additional resources from the private sector (both domestic and foreign), and which finance the supply of public goods that are undersupplied by the market.

The financial needs of the public sector in its role as facilitator and regulator of economic activity are defined by the costs of establishing the necessary institutions and incentive systems for advancing sustainable development. These costs include design, information, administration and enforcement costs, as well as the cost of supplying the basic environmental infrastructure (legal, human and physical). Like the private sector, the public sector may find that a good part of the needed financial resources can be found within the sector through win–win interventions such as the phasing out of distortionary subsidies, redeployment of existing resources, revenues generated by incentive systems and the like.

The need for external financial resources

Despite the prospects for reducing financial needs and generating additional funds from domestic sources, the need for the infusion of external financial resources is not eliminated, though it can be substantially reduced. External financial resources are needed for many purposes:

1   Owing to domestic capital constraints there is a need for external financing to bridge the gap between the domestic demand (both private and public) and the domestic supply. While correction of capital market imperfections (eg, interest rate ceilings) is the first-best solution to the capital constraint, it is neither sufficient nor achievable overnight without undue disruption.
2   External funds are needed to resolve 'cash flow' problems arising from the time distance between the benefits and costs of projects and policies.
3   Financing is often needed to cushion the short-term impacts of policy reforms: to pay compensation to those adversely affected or to build consensus for the reforms. Availability of external sources of funding for this purpose can encourage and provide leverage for policy reforms.
4   External resources are necessary for financing the foreign exchange components of investments, and to build investors' confidence as well as to leverage domestic sources of financing; they may also have demonstration benefits.
5   Cleaning up past contamination (eg, hazardous waste sites) and restoring damaged natural resources are often extremely costly and capital- and technology-intensive. Large-scale clean up and resource restoration generally cannot be accomplished with domes-

tic resources without distortionary or excessive taxation and crowding out of other investments as the East European experience of the past few years demonstrates. Therefore, such clean up should be limited to sites with significant health impact or productivity losses and financed with external financial resources to the largest extent possible.

6 Most importantly, there is a need for external financing (in the form of grants and loans) to internalize global externalities: to pay the incremental costs of projects that have both local and global benefits; projects that would not be undertaken otherwise. This type of external financing does not represent development assistance or resource transfer, but payment for conservation services provided by developing countries to the global community over and above what they otherwise have the economic incentive to provide. This financial need may arise from international conventions or simply from pressures from developed countries or the global community to conserve resources of global value. It may also arise from the host country itself wanting to avoid irreversible losses of environmental assets in earlier years (when poorer) that may be highly valued in later years (when richer).

Financing requirements of Agenda 21

The United Nations Conference on Environment and Development (UNCED) Secretariat estimated that implementation of all activities under Agenda 21 from 1993 to 2000 would require additional resources of US$125 billion a year, or 1 per cent of the North's gross national product (GNP). In addition, governments and the private sector in the South would need to expend another US$500 billion a year to put their economies on a sustainable development path. While only tentative estimates, these figures help put into perspective the progress achieved during and since UNCED to secure the resources for the transition to a sustainable economy.

The UNCED Secretariat found the external finance figure of US$125 billion by estimating the cost of addressing sector- and resource-specific environment and development problems. The sectoral distribution is given in Table 5.1. The total estimate of external financial needs is within the same order of magnitude of estimates by other sources. The Worldwatch Institute has estimated the concessional finance needs of sustainable development at US$145 billion annually (1988 estimate) (Roodman, 1996). The WIDER Programme of the UN University put the figure at US$60 billion in 1993, rising to US$140 billion by the year 2000. The World Resources Institute estimated the additional financial resources needed at the more modest level of US$20–50 billion annually (WRI, 1987). Even the most modest of these estimates is several orders of magnitude in excess of what has been made available in the post-Rio years and does not appear to be within the realm of possibility in terms of conventional sources of international development financing.

Table 5.1 *Financing Sustainable Development: Agenda 21 Estimates of Needed Additional Concessional Funds*

Annual costs $m for the period 1993–2000 Sector/Policy	Amount ($m)
Accelerating sustainable development	9000
Combating poverty	15000
Demographic dynamics and sustainability	4000
Improved health	6500
Improved urban environment	29300
Protecting the atmosphere	21230
Planning of land resources	50
Combating deforestation	5670
Fragile ecosystems	
• desert areas	4885
• mountain ecosystems	2400
Biodiversity	1750
Biotechnology	200
Oceans	902
Fresh water resources	17040
Toxic chemicals	225
Hazardous wastes	1250
Solid wastes	1250
Radioactive effects	64
Sustainable agriculture	5100
Total	125,816

Source: Markandya (1994).

Available resources

In the long run the available domestic resources are defined by the country's revenue mobilization capacity, which is determined by the national income and by the private and public sectors' propensity to save.[1] The percentage of GNP saved and invested varies among countries from a low of 5–10 per cent to a high of 30–40 per cent. Sustainability requires that the formation of new capital (human, man-made, natural and environmental) equal the sum of rents from natural resource depletion and environmental damages.[2] For sustainable development, capital formation needs to be even higher. To this, one should also add the cost of rehabilitation of degraded resources and environmental clean up to the extent that it is worth doing. Therefore, it is possible to determine whether a country saves and invests sufficiently to sustain (or raise) current living standards and environmental quality by comparing aggregate savings (net investments) to rent generation (revenue depletion) and environmental damage incurred. By this measure (which is quite generous because it assumes perfect substitutability between different forms of capital), many developing (and quite a few developed) countries would not qualify as sustainable economies.

While there is a wide scope for increased domestic resource mobilization (higher rates of savings), the UNCED-estimated domestic financing gap of US$500 billion per anum cannot be viewed as entirely available to be raised through increased savings alone, for it accounts for almost 10 per cent of the developing world's GNP. At least half of the amount will need to come from redeployment and more efficient use of existing resources and from removal of barriers to economic growth and sustainable development, the subject of the following section.

As discussed at the outset of this chapter, external financial resources are also needed to supplement and to leverage domestic resources. Official development assistance (ODA) amounts to under US$60 billion or about 0.30 per cent of the GNP of OECD countries (OECD, 1996b). This figure is clearly inadequate when compared with the estimated financial needs of developing countries and with the outflow of resources for debt servicing at the level of US$60–70 billion annually. The goal of Agenda 21 was to raise additional external funds for sustainable development in part by increasing bilateral and multi-lateral ODA to 0.7 per cent of the GNP of OECD countries. Were this goal feasible, half of the estimated external financing need would have been met. The chances of this happening, however, are minimal considering the political difficulties of maintaining even the current levels of ODA. While some additional concessional financing could be forthcoming for special programmes such as population, literacy and environment, ODA is not expected to contribute substantially to closing the external financing gap.

Various approaches to debt relief, such as debt rescheduling, debt-for-equity, or debt-for-nature swaps and debt forgiveness have contributed to a reduction of the outflow of financial resources from developing countries and can continue to make contributions to external financing for those countries which are actually servicing their debts. In this regard, debt-for-policy reforms or debt-for-sustainable development may have a greater promise than the narrowly conceived debt-for-nature swaps. Again, this is not expected to be a major source of external financing of sustainable development.

In contrast to the stagnation of official development assistance, private capital flows to developing countries have grown unexpectedly and rapidly. While private capital flows are not a substitute for ODA, they are a useful, indeed necessary, complement and help free resources for more targeted assistance to the poorest countries. Private capital flows to developing countries have grown from being less than ODA in 1991 to being 3–4 times the level of official aid today. The share of private capital flows in aggregate resource flows to developing countries has almost doubled from about 40 per cent in 1990 to about 80 per cent in 1996. The role of private capital flows in capital formation in developing countries has increased dramatically. Today they account for 15 per cent of fixed investment in developing countries compared to only 3.7 per cent in 1990. Unlike ODA, private capital flows did not gravitate to the poorest countries. About 80 per cent of private capital flows and three-quarters of foreign direct investment (FDI) since 1990 went to 12 middle-income countries. What does the rapid growth of private capital flows mean for sustainable development? As indicated already, private capital flows (including FDI) are not substitutes for, but complements to ODA, since poor countries which need them most attract the least. Moreover, private investment is not automatically channelled to sustainable development activities. On the contrary, social and environmental areas traditionally have been among the activities least attractive to foreign investors, partly because of government regulations that limited foreign (and even domestic) private-sector involvement. Moreover, without enforcement of environmental regulations and freedom to charge user fees or raise tariffs to cover costs (including an acceptable return to capital) these sectors are not attractive to private capital.

All three conventions dealing with global issues – climate change, biodiversity, and ozone – have recognized the need to transfer financial resources to developing countries to enable them to comply with their provisions. However, only the Montreal Protocol provided specific amounts (US$260 million in 1991–1993 and US$480 million for 1994–1996). In addition, US$1 billion a year has been made available through the Global Environmental Facility to finance the incremental cost to development projects of environmental components with global benefits. Neither these special official funds for global environmental issues nor the considerable and growing assistance from environmental NGOs is likely to narrow substantially the external financing gap, although they make important contributions to specific areas.

The financing gap

The UNCED figures given above are indeed estimates of domestic and external financing gaps. Our assessment is that these figures are gross overestimates because they are based on a business as usual scenario. Sustainable development under a business as usual scenario, however, is unattainable, even if these resources become available. Sustainable development calls for fundamental reforms to reduce barriers to efficient use of resources, conservation and technical development, and to redeploy existing resources in a more efficient and targeted way. If these reforms do take place, the financing gap can be significantly reduced but not eliminated. Additional resources would be necessary to augment more efficiently used existing resources in an environment that enables, rather than hinders, technological development and transfer.

A second distinction must be made between financial resources needed to meet short-term cash flow problems and incremental resources needed to augment existing resources. Cash flow problems are temporary financing gaps arising from the lumpiness of new investments, stretched-out return streams, and imperfect capital markets. Such gaps between expenditures and returns can usually be addressed through bridge loans, revolving funds and government-guaranteed loan schemes. In the case of technology development there are the added problems of uncertainty of returns, long gestation and the inability of investors and innovators to capture the full return on their investments owing to the public good aspects of technology development. These two factors blur the distinction between the cash flow gap and true resource gaps, and can usually be addressed through incentives for increased venture capital, introduction of a patent system for new technologies, and partial public funding of research and development with significant public good aspects.

The need for augmentation of resources, as distinct from the cash flow gap, arises from the imbalance between a country's need for capacity building (both for human resources and institutions) and provision of basic infrastructure for technology development on the one hand, and the ability of the country to mobilize resources on the other. The latter is usually due to a combination of low income levels and a poor tax collection system. Augmentation of resources can be accomplished through existing mechanisms such as the fiscal system, user charges, resource rent capture and privatization as well as through new innovative mechanisms such as environmental taxes, betterment charges and tradable emission permits (see Figure 5.1). Yet domestic resources in much of the South may continue to be inadequate for financing the development transfer and commercialization of environmentally sustainable development owing to limited tax and capital base, underdeveloped taxation systems, capital markets and diversion of substantial resources to servicing foreign debt. These special conditions of developing countries are discussed in Chapter 8.

Finally, part of the inadequacy of domestic resources in the South and the need for external augmentation arises from the added expenditure needs for conserving resources of global value, such as biodiversity and the global climate. While developing countries also stand to benefit from policy changes, institutional reforms and technological investments which would preserve the 'global commons', at their current level of income and discount rates, they can ill afford the necessary expenditures if they cannot be recovered from adequate domestic returns. Here, there is a need for incremental cost financing of investment and technologies that generate global benefits through innovative international financing arrangements such as the Global Environmental Facility, international payments for conservation services, and various joint implementation activities between North and South such as carbon credits and offsets and joint biodiversity/biotechnology development ventures (see Figure 5.1).

REDUCING FINANCING NEEDS

The objective of this section is to identify means to reduce financial resource needs. Subsequent sections will focus on mobilizing additional resources from existing sources, and on developing new sources and mechanisms for closing the financing gap. Contrary to the prevailing pessimism, this author has found that there is no scarcity of financial

A. Funding gap under business as usual scenario:

B. True funding gap following reforms and use of economic instruments:

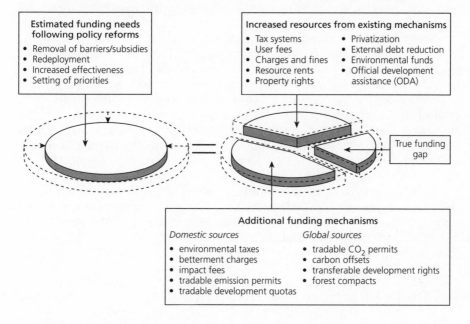

Figure 5.1 *Financing Needs and Sources for Sustainable Development*

resources to pursue sustainable development. First, the financial needs and hence the financing gap have been grossly overestimated under a business as usual scenario that attempts to 'buy' (or mandate) rather than induce and lever sustainable development by removing barriers and providing incentives. Second, there is enormous potential for redeploying and making more efficient use of existing resources. Ignoring this opportunity and seeking additional resources amounts to 'throwing good money after bad money'. As Figure 5.1 highlights, there is a difference between the apparent funding gap and the true funding gap; the objective of the policy-makers ought to be to whittle down the apparent funding gap to its irreducible minimum, and then raise revenues to finance it.

Third, resource scarcity, including that of financial resources, is a fact of life. Priorities must be set and choices made in life and sustainable development is no different. Fourth, there is great scope for saving funds (reducing expenditures) and generating additional resources through existing fiscal and financing mechanisms such as the taxation and public expenditure systems, the pricing of utilities and public services, the pricing and taxation of natural resources, the privatization of public enterprises, the reform of property taxes, the collection of charges and fines, the conversion of external debt, and the operation of special environmental funds.

Finally, there are literally dozens of new and innovative financial mechanisms for raising additional domestic and external resources for sustainable development, including the economic instruments discussed herein. For a quick overview of such instruments already in use, see Appendices 1–4.

Again, what is lacking is not money to finance sustainable development but the political will to act innovatively and decisively to translate sustainable development from a political slogan to an operational objective and, ultimately, a reality. Without correction of the pervasive policy and market failures that fuel the prevailing anti-environment and anti-sustainability behaviour and culture (despite the rhetoric), additional financial resources made available even at zero cost, will 'simply pull the global economy a little further along an ultimately unsustainable track instead of switching it to a track that leads to sustainability'. (Vincent, 1994)

Part of the financing gap could be closed through removal of barriers and distortions, more effective use of existing resources including domestic development funds, environment protection budgets, international development assistance and prioritization. We will consider each in turn.

Removing barriers and distortions

As previously discussed, the apparent financing gap is inflated by the existence of multiple barriers to sustainable development. These barriers were introduced in Chapter 2: policy failures, market distortions and institutional failures.

Eliminating *policy failures* should begin by phasing out economically costly and environmentally harmful subsidies which distort the economy and subsidize waste and environmental degradation. This is the single most cost-effective means of financing sustainable development. Examples include subsidies for fossil fuels, electricity, water, pesticides, logging, land clearing, construction materials and capital-intensive industries (see Table 5.2).

It is often argued that subsidies are necessary to assist the poor. Empirical evidence, however, indicates that these subsidies often harm the more vulnerable groups. In the case of 'free water', for example, the poor are often forced to purchase more expensive, privately provided water as the underfunded state system attains limited coverage and experiences regular shortages. Those fees have been demonstrated to be equal to or greater than the resources needed to finance the public provision of such resources. According to Steele and Pearce

Table 5.2 *Selected Subsidies with Harmful Side-effects, by Activity*

Activity	Examples of subsidies	Side-effects
Mineral production	Low or zero royalties on oil and other minerals; aid for coal production in Germany, Russia, and other countries	Stimulatory effects of low royalties are minimal; but those of subsidies to uncompetitive industries are significant, abetting pollution and waste
Logging	Low timber royalties in developing countries; below-cost sales in North America and Australia	Stimulatory effect of low royalties are minimal; but below-cost sales worsen deforestation, siltation and floods
Fishing	Billions of dollars per year in subsidies for fuel, equipment and income support for fishers worldwide	Promote overfishing, thus hurting catch, employment and marine ecosystems in the long run
Agricultural inputs	$13 billion a year lost on public irrigation projects in developing countries; billions more lost in industrial ones; subsidies for pesticides and fertilizers in some developing countries	Encourage water waste and salinization, higher rates of pesticide and fertilizer use, soil degradations and water pollution
Crop and livestock production	$302 billion in annual support for farmers in western industrial countries; low fees for grazing on public lands in North America and Australia; tax breaks for forest clearance in Brazil until 1988	Encourage environmentally destructive farming and overgrazing
Energy use	$101 billion in fossil fuel and power subsidies in developing countries each year; comparable losses in rest of world	Contribute to energy-related problems ranging from particulate emissions to global warming

Source: Worldwatch Institute, as cited in Roodman (1996).

(1996, p 159) inadequate access to public services is associated with subsidization in many developing countries; for instance, as much as 96 per cent of the rural population in Bangladesh without access to sanitation services in 1990 and 86 per cent of Indonesians without access to electricity, both subsidized services. While removal of these subsidies is made difficult by vested interests and political economy considerations, their gradual phasing out over a period of years is not without precedent. The phasing out of pesticide subsidies in Indonesia, of oil subsidies in Thailand and of ranching subsidies in Brazil, offer grounds for optimism.[3] The World Bank (1997a) offers further

Table 5.3 *Global Estimates of Subsidies (US$ bn, 1995)*

Item	Global	Industrial countries	Transition economies	Developing countries
Energy				
Fossil fuels	82	9.9	23+	25+
Electricity	206+	94+	–	112
Road transport	112+	95+	5+	11+
Water	56+	–	–	56+
Agriculture	352	342	–	10
Subtotal	870+			

Source: Gandhi et al (1997).

examples. Fertilizer subsidy reduction resulted in 2 per cent savings in total government revenue per year in Bangladesh. Energy intensity in China declined by 30 per cent following a drop in coal subsidies from 61 per cent in 1984 to 11 per cent in 1985. And, the removal of irrigation subsidies in Hungary in 1990 resulted in the equivalent of US$2 million (1986) in reduced annual government spending. Globally, distortionary subsidies are still estimated to exceed US$800 billion (see Table 5.3) despite a significant reduction in recent years.

Phasing out of subsidies makes four contributions to sustainable development:

1) It frees up budgetary resources to spend on poverty alleviation, resource conservation, women's education and other similar investments that advance sustainable development.
2) It removes a major economic distortion thereby improving efficiency and raising economic growth, a sine qua non condition for sustainable development.
3) It improves income distribution since most taxes are regressive and subsidies disproportionately benefit the rich (eg, capital and energy subsidies).
4) It improves the environment not by spending new money, rather by saving money and realigning the incentive structure in favour of environmentally sound practices, encouraging movement from pesticide use to integrated pest management, and from energy supply expansion to energy demand management.

Market failures are the second set of barriers that prevent a country's economy and technology system from getting closer to a sustainable development path as already discussed in Chapter 2. Recall that the most severe forms of market failure are unaccounted externalities. For example, the environmental externalities of burning fossil fuels include local pollutants (CO, NO_x, suspended particulate matter (SPM)) which affect human health; regional pollutants (SO_2) which affect agriculture and property downwind; and, global pollutants (CO_2, methane, etc) which may contribute to global warming. Failure to regulate, or cost and charge, such negative externalities results in overconsumption of fossil fuels, excessive rates of emissions and discouragement of the development, transfer and adoption of more energy-efficient production technologies, of pollution control and abatement processes and equipment (eg, desulphurization of coal, electrostatic precipitators) and of alternative, less polluting fuels. Similarly, failure to introduce standards or charges for liquid and solid waste discourages the development, transfer and adoption of waste minimization, waste treatment and recycling technologies. Markets also tend to be myopic, underinvesting in resource conservation and technological development. Tax relief for long-term capital gains and private–public sector cost sharing of research and development for environmentally sustainable technologies would help remove this barrier to sustainable development.

Institutional failures such as insecure property rights affect agricultural land, forest, fisheries and pastures, and result in excessive and wasteful resource use and underpricing of scarce resources. The result is under-investment in improved-recovery technology, in development of substitutes and in resource conservation. Failure to protect intellectual property rights results in further disincentives for invention and innovation.

Clearly, the removal of policy and institutional failures and the correction of market distortions would go a long way in narrowing both the technology and the financing gap for sustainable development, while saving budgetary resources that can be used to support activities and investments that promote rather than hinder sustainable development. For example, removal of fossil fuel subsidies will not only reduce the emissions of local and global pollutants but will also free up budgetary resources for investing in renewable energy, development of more energy efficient technologies and the enhancement of sinks (eg, reforestation). This brings us to the next means of closing the financing gap: the redeployment of existing resources.

Making more effective use of existing resources

No government or development assistance agency can claim that its current allocation of budget and development funds coincides fully with the allocation that would best advance Agenda 21. The current allocation of resources is largely a legacy of pre-UNCED decisions, the Cold War, inertia and vested interests. While it would take time to redeploy existing resources sufficiently to coincide fully with the priorities and objectives of Agenda 21, a partial adjustment is possible even in the short run. For example, more of the educational budget and human resource development funds can be directed towards the education of women to induce a reduction in fertility and child mortality and improve resource management at the family level, and towards the building of human resource and institutional capacity for furthering sustainable development in the coming years. Another example of desirable and feasible reallocation of funds that would advance Agenda

21 is to reduce emphasis on supply expansion and to increase resource allocation to demand management, increased use efficiency and resource conservation, and to improve operation and maintenance of existing systems of water and energy supply.

Nor is the current resource allocation economically efficient and socially equitable. A large share of scarce financial and capital resources is tied up in the construction of prestigious megaprojects (airports, highways, refineries, long-range power lines, steel mills, etc) which generate low returns and little employment. At the same time, low visibility projects (such as repair of rural roads, safe water and sanitation, soil conservation and watershed protection) which would generate both high returns and considerable employment are not undertaken owing to lack of financial resources.

In many mixed and formerly planned economies, public utilities, state enterprises and parastatals absorb a significant portion of the state budget without contributing to welfare improvement. In addition, reduced competition, a soft budget constraint and underpricing of products and services compounds the misallocation and inefficient use of resources and results in substantial welfare losses. Privatization of state enterprises is likely to save a substantial portion of the national budget for sustainable development investments, as well as to improve economic efficiency and reduce waste in the provision of public services and other products currently produced by state enterprises. Efficient private provision of public services can be effected through competitive bidding with adequate safeguards for equity and environmental protection.[4]

Privatization of money losing state enterprises would generate three direct sources of funding for investments in sustainable development and other uses:

1   additional government revenues from the sale of state enterprises;
2   savings in government expenditures by no longer having to finance state enterprise deficits; and
3   additional tax revenues from an expanded tax base which the more efficient production would bring about.

Another sector where significant resources can be redeployed to advance sustainable development is the military sector.[5] First, in the post-Cold War years, ethnic conflicts notwithstanding, some shift of resources from the military to other sectors is a viable option for most countries. A 10 per cent reduction of military expenditures worldwide could generate as much as $100 billion per year, or a quarter of the financing gap for sustainable development once the barriers are removed. Second, the military could redeploy its considerable human, organizational and technological resources to transform itself from an environmentally destructive force into an agent of environmental recovery and sustainable development. Third, much of the military knowledge, skill and technology can be redeployed for commercial uses, thus alleviating part of the technological gap and corresponding financing gap. Military conversion is already underway in many formerly planned economies, but there is also considerable scope for conversion in market economies.[6]

A last but significant type of more effective resource use is the re-targeting of existing funds from low- or unsustainable-return technologies, like import substitution and waste treatment to high-return, low impact technologies such as renewable energy, waste minimization and pharmaceuticals from local biodiversity resources.

For development assistance agencies and environmental support groups, the challenge is to lead by example: to redeploy their own resources in such a way as to integrate environment and development in the spirit of Agenda 21. Ultimately, the implementation of Agenda 21 depends on the capacity of developing countries to reform their policies and restructure their economies to speed up growth while slowing down, and eventually reversing, environmental degradation. The necessary changes call for analytical and integrative skills, as well as an institutional infrastructure, which are in scarce supply in most developing countries. Development assistance agencies need to recast and restructure their existing projects and resources to achieve the critical means necessary for elevating developing country capacity to levels that would enable a transition to a sustainable economy. This requires more investment in policy research, reform advocacy and policy dialogue as well as technical assistance, demonstration and pilot projects and catalytic and strategic interventions.

Setting priorities

While the financing gap can be reduced by removing barriers and distortions and by making more effective use of existing resources, the basic scarcity of resources remains, necessitating priority setting and efficient allocation, not only across uses but also over time. Not all apparent needs can be addressed simultaneously, even where financial resources are not binding; human, institutional and administrative resources may be binding. If sustainable development is to be the operative objective of policy and public investment, the use of limited financial (and other) resources must be allocated among competing uses in order to equate the present value of 'sustainable' returns at the margin between uses at the same and different points in time. By 'sustainable' returns we do not mean that each activity must by itself be sustainable but that each activity should contribute towards making the economy sustainable by accounting for all of its costs and benefits.

In practical terms, the highest priority investments are those that safeguard and enhance the country's resource base, and the natural, human and man-made productive capital. High priority policies and investments often include averting irreversible damages to ecosystems, protecting critical watersheds, the education of women, employment of the labour force, security of property rights, poverty alleviation, encouragement of high rates of savings, a conducive environment for domestic and foreign investments and the development of mechanisms for internalization of environmental costs. Within these broad areas, specific priorities vary from country to country, according to the level of development, the structure of the economy, resource endowment and inherited legacies and problems. Where fundamental reforms are needed to put the economy on a sustainable path, substantial financial resources are needed to secure the support of influential sectors of society or to cushion short-term, adverse impacts on vulnerable socioeconomic groups.

The key is to remove perverse incentives and replace them with positive ones, without imposing undue hardships or creating strong opposition to the reforms. The objective of reforms should be correction of policy and market failures, not punishment or hardship. If indeed reforms are beneficial over the long haul, that is they have a positive net present value, the highest priority use of financial resources is to provide leverage for, and support these reforms.

RAISING ADDITIONAL REVENUES

Policy reforms to remove barriers to sustainable development, better prioritization of needs and redeployment of existing resources will significantly reduce the funding gap of sustainable development but they will not eliminate it altogether. Raising additional revenues is both necessary and possible from both conventional sources and from innovative economic instruments. The objective of this section is to review selected instruments in terms of their revenue-raising function without forgetting that getting incentives right is their primary function.

Environmental taxes

In addition to fiscal policy reform that shifts the tax burden from environmentally friendly to environmentally destructive activities, it is possible to gain further revenues from fiscal systems already in use through more effective management and better design of these instruments. One such example is the ozone-depleting substance tax in use in the USA. The original tax of US$3.02 per kg was applied to eight chemicals in 1989 and increased to 20 chemicals in 1990. In 1995 the tax rate was increased to US$11.80 per kg and set to increase automatically by 45 cents each year. The results in terms of environmental effectiveness have been unequivocal, with production of these chemicals dropping to 'less than half their pretax level', according to the World Bank (1997a). But more astounding, the annual revenues of the tax have risen consistently to reach over US$1 billion in 1994 (International Institute for Sustainable Development, 1994).

The 1990s have witnessed the unilateral introduction of carbon taxes in an effort led by the Nordic countries, the Netherlands and Germany to increase environmental tax rates in general to more meaningful levels. For example, Sweden introduced taxes on carbon dioxide ($0.4 per kg), sulphur, ($4.55 per kg) and nitrogen oxide ($6.05 per kg) in the early 1990s, which not only generated $2 billion in tax revenues but also reduced the use of transport fuels by 2 per cent and induced a fuel shift among power stations from coal to biofuels. Finland introduced an even higher tax on carbon of $6.10 per ton on all fuels since 1990. However, a European Community carbon-tax proposal at a graduated rate from $1 to 10 per ton of carbon over a period of several years failed to receive approval. Extra-budgetary pollution taxes or charges have been introduced throughout Central and Eastern Europe with the revenues earmarked for environmental purposes and deposited in specially designed environmental funds (see below).

In developing countries, pollution charges have been introduced, largely as sources of environmental revenues, in several countries including Malaysia, Republic of Korea, Indonesia, Thailand, India, China, Brazil and Mexico. The most notable examples of pollution charges, aimed to act both as incentives and revenue sources, are the differential tax between leaded and unleaded petrol in Thailand and the reform of the long-standing pollution levy system in China to improve efficiency and compliance. China has also recently introduced a sulphur tax on an experimental basis. While China's pollution levies generate 15–20 per cent of China's capital expenditure for pollution control, their rates are still far below the marginal cost of pollution control. This is true of environmental taxation in general. For example, the World Bank estimates that Indonesia can generate between $0.6 and 1.1 billion (or 3–5 per cent of government domestic revenues) from pollution and congestion charges in selected urban centres (see Table 5.4). Hammer and Shetty (1995) estimated that the proper tax rate on petrol in Malaysia would generate about 7 per cent of the total government revenue.

Tradable permits

Tradable permits could be a major factor of environmental finance because they reduce compliance costs (by 60 per cent in the case of sulphur emissions in the United States) and when they are auctioned off they generate government revenues. It is accurate to say that no fully functioning tradable emission permit systems exist outside the United States. Nevertheless, the 1990s (especially post-Rio) have seen a growing interest among transitional and developing countries and a number of experimental introductions, though actual trades are still rare. Tradable emission permit systems have been designed for Almaty, Kazakhstan (one trade known) and Santiago, Chile (no trades yet). Study and experimentation are known to be underway in the Opole region of Poland, in Sokolov, the Czech Republic and Shanghai, China. Interest is also being expressed in Thailand, El Salvador and Mexico.

Table 5.4 *Indicative Revenue Potential from Forestry and Externality Taxation, Indonesia, ca 1993*

Initiative	Incremental revenue potential (billion US$)	Share of 1993 gov. dom. revenues (per cent)
Forestry: Raise stumpage fees to recover 75% of logging rents	1.5–2.0	6–8
Pollution: Pollution charges for Jabotabek urban area	0.2–0.5	1–2
Congestion: Congestion charges for urban and inter-urban Indonesian roads	0.4–0.6	2–3

Source: World Bank (1994b).

The major obstacles to the wider introduction of tradable permits systems is the lack of inventory of emissions and sources and the weakness of monitoring and enforcement systems of many developing countries. It is reasonable, however, to expect further experiments and a few actual trades taking place over the next five years.

Charges and fines

In many developing countries the bulk of revenues for environmental investment comes from fines imposed on violators of environmental regulations and, to a lesser extent, from pollution charges. Yet none of these instruments comes anywhere close to their potential as a source of revenues and they hardly ever act as incentives for behavioural change. Regulations are not consistently enforced and when they are, the fines imposed on violators are far too low by comparison with the expected gain from non-compliance and the resulting environmental damage or social cost. Both their erratic use and inflation erode their significance as financing sources. Where fines for non-compliance are set high enough to provide incentive effects, as in Poland, they are rarely paid or collected (Panayotou, 1995b).

Charges, on the other hand, are usually introduced purely as financing mechanisms to defray part of the cost of administering the command-and-control regulation system, and they are not related to any meaningful measure of environmental damage or abatement cost. In other words, they are not Pigouvian (corrective of incentives). The exclusive emphasis on revenues directly raised by charges in general (as in cost recovery) and of pollution charges in particular, is misplaced, since their incentive effect could reduce financing needs and or induce

---

Box 5.1 The Polish Charge System

The role and purpose of environmental charges in Poland is described in the National Environmental Policy of Poland, approved by Parliament in 1991. According to Anderson and Fiedor (1997), 'the stated intent of the government [is] that charges should serve a complementary role in the national administrative/regulatory system of environmental management'. Charges should:

- encourage polluters to minimize the social costs of meeting stated environmental goals;
- bear some relation to the marginal damages resulting from pollution emissions or discharges; and
- generate revenues which can then be recirculated for environmental investments and related purposes.

While the Polish pollution charges are among the highest in the world, they are not high enough to provide an incentive to change production processes. There are numerous low-cost win–win actions which can and are taken to reduce pollution and the charges paid, but the revenue-raising potential of the instrument remains the focus. An estimated $450–500 million is collected annually and distributed to the National Environmental Fund, regional and local funds, an amount which accounts for almost 'one-half of the annual capital costs of environmental investments in Poland'.

Source: Anderson and Fiedor (1997).

---

private environmental expenditures in excess of public revenues raised (see Box 5.1).

A practical problem does arise, however, in the case of pollution charges, which are not seen as a means of cost recovery or payment for service or resource use and can potentially raise large amounts of revenue. Environmental ministries prefer to view pollution charges as user fees and want the revenues earmarked for environmental investments to abate pollution and to rehabilitate degraded environments. Finance ministries prefer to view pollution charges as taxes and hence as a source of general revenue to be allocated between alternative uses in order to maximize the social rate of return without regard to the origin of the revenues. Earmarking, often simply viewed as a distortion by finance ministries, is exemplified by the development of environmental funds in recent years as an extra-budget mechanism for financing environmental investments.

User fees, cost recovery and full-cost pricing

A significant source of increased financing from existing mechanisms is improved cost recovery from public investments through user fees. Again, only a small fraction of the cost of irrigation water and industrial energy is paid by users; the rest is covered by the diversion of scarce financial resources from other, often more productive, uses. The same is true of residential energy and water use. Full-cost pricing of public utilities and services can be equally important in the augmentation of resources (financing effect) as it is to the removal of barriers (incentive effect) and the redeployment of existing resources (efficiency effect). While full-cost pricing implies higher prices for consumers and producers in the short run, the long-term benefits in terms of sustainable economic growth often outweigh these costs. Some short-term cushioning of the impact on low-income groups might be necessary.

Cost recovery in irrigation has increased from an estimated 10–20 per cent in the 1980s (Repetto, 1988) to about 20–25 per cent today (Moor, 1997). Still, $20–25 billion go to irrigation subsidies in developing countries every year and another $20 billion to drinking water supply. Removal of water subsidies would reduce water use by 20–30 per cent (in parts of Asia by as much as 50 per cent) and make it possible to supply most of the 1.2 billion people without access to safe drinking water without large, environmentally destructive water development projects.

Resource rent capture

Almost all developing countries exploit, and many export, natural resources such as minerals, forest products, petroleum and fish. While the rate of resource exploitation in most countries is excessive and possibly unsustainable, little of the growing scarcity rent is captured by governments and reinvested in the protection and enhancement of the resource and the enlargement of the country's stocks of human and man-made capital, as sustainable development requires.

For example, a fraction of the scarcity value or stumpage of tropical timber is captured by governments (see Panayotou, 1993a), and a good part of whatever is being captured is returned to logging companies through public construction of logging roads and log-processing subsidies which encourage increased logging. Log export bans depress the domestic price of logs and subsidize their wasteful use by inefficient plywood mills in the name of increasing the gross value added even as the net value added shrinks and wasteful logging intensifies (see Panayotou and Ashton, 1992). The failure to charge logging its full opportunity cost in terms of forgone non-timber forest products and environmental services (watershed protection, biodiversity, etc) results in further undervaluation of timber, wasteful use and uncollected rents. Even the means of collecting rents may result in considerable waste. For example, taxes on the amount of timber removed from the logging site (rather than on the amount of marketable timber on the site) result in high grading, partial recovery of logs and highly destructive logging and relogging. The result is resource exploitation that is excessive and inefficient and tax revenues (and foreign exchange earnings) that are too low and used wastefully (Panayotou and Ashton, 1992).

Billions of dollars a year in additional foreign exchange earnings and government revenue can be obtained through a more efficient resource concession and taxation system. Such a system would provide for longer-term concessions awarded through competitive bidding and taxed efficiently through area-based taxes. With such improvements, not only could wasteful logging be reduced but there would also be more government revenues to invest in forest protection and reforestation. Higher rates of collection of resource rents by governments, however, does not automatically advance sustainable development; it might even retard it if the government's propensity to save and invest in sustainable development activities is lower than that of the private sector. How the revenues from resource rent capture are spent is as critical as the level of these revenues. Given the high transaction costs and leakages in collecting and expanding public revenues, sustainable development may advance more by providing private investors with incentives to reinvest resource rents than through direct public expenditures.

Resource taxation has generally increased from 7–20 per cent of resource rents in the 1970s and early 1980s to over 50 per cent of the rents at present, through successful reforms especially of the forest sector policies. Examples include Indonesia, the Philippines and Honduras. The Philippines raised the charge on timber cut from 1 per cent of the market price in the late 1980s to 20 per cent in the early 1990s. Indonesia was able to mobilize an additional billion dollars of revenues by reforming its forest tax policy. Yet the World Bank estimates that by raising its stumpage fees to cover 75 per cent of the resource rents, Indonesia would be able to obtain another \$1.5–2.5 billion; a 6–8 per cent increase in government revenues. Low stumpage charges are also found in China, Cameroon, Kenya, Nigeria and Surinam among others. Indonesia has been particularly successful in capturing rents from petroleum and mineral extraction. Others, such as Russia and the oil producing countries of Eastern Europe and Central Asia, stand to gain between \$10 and 20 billion in additional revenues through more efficient pricing and royalties and taxes that capture a larger part of resource rents. Venezuela can increase government revenues by 6 per cent by raising petroleum prices to world levels, and Chile can earn over a billion dollars from introducing a contribution of a resource royalty and additional profits tax on copper extraction.

Property rights and property taxes

Taxes on property, especially land, is a growing source of revenue in developing countries and in some countries they are the only source of municipal and local government finances. Yet property taxes tend to be very low by comparison to developed countries and over time tend to lose their value to inflation. In the tax base, property values are not frequently upgraded. Land use changes and ownership transfers are not always recorded (and taxed) and when taxes are paid they are often based on outdated (and hence too low) property values. Land use taxes are uncommon and capital gains and windfalls are rarely taxed.

Furthermore, insecure property rights over natural resources, especially land, have been a major cause of farmers' lack of access to capital markets and of under-investment in land improvement, in soil conservation and in tree planting. This in turn leads to low agricultural productivity, low farming incomes and encroachment on forests to obtain additional land for cultivation. This also results in low tax revenues and high public expenditures on poverty alleviation, forest protection and mitigation of off-site effects such as the sedimentation of dams and reservoirs from soil erosion.[7]

Issuance of secure land titles to farmers with insecure ownership results in a doubling or tripling of the value of the land, while the costs of the necessary cadastral surveys, title registration and other related expenses are only 2–3 per cent of the pre-title value. Thus, improved security of ownership over land and other natural resources — a necessary condition for sustainable development — can be self-financed and at the same time generate enormous private and social benefits. Estimates of productivity gains from land titling range between 10 and 30 per cent; investments in land improvements, soil conservation and tree planting range between 60 and 200 per cent (Feder et al, 1986). This also has the added attraction of increasing tax revenues because of the expanded tax base and savings in government expenditures on poverty alleviation and forest protection.

Privatization of state enterprises

As the experience of Eastern Europe, the former Soviet Union and many socialist economies in the developing world amply demonstrates, the environment has suffered as much as the economy in the hands of state enterprises. Privatization, economic restructuring and price reform are well established and widely accepted as necessary conditions for revitalizing the economy and spurring economic growth; that they are equally important to environmental improvement and sustainable development is less well known and recognized (Panayotou, 1995b).

Private provision of public services such as water supply, waste water treatment, solid waste collection, power generation and telephone services would generate similar savings as long as competitive bidding and adequate safeguards against monopoly pricing are adopted (Panayotou, 1997b). At the same time, unaccounted environmental and social costs must be internalized through regulation or, preferably, through economic instruments.

The 1990s have witnessed unprecedented interest and action towards tapping the resources of the private sector by: (a) undertaking policy reforms to provide a more stable and predictable policy environment and a more transparent legal and environmental framework; (b) adopting financing and management innovations, such as build-own transfer (BOT), build-own operate (BOO) and build-own lease (BOL); and (c) privatizing sectors such as power generation, telecommunications, transport infrastructure, water supply and sanitation, and even environmental monitoring, all of which were previously in the inclusive domain of the public sector. Recent privatizations include telecommunications in Costa Rica, power generation and water supply in Argentina, water supply and traffic management in the Philippines, and the urban rail system development and waste management in Thailand. A World Bank (1996a) review of the post-privatization performance of 60 companies reveals an 11 per cent improvement in efficiency, 44 per cent improvement in investment and 45 per cent improvement in profitability; employment and tax payments also increased.

Privatization and other forms (such as joint ventures and partnerships) of involving the private sector in financing sustainable development are likely to accelerate in coming years as governments seek to mobilize resources to improve infrastructure and public services. The global market for environmental investments alone is projected to exceed $600 billion per year by 2000 (IFC, 1992).

Environmental funds

Environmental funds are specialized funds or institutions designed to collect earmarked revenues and disburse them for environmental and conservation purposes. Examples include trust funds, foundations, endowments, revolving funds, green funds and other grant- or loan-making entities. National environmental funds are a special type of fund that collect and disburse public money in support of national environmental strategy, environmental action plans or environmental policy. They are usually funded or capitalized from pollution charges, fees and fines, budgetary contributions, debt-for-nature swaps or contributions from donor agencies. Green funds, on the other hand, are private, social-purpose funds made available by private investors for lending to environmentally sound enterprises and projects.

Environmental funds may be general or specific in scope: at one extreme, they simply provide a supplement to the general environmental (or sustainable development) budget; at the other extreme, they are tied to a single-purpose use. For example in Poland, the National Environmental Fund (NEF), a depository for environmental charges and fines used for wide ranging environmental activities, is a general fund while the privatization escrow funds are tied to particular enterprises and used for the sole purpose of cleaning up past contamination. Funds might also be local (eg, municipal), national, global or mixed. The Global Environmental Facility (GEF) is a global fund, the above mentioned Polish NEF is a national fund while another Polish fund, the Ecofund, created through debt-for-nature swaps, is a mixed fund as it funds national projects of global significance.[8] Funds, in effect, disburse subsidies through grants, reduced interest payments, direct loans, loan guarantees, equity investments and co-financing with commercial banks, public financial institutions, private enterprises and NGOs, in order to achieve environmental policy goals.[9]

Environmental funds have both advantages and disadvantages. On the positive side, they combine a diversity of funding sources (public, private, domestic and international) which provide a degree of independence; they are a source of stable financing and can move funds easily without the bureaucratic constraints of the general budget; they provide a framework for the coordination of donors and the balancing of national and international priorities; and they encourage the participation of a wide range of interests (including government, business, local communities and environmental groups), thereby ensuring public support, transparency and accountability (Dillenbeek, 1994).

On the negative side, environmental funds are potential sources of inefficiency and distortion and may weaken rather than strengthen the environmental ministries. Efficiency requires that public funds be allocated in order to equalize social returns among alternative uses at the margin; this requires flexibility in shifting funds between uses as priorities (and social returns) change. Earmarking limits this flexibility, introducing rigidities and inefficiencies in resource allocation as changes in revenue rather than changes in demand determine the supply of public services (Opschoor et al, 1994). Another danger is the potential bias of fund allocations in favour of supply expansion rather than demand management; in favour of end-of-the-pipe solutions rather than prevention and waste minimization; and in favour of capital-intensive solutions rather than policy reform and behavioural changes.

The strongest argument in favour of environmental funds and earmarking is that environmental taxes and charges are the prices for using environmental services, such as the environment's assimilative capacity and therefore the revenue from these sources should be used to maintain these environmental services rather than for general revenue purposes, as with other taxes (Panayotou, 1994a). A second argument is that environmental funds are a practical application of the polluter pays principle in which pollution charges are collected from all polluters and the revenue is then allocated (recycled) to those polluters that are prepared to undertake remedial measures accounting for environmental policy priorities. A third argument in favour of environmental funds is that earmarking enhances the political acceptability of environmental taxes and charges (Opschoor et al, 1994).

Environmental funds are of particular relevance to economies in transition because of the underdevelopment of the government budgeting process and of private capital markets. However, care must be taken to define their mandate clearly to avoid crowding out private investments and to phase them out as the restructuring process resolves these transition-related problems. Environmental funds emerged as a major new trend in environmental and conservation finance in the early 1990s. To date, national environmental funds have been set up in over 20 developing countries (eg, Argentina, Mexico, Peru, the Philippines, Chile, Thailand, Bolivia, Honduras, Uganda and others) and in most transition economies in Eastern Europe (eg, Bulgaria, Czech Republic, Hungary, Poland and Russia). Table 5.5 gives several examples of environmental funds in both transitional and developing economies.

National environmental funds in transition economies, being largely a legacy of central planning, tend to be comprehensive funds in

Table 5.5 *Examples of Environmental Funds*

	Revenues	Main Expenditures	Beneficiaries	Disbursement
Earmarked Tax Funds				
Hungary – CEPF	Fuel tax, product charges, traffic transit fee, pollution fines, EU PHARE grant	Air pollution abatement, waste management, water pollution control, public awareness building	Public transportation companies, municipalities, industrial enterprises, research institutes	Grants, low-interest loans
Poland – NFEPWM	Air and water pollution charges, water use and waste charges	Air and water pollution abatement, soil protection, environmental monitoring and education	Industrial enterprises, municipal companies, universities	Soft loans, loan guarantees, grants
Russia – FEF	Pollution charges, fines	Pollution control, environmental R&D, institution building	Municipal companies, industrial enterprise, research institutes	Grants
Directed Credit Funds				
China – Tianjin IPCF	IDA credit, pollution charges	Waste reduction and recovery, pollution prevention (cleaner technology)	Industrial enterprises	Market-rate loans plus grant (10–30%)
Russia – PAF	IBRD loan	Waste recovery	Public and private industrial enterprises	IBRD rate plus 400 BPs
Slovenia – Eco-Fund	Budget allocation, IBRD loan	Urban pollution abatement	Households, cooperatives, commercial and industrial enterprises, municipalities	LIBOR plus 200 BPs
Green Funds				
Bolivia – FONAMA	DNSs by international NGOs, foreign government contributions	Support to protected areas in nature conservation	Local communities, NGOs	Grants
Colombia – ECOFONDO	DNSs, NGOs, foreign governments	Nature protection, environmental education, integrated watershed management	NGOs, local groups	Grants

Source: World Bank (1997b).

the sense that they finance a broad range of environmental investments. They are usually located within environmental ministries,
although in some countries, such as Poland, the Fund is a separate
agency with an autonomous management structure. Most transition
country NEFs rely on environmental taxes, charges, and fines for the
revenues. Emission charges are the principal source of revenues for
NEFs in Poland, Russia, Estonia, Czech Republic, Slovakia and China.
Hungary uses a variety of instruments to capitalize its fund, including
non-compliance charges, product charges and a transit traffic tax, while
Bulgaria uses car import taxes as well as non-compliance charges
(Lovei, 1995a).

In developing countries NEFs tend to be more specific and, because
environmental taxation is not as well developed as in transition
economies, they rely on external sources or other fees for funds. Pearce
(1997) reports that in Algeria the main source of the fund is a tax on
airline tickets, in Belize a tax on foreign tourists and in Costa Rica a tax
on petrol, while Brazil's municipal environmental funds are financed
by World Bank loans. It is reasonable to expect further development
and proliferation of environmental funds in the foreseeable future. A
key to their future success is more efficient management, reduced
administration cost and use of rigorous benefit–cost analysis of projects
as the principle criterion for disbursing funds.

External development assistance

Poor developing countries can be given incentives for policy reform in
the form of matching funds for domestic resources generated for
sustainable development investments through reduction of subsidies
and industrial protection, privatization of state enterprises, increased
resource rent collection, improved tax administration or stricter
scrutiny of public projects with negative environmental and social
impacts.

Multilateral lending institutions, such as the World Bank, attempt
to do this through conditionality, but this has negative connotations
which are resented by some developing countries who perceive conditionality as a challenge to their sovereignty. Matching funds for policy
reform is a positive concept that levers, or rather, motivates policy
reform. The perception would be of a country initiating the reforms
and outside funding as an added or supplemental benefit.

Matching funds need not be dollar for dollar. For example, consider
a country that has traditionally been subsidizing fossil fuels and is now
considering the phasing out of these subsidies, thereby saving $100
million to be invested in solar energy for rural electrification. The
knowledge that another $10 million will be made available by a multi-
lateral or bilateral agency in support of such a policy change might
increase the chances that such a reform does take place. The $10
million of matching funds might be regarded as payment for incremental costs justified by the global benefits stemming from reduced

greenhouse gas emissions (and hence financed by GEF) or regarded as development assistance for restructuring the energy sector and investing in rural development (financed by bilateral or multilateral development financing sources). Although the source of funds would vary according to the expected beneficiaries, the objective is the same: to motivate an economically and environmentally favourable policy change that would advance sustainable development. The additional resources are not so much the external matching funds as the domestic funds saved from wasteful use and the higher rates of return to private and public investment generated by the policy reform, which the matching funds will have generated, set in motion.

Chapter 6
Economic and Financing Instruments for the Global Commons

The scope of economic instruments is not limited to the management of domestic environmental problems, but extends to the management of the global commons, such as the conservation of tropical forests, the preservation of biodiversity and the protection of the global climate and the ozone layer. As in the case of local environmental problems, the cost of controlling global pollutants or conserving resources of global importance varies significantly among countries, as does people's willingness to pay for accomplishing global environmental objectives.

The demand for global environmental policy comes mainly from the developed countries, which have sufficiently high incomes and low discount rates to be concerned with environmental amenities and distant threats to their lifestyles. The lowest-cost supply comes mainly from developing countries either by virtue of their greater biodiversity, lower energy efficiency (and thereby greater scope for efficiency gains) or lower opportunity costs. Under these circumstances equal or proportional emissions reductions by all countries would be excessively costly, if not totally unacceptable to developing countries.

Economic instruments can also be used as vehicles for the internalization of global environmental benefits to developing countries. In terms of efficiency, the cost of a given global environmental improvement would be minimized (cost-effectiveness); in terms of distribution, the wealthy beneficiaries would pay and the poor countries would benefit (equity) along the lines of the beneficiary pays principle.

In the absence of a global government with taxation power, developed countries' willingness to pay for conservation could be captured through new innovative trading arrangements between developed and developing countries. Developing countries need financial resources and efficient technology to pursue sustainable development; in exchange they can offer:

1   unmatched biological diversity which can best be preserved in situ;
2   forests which are of global significance in terms of their impact on global climate atmospheric balance and biodiversity habitat;

3   environmental amenities which include wildlife and other natural
    assets of recreational, educational and scientific value; and
4   low-cost reduction of carbon emissions.

The South could offer to trade environmental conservation for financial and technological resources on behalf of the global community. It
has a comparative advantage to do so because protection and maintenance of natural resources is labour-intensive and requires proximity
and intimate knowledge of the resource, as well as interest in preserv-
ing national sovereignty.

But how are such trading arrangements actually to be effected?
While there is a well-developed market for financial and technological
resources, there is no such market for the conservation of natural and
biological resources. This is due to the nature of these resources (global
externalities), the lack of well-defined (and fully recognized) property
rights and the difficulty of enforcing contracts across borders in the
absence of a 'global authority' which supersedes national sovereignty.
Moreover, the object of conservation and exchange is difficult to define
and monitor.

Despite these difficulties, some exchanges of this nature have
taken place. Examples include debt-for-nature swaps, the Global
Environmental Facility, the bioprospecting rights purchased by the
Merck Pharmaceutical Company in Costa Rica and the EcoFund in
Poland created through debt-conversion and several carbon-offset
arrangements between northern power utilities and southern energy
companies or forest concerns. However, as these exchanges circum-
vent rather than enhance the market, they remain more the
exception than the rule. Just as other goods and services are traded,
market mechanisms need to be developed for trading conservation
and global climate protection. Transferable development rights and
internationally tradable emission permits are such mechanisms
which have been suggested and are being studied. In what follows,
we briefly review first global environmental financing institutions
and international environmental taxation followed by a more
detailed discussion of innovative economic and financing instruments for the global commons.

GLOBAL ENVIRONMENTAL FINANCING INSTITUTIONS

The most important of the global environmental financing institutions
is the Global Environmental Facility (GEF) established in 1990 with $1.3
billion to provide grants and concessional funds over a three-year pilot
phase. GEF is now an established institution with regular capital replen-
ishment (the latest of $2 billion over three years) through individual
country contributions (mainly from developed countries). The facility
assists developing countries to address four areas of global environmental concern: global warming, loss of biodiversity, pollution of

international waters and depletion of stratospheric ozone. The last area is addressed by an associate 'institution', the Montreal Protocol. GEF draws on the expertise and experience of three global institutions: United Nations Development Programme (UNDP), UNEP and the World Bank. The Global Environmental Facility and the Montreal Protocol investment programme implemented through the World Bank during 1991–1996 stood at $725 million. On average, GEF is funding 20 per cent of the total costs ($2.8 billion for the period 1991–1996) of projects in developing countries with global benefits. The GEF contribution varied from a low of 7 per cent in climate change projects to a high of 65 per cent in biodiversity protection projects. Almost half of GEF funding went to the protection of biodiversity and leveraged additional funding from other sources. The cumulative funding for biodiversity-related activities managed by the World Bank increased from under $50 million in 1989 to over $1.2 billion in 1995; since Rio it doubled.

The Global Environmental Facility has increasingly been using its resources to leverage additional funds, especially from the private sector. The International Finance Corporation/GEF Poland Efficient Lighting Project and the IFC/GEF Small and Medium Enterprises Project are two examples. By putting relatively small amounts into venture capital funds, GEF is able to mobilize four or five times as much in equity financing in the private sector, which in turn mobilizes a multiple in loan financing. By one account GEF is able to mobilize 10–20 times the amount of funds it invests in biodiversity and other conservation investments (A. Steer quoted in UN/DPCSD, 1996).

INTERNATIONAL ENVIRONMENTAL TAXATION

Existing international financing mechanisms rely largely on voluntary contributions by nations, and as such they provide inadequate and erratic or unstable resource flows for international environmental investments. International environmental problems such as global warming, biodiversity loss and ozone depletion are global public goods that call for global environmental taxation, which, in turn, requires sovereign nations to yield their sovereign powers of taxation to a supra-national authority. Three such taxes have been proposed:

1   an international foreign exchange transactions tax, known also as Tobin tax;
2   an international carbon tax on energy fuels; and
3   an international air transport tax.

Of these three taxes, the Tobin tax is expected to generate the largest revenues (in the hundreds of billions of dollars) but has no positive environmental effects. The carbon tax would generate the largest environmental benefits (by discouraging high-carbon fuels) and at the same time generate substantial revenues ($55 billion per year according to Shah and Larsen 1992), but, unlike the other two, it is distribution-

Table 6.1 *Potential Revenue of a Carbon Tax in Selected Countries, 1991*[1]

Country	US$ (millions)	Percentage of government revenue	Percentage of GDP
Germany	1773	0.54	0.16
Japan	2371	0.73	0.10
United States	12,461	1.37	0.28
Brazil	503	0.50	0.17
China	5699	8.81	1.87
India	1454	3.85	0.57
Indonesia	263	1.62	0.35
Mexico	772	3.16	0.55
Nigeria	90	2.33	0.37
Poland	1257	5.07	1.97
Former Soviet Union	10,129	–	–
World	54,810	–	0.31

Source: Shah and Larsen (1992).[2] Appeared in Gandhi et al (1997).

ally regressive. Table 6.1 shows the potential revenues from a carbon tax in selected countries. The air travel tax, though progressive in its incidence, generates limited revenues and limited environmental benefits.

While the debate on these instruments of international taxation has intensified in the post-Rio years, little progress has been made towards serious consideration of any one of them, largely because of the reluctance of sovereign nations to yield sovereign taxation powers to a supranational authority. Nevertheless, there appears to exist considerable public support for some form of international resource mobilization for the environment. In a Gallup Survey (Dunlap et al, 1993) in 30 major countries following the Earth Summit, industrialized country citizens (by a majority of 70–90 per cent) favoured contributing money to an international environmental agency. Over two-thirds of the respondents expressed support for such a global institution and indicated willingness to let their own governments grant it the necessary authority. In the absence of political will among governments to do so, an alternative institutional arrangement must be found which yields the minimum possible delegation of tax authority. Among the alternatives proposed are the harmonization of national taxes through international agreements, and non-sovereign international taxes along the lines of the European Union taxes, which involve a minimal delegation of sovereignty by member states who are allowed to keep a percentage of the tax revenues for their own use (Herber, 1997). Ultimately, progress would depend on galvanizing global political consensus on the need to mobilize stable and predictable global resources to address global environmental problems. A gradual approach of first introducing a modest OECD carbon tax may help build consensus for a global application at a later stage.

TRANSFERABLE DEVELOPMENT RIGHTS

The treatment of biodiversity as a global rather than national resource and the pressures to conserve it are perceived by developing countries as a challenge to their ownership and sovereignty over these resources. If, however, the primary purpose of efforts to protect biodiversity is conservation, not redistribution of resources, the first step is to recognize the ownership of developing countries over these resources and their right to develop them in order to maximize their own benefits. Much of the conflict between developed and developing countries concerning the conservation of biodiversity arises from a failure to distinguish between ownership and spatial exercise of development rights.

One form of attenuation of property rights is the complete separation of development rights from ownership rights, through the instrument of transferable development rights (TDRs). Without challenging property ownership (and entitlement to the benefits from ownership), all or certain types of development are prohibited on a site in the name of public interest. However, property owners are allowed to transfer to other sites or sell their development rights to others and thereby recover their full market value. Allowing extra development (beyond building or zoning regulations) ensures demand for such rights to the holders of transferred development rights. Both the ratio of transferred development rights to additional development entitlement and the percentage by which existing regulations can be exceeded in each zone are specified by law. The instrument of TDRs has been used extensively in the conservation of historical buildings, archaeological sites, cultural heritage, wetlands and coastal areas, and is today under consideration by a number of countries as an instrument for the conservation of greenbelts, forests and biodiversity.

The concept of TDRs makes possible the creation of conservation areas without the need for assessment of land values and compensation: it simply creates a market with the demand and supply of development rights that results in an equilibrium price at which exchange or transfer takes place (see Box 6.1).

In principle, there is no reason why TDRs cannot be used internationally as an instrument of payment by the North for conservation and supply of environmental services by the South. Tropical countries could set aside habitats for biodiversity conservation and divide each habitat into a number of TDRs, corresponding to an area unit, say, a hectare. Each TDR would state the location, condition, diversity and degree of protection of the habitat and any special rights that it conveys to the buyer/holder. TDRs could then be offered for sale both locally and internationally at an initial offer price that covers fully the opportunity cost of the corresponding land unit (ie the net present value of the income stream of the forgone development opportunity).

It is preferable to start at a relatively high price to test the market, since undervaluation is irreversible (following sale) while overvaluation is reversible (following non-sale). If the price turns out to be too high

Box 6.1 A Proposed Application of TDRs in Biodiversity Conservation in Akamas Peninsula, Cyprus

The Akamas Peninsula has an area of 250 square kilometres and is situated in the northwest of Cyprus; it is considered to be the last virgin territory in the eastern Mediterranean. This unique area has remained almost untouched by development despite the quadrupling of the number of tourists who have visited the island in the last ten years alone.

Due to the variety of its geomorphological features and the microclimate of its individual localities, Akamas displays a large concentration of biotopes, making up a unique ecosystem. The area supports an indivisible natural resource base comprising a rich flora and fauna, beautiful beaches and landscape, and interesting historical, archaeological and cultural heritage.

The flora of Akamas includes at least 20 endemic and other rare species. About 14 different kinds of orchids and *Tulipa cypria* (a rare endemic species) are also found in the area. Akamas also hosts the loggerhead-turtle (*caretta caretta*) and the green turtle (*chelonia mydias*), both under threat of disappearing from the Mediterranean, as well as a rare species of vulture (*Griffon vulture*), a fresh water crab (*Potamion potamios*) and endemic species of birds and butterflies. In addition, the area is used as a temporary stop-over by a multitude of birds when migrating from one continent to another.

The remarkably rich natural resources of Akamas are undergoing severe pressures and are threatened with degradation from a variety of sources including:

- day visitors in the area destroying flowering plants, forests, and animal species;
- property owners putting pressures on the government to open up the area for tourist development; and
- inhabitants in nearby villages demanding some kind of development.

The government has responded by zoning part of the Akamas area as a non-development area, stopping short of declaring it a national park. This response has intensified the conflict. On one side, local and international environmental groups such as the Friends of Akamas and Greenpeace find this response inadequate protection for the last unspoiled part of the island and demand stricter policies and the declaration of the area as a national park.

In the opposite camp are the inhabitants of villages surrounding Akamas, who own land in the area. They are demanding that the government provide them with roads and other infrastructure for tourist development as it has in the rest of the island. Being among the poorest people on the island, they see tourist development as their only chance for a better life; they have allied themselves with developers in lobbying the government to open the area to tourist development, and they are especially distressed because the prices of their land have dropped significantly following the government restrictions on development. Appropriation of the land by the government and compensation of land owners is out of the question because of the large amounts involved were this land to be compensated at its market value (as coastal property suitable for tourist development).

The result of these unresolved conflicts is a stalemate which neither protects biodiversity nor allows development to proceed. Akamas is neither a protected national park nor a managed tourist development zone. This uncertain situation is open to pressures for readjustments, exemptions and relaxations which prey on nature in a silent but equally destructive way.

To resolve these development versus conservation conflicts, which are not unique to Akamas but arise throughout the island, the concept of transferable development rights has been proposed by the Enalion Environmental Management Centre (Panayotou et al, 1991). The concept of transferal of development rights would ensure that areas of natural beauty be preserved in their natural state. It has been introduced in Cyprus for the first time in recent legislation for the preservation of buildings of unique cultural and historical value. It is now proposed that sites of natural beauty or those that are rich in ecological and biological resources could also be preserved through the use of this mechanism, without depriving their owners of their development rights and without paying compensation. The coastal area and, in fact, all of Cyprus could be divided into development areas and conservation areas. Land owners in conservation areas would retain their rights but they would not be allowed to exercise them on the site. They would instead be allowed to sell or transfer these rights to property in development areas, thus sharing in the benefits of development without actually developing their own land, which would remain in their hands in a natural state. It is estimated that the NPV of preservation benefits in terms of improved quality of tourism in the development areas combined with ecotourism on the conservation area would exceed the NPV forgone earnings from not developing Akamas into a mass tourism area like other parts of the island.

Source: Panayotou (1994b).

to clear the market (ie to exhaust the supplied TDRs for a particular habitat), the price can be lowered to attract additional demand. Alternatively, the quality of the TDR can be enhanced by enlarging the area to include additional biodiversity values or by improving its protection and management.

The potential buyers of TDRs include local and international environmental organizations, local and international foundations and corporations, developed country governments, chemical and pharmaceutical companies, scientific societies, universities and research institutions and even environmentally minded individuals from developed countries. The motivation for purchasing TDRs would naturally vary among prospective buyers. Some may derive direct use values such as prospecting for new chemicals or pharmaceuticals. Others may be expressing their non-use values through the purchase of TDRs. Still others might buy and hold TDRs if they expect them to increase in value as a result of decreasing supply and demand expansion from population and income growth, change in tastes or rising environmental awareness. Certainly every new discovery of a valuable new species, or even a new use of an existing species in a particular habitat, would increase the value of the TDRs of that site.

Despite the variety of increasing benefits that TDRs may confer on prospective buyers and holders, it is unlikely that there will be sufficient demand to preserve all the habitats that are worth conserving (eg based on contingent valuation of willingness to pay), for reasons ranging from myopia to free-riding. Given the public good nature of biodiversity conservation, the governments of developed countries (the main beneficiaries) could take 'pump priming' action to stimulate the demand for TDRs.

One way developed countries can stimulate the demand for TDRs is by providing credits to domestic firms and property owners for the acquisition of TDRs from developing countries against domestic environmental regulations such as building codes, forest harvesting and replanting regulations, environmental emission standards and CO_2 emissions.

A criticism of this method of stimulating demand for TDRs might be that the conservation of biodiversity in the tropics is thereby accomplished at the expense of the domestic environment in developed countries. One way around this problem is to tighten environmental regulations from current levels and then provide offset credits for buyers and holders of TDRs. Another method is to introduce a conservation tax and then allow people the option of paying this annual tax or purchasing and holding TDRs from conservation areas in lieu of the tax.

The great advantage of this mechanism for the conservation of tropical forests and biodiversity is that it makes the opportunity costs clear and provides a vehicle for the beneficiaries to pay them (Panayotou, 1994b). It also provides developing countries with substantial transfers of financial resources for sustainable development without compromising national ownership or sovereignty over tropical forests. Not only can TDRs be bought back, they can be leased on an annual basis rather than sold outright. Essentially, what the country is selling or leasing is not the rights to exploiting or developing its forests, but conservation services. Biodiversity conservation can be combined with carbon sequestration and traded as a bundle of environmental services (see Box 6.2).

INTERNATIONALLY TRADABLE EMISSION PERMITS

The virtually unlimited opportunities for low-cost reduction of greenhouse gas emissions are a grossly undervalued resource potentially in high demand in the North which the South has a comparative advantage to supply in exchange for financial and technological resources. While reductions of CO_2 emissions from fossil fuel consumption in Japan and the EU might cost over \$50–100 per ton, in developing countries, such as India and China, they might cost under \$20 per ton. If CO_2 emission reduction were a conventional commodity, there would be no doubt about where developed countries would seek to obtain these supplies.

Allowing emissions trading across nations would obtain a given reduction of emission at the lowest possible cost; it would be efficient. It would also encourage technology transfer and flow of financial resources from North to South in the interest of both the protection of global climate and sustainable development. For most developing

countries, tradable emission permits would be a major source of financial inflow and technology transfer and would provide a strong
incentive to become more efficient in order to save emission permits to
sell to other countries or for their own industrial expansion.

Although it would seem like a natural market to emerge, two obstacles stand in the way of emissions reduction trading today. First, until
recently, there was no binding obligation of countries to contain their
emissions. The Kyoto Protocol adopted in December 1997 by the
Conference of the Parties to the Climate Convention established
binding commitments by Annex I countries (mostly developed
countries) and allows trades among them, though the arrangements
and institutions necessary for emissions trading have been left to be
worked out in the next Conference of the Parties scheduled for
November 1998 in Buenos Aires. In addition, a special mechanism has
been established known as the Clean Development Mechanism (see
below) to facilitate trades between Annex I and non-Annex I countries,
a form of joint implementation (see below). Still, this is far from a
global emissions trading system. The Climate Convention could
change that, especially if amended to set an aggregate ceiling on greenhouse gas emissions, allocated among countries according to
population size or a combination of population size and some other
variable such as GDP or historical level of emissions. Any allocation
mechanism that has any chance of being accepted by the South would
result in excess demand for emission permits by the developed
countries and excess supply by the developing countries, setting the
stage for emissions trading. At the same time, in its best interest, the
South would probably be willing to work closely with the Climate
Convention to raise global abatement standards and regulations as this
would add considerable value to their permits and thereby increase
their potential revenue. Consequently this action would force developing countries into reducing 'extravagant' emissions due to inefficiencies
because of higher opportunity costs. Even if allowable emissions were
frozen at historical levels, growth would generate demand for
additional emission permits. These permits could be more easily
obtained from developing countries through improved energy
efficiency rather than from developed countries, such as Japan or
Germany, where further improvements in efficiency or reductions in
emissions can only come at a high cost.

A global emissions trading system promises huge economic and
environmental benefits but faces political and technical problems.
Significant progress has been made since Rio in better understanding
the problems involved and developing options such as alternative
formulas for permit allocation. The United Nations Conference on
Trade and Development (UNCTAD) is carrying out an extensive
research effort for the design and implementation of internationally
tradable emission permits and is developing a pilot emissions trading
project in cooperation with the Earth Council (Joshua, 1996). The
establishment of binding emission reduction commitments at Kyoto is

certain to accelerate progress towards an international emissions trading system which, if properly designed and implemented, promises to effect significant transfers of financial and technological resources to developing countries.

JOINT IMPLEMENTATION AND CARBON OFFSETS

Joint implementation projects are an important step towards an international system of tradable permits for greenhouse gas emissions. Such a system can be implemented gradually, first among OECD countries and later globally.

Joint implementation is a bilateral arrangement between a developed and a developing country to collaborate on a global commons problem in recognition of the potential mutual benefits arising from differential opportunity sets, determined by differences in the level of development, technology and preferences.[3] A developing country with low-cost carbon emission reduction opportunities and in need of new technology and financial resources could cooperate with a developed country with both the technology and the financial resources for emissions reduction. The developed country, in turn, gains lower-cost carbon emission reduction (or sequestration) opportunities to meet its obligations under the Global Climate Convention.

The cooperation, or rather, joint implementation, may take the form of the developed country transferring financial resources and technology to the developing country in exchange for carbon reduction credits against the developed country's international obligations. This helps the developing country to become more energy efficient as it switches fuels (eg from coal to natural gas) and more protective of its forests by planting trees in degraded watersheds. These exchanges, or carbon offsets, as they are known, can take place between the two countries' governments or private sector entities with government endorsement. The expectation is that the investor country would eventually receive credit against its own commitment to reduce GHG emissions under the Framework Convention on Climate Change (FCCC), while the host country derives development and local environmental benefits from the investment. Likely projects include energy efficiency investment. Table 6.2 presents some examples of joint implementation activities which have been approved under the United States JI initiative.

One type of carbon offset is between a developed country utility and a developing country forest company or a forest department. The power utility finances a shift to reduced impact logging techniques, enrichment planting (or reforestation) or forest conservation in a developing country in exchange for credit for the carbon saved or sequestered by the funded forestry activity. As long as the marginal cost of these activities is less than the cost of additional pollution abatement at the power utility, and assuming no or low transaction costs,

Table 6.2 *Joint Implementation Projects under the US Initiative on Joint Implementation*

Country	Type of project	Parties
Round 1 Feb 1995		
Belize	Protected areas and forest management 6 kha	Belize Programme for Belize, Wisconsin Electric Power Co, US Nature Conservancy
Costa Rica	Forest management 71 kha + buffer zone 20 kha	FUNDECOR (CR), CR Ministry of Natural Resources, Wachovia Timberland Investment Management
Costa Rica	Wind Plant 20 MW	Plantas Eolicas (CR), Charter Oak Energy (US), KENETECH Windpower, Merrill International
Costa Rica	Preventing deforestation	Nat Fish and Wildlife Foundation (CR), COMBOS (CR), CR Min of Nat Resources, Tenaska Washington Ptnrs (US), Trexler Associates (US), Council of the OSA Conservation Area (US), Rainforests of the Austrians
Honduras	Solar panels	COMARCA (H), AHDEJUMAR (H), Enersol Assoc (US)
Czech Republic	Gas for lignite in district heating	Center for Clean Air Policy (US), Wisconsin Electric Power, Edison Devpt Co, NIPSCo Devpt Co
Russian Federation	Sequestration of CO_2	Oregon State Univ, US EPA, Russian Federal Forest Service, Russian International Forestry Inst.
Round 2 Dec 1995		
Honduras	Biomass power station	Biomass Generacion, Nations Energy Corp, Edison Electric Inst, Add-on-Energy
Costa Rica	Hydroelectricity 16 MW	New World Power Corp, Compania Hidroelectrica Dona Julia, CR Ministry of Natural Resources
Costa Rica	Wind Energy	New World Power Corp, Energia del Nuevo Mundo, Molinos de Viento del Aranal, CR Ministry of Natural Resources
Costa Rica	Wind Energy	Power Systems Inc, Aeroenergia SA, Energy Works
Russian Federation	Methane capture from pipelines	Trans-pacific Geothermal Corp, C and R Inc
Costa Rica	Forest restoration	Guanacaste Conservation Area, National Inst of Biodiversity, Nature Conservancy
Nicaragua	Geothermal energy	Trans-pacific Geothermal Corp, C and R Inc
Costa Rica	Tree planting	Newton Treviso Corp, Cantanal Agric Center of Turrialba

Source: Steele and Pearce (1996).

Table 6.3 *Examples of Activities Implemented Jointly between Developed and Developing Countries.*

Country/Area	Project type	Greenhouse gas offset (tons of carbon)	Total project cost	Foreign sponsor contribution
Malaysia	Improved forest management	80,000–160,000	600,000	600,000
Malaysia	Reforestation	6,300,000	16,500,000	1,300,000
Czech Republic	Fuel switching and energy efficiency	3500 (per year)	1,500,000	600,000
Czech Republic	Reforestation	3,100,000	29,500,000	5,700,000
Amazon Basin	Forest protection	64,000,000	3,400,000	3,000,000
Guatemala	Tree planting, forest protection	16,500,000	15,800,000	2,200,000
Paraguay	Forest protection	14,000,000	3,900,000	2,000,000
Ecuador	Reforestation	9,700,000	17,000,000	1,100,000
Belize	Forest protection, improved forest management	1,300,000	2,600,000	2,600,000
Russia	Reforestation	35,000	250,000	250,000
Costa Rica	Various	200,000	2,000,000	2,000,000

Sources: Applied Energy Services Incorporated (AES): 'AES: Greenhouse Gas Offset Programs' Fall Update 1993, Arlington, Virginia; United States Initiative on Joint Implementation (USIJI); *About USIJI – A Program Profile*, Washington, DC; USIJI (1996) United States Initiative on Joint Implementation (USIJI) *Activities Implemented Jointly: First Report to the Secretariat of the United Nations Framework Convention on Climate Change*, US Government Document, DOE (P0048), Washington, DC, 1996.
As published in Panayotou (1997c).

these trades will continue.[4] The potential benefits are substantial, arising from differential costs of CO_2 reductions between developed and developing countries, and shared between the parties involved, both private and public. Table 6.3 presents some examples of activities implemented jointly between developed and developing countries. While this is only a partial list, the amounts involved are substantial, as are the global and local environmental benefits. Joint implementation is potentially a very important source of additional financial flows for sustainable development investments with both local and global environmental benefits, provided it is incremental to existing flows and does not distort the host country's development priorities.

Because of these concerns, the first conference of the Parties to the Climate Convention in Berlin in March–April 1995 established a pilot phase for Activities Implemented Jointly during which no crediting is allowed. During the pilot phase, experimentation is encouraged, as long as: (a) it has the approval of the governments of participating countries; (b) it supports national environment and development priorities; (c) it results in additional measurable gains; and (d) it is incremental to current ODA.

While several pilot offsets have been initiated in recent years (eg, New England Electrical System with the Sabah Foundation and Applied Energy Systems of Virginia with Guatemala), North–South carbon offsets have not yet been sanctioned by governments or the global community as a legitimate means of meeting CO_2 reduction obligations under the Climate Convention.

Despite criticism of carbon offsets and other joint implementation mechanisms, there is sufficient interest by both the North and the South to warrant further study and experimentation. Carbon offsets is one mechanism by which the global value of carbon sequestration can be internalized by the local populations of developing countries. Joint implementation, if properly designed and implemented to be efficient and equitable, is indeed an application of the cost-effectiveness and beneficiary pays principles of efficiency and equity, respectively.

The following developments during the pilot phase are indicative of the potential of joint implementation as a mechanism of cooperation between North and South and as a financing mechanism for sustainable development:

- On the demand side, at least 12 countries have included joint implementation in their national climate action plan, mandated by the Climate Convention: Australia, Canada, Costa Rica, Denmark, Finland, Germany, Iceland, Japan, the Netherlands, Norway, Sweden and the United States.
- On the supply side, at least a dozen countries have signed statements of intent to cooperate with the United States, among them: Bolivia, Chile, Pakistan, South Africa and all seven countries of Central America (Zollinger and Dower, 1996).
- As of July 1996, 17 countries are listed in the pilot phase as having launched or proposed projects ('activities implemented jointly'); 32 projects mainly in Central America and Eastern Europe have received official bilateral approval (UN-FCCC, 1996).
- Of more than 50 proposals submitted to the US Initiative on Joint Implementation, 15 have been approved, and of these, four have been fully financed. Of more than 40 submissions to the International Utility Efficiency Program in Washington, DC, nine are being considered for implementation (Zollinger and Dower, 1996).
- The International Business Action on Climate Change, a private sector initiative by the World Business Council for Sustainable Development (WBCSD) has received over 80 submissions, potentially worth $3 billion, although few are developed enough to be considered as pilot projects (WBCSD, 1996).
- The Netherlands has set aside $51 million for joint implementation programmes in Eastern Europe.
- Norway has set up bilateral joint implementation demonstration projects and recently purchased 200,000 tons of carbon in certified transferable offsets from Costa Rica at the cost of $2 million (see Box 6.2). Norway also co-finances World Bank and IFC investments and research on activities implemented jointly.

Box 6.2 The Costa Rican Environmental Service Payments Scheme and Certified Tradable Offsets

In an effort to halt deforestation and encourage reforestation, the Costa Rican government, during the 1980s, introduced incentives in the form of tax credits for landowners maintaining forests on their lands. To allow smallholders, who usually paid no taxes, to benefit from the scheme, the government allowed the reforestation tax credits to be traded. This created the first rudimentary market for environmental services in the country. In the 1990s, this scheme was reformed and expanded into a comprehensive system of payments for environmental services, both local and global. The government identified four sets of services which are provided by forested private lands that are external to the owner and for which he/she receives no payment and therefore faces inadequate incentives to provide them:

1 watershed protection services (local/national);
2 ecotourism attraction (local/national);
3 biodiversity conservation (global); and
4 carbon sequestration (global).

The government sought both instruments for internalizing these values to the landowners, (ie instruments for effecting commensurate payments) and financial resources to finance these payments. It was recognized that at a minimum, farmers must be compensated for the opportunity costs (forgone benefits from current land uses, mainly cattle ranching) estimated around $30 per ha per year. This set the lower bound for the payments. The upper bound was set by the value of the environmental services provided to both the local/national economy and to the global community. This value was conservatively estimated to be in the range of $40–60 per ha per year (more generous estimates put the value of environmental services of forests in Costa Rica in the range of $100–200 per ha per year). The government settled on an incentive payment of $50 per ha per year, higher than the average opportunity cost and lower than the 'value' of environmental services provided.

Funding for the payment of environmental services contracts is obtained from a sales tax on fossil fuel and from the Carbon Fund which serves as a depository for revenues obtained from carbon sales to the international community. The Carbon Fund buys environmental services from farmers and resells them to beneficiaries. The Carbon Fund has established Certifiable Tradable [Greenhouse Gas] offsets or CTOs, which is a financial instrument for transfer (sale) of carbon offsets in the international market. CTOs are pre-approved, transferable and guaranteed by Costa Rica for 20 years. The first CTOs for 2000 tons of carbon were sold in July 1996 to Norway for $2 million. The Centre for Financial Products purchased 1000 CTOs for resale in secondary financial markets. The Centre has an exclusive contract to broker 4 million tons of Costa Rican Carbon over the next 20 years with a floor price of $10 per ton generating at least $40 million in revenues. Costa Rica expects to eventually supply 15 million tons of carbon to world markets.

Source: Castro and Tattenbach (1997).

Box 6.3 Kyoto Protocol, Article 12: The Clean Development Mechanism

1   A clean development mechanism is hereby defined.
2   The purpose of the clean development mechanism shall be to assist Parties not included in Annex I in achieving sustainable development and in contributing to the ultimate objective of the Convention, and to assist Parties included in Annex I in achieving compliance with their quantified emission limitation and reduction commitments under Article 3.
3   Under the clean development mechanism:
    (a)   Parties not included in Annex I will benefit from project activities resulting in certified emission reductions;
    (b)   Parties included in Annex I may use the certified emission reductions accruing from such project activities to contribute to compliance with part of their quantified emission limitation and reduction commitments under Article 3, as determined by the Conference of the Parties serving as the meeting of the Parties to this Protocol.
4   The clean development mechanism shall be subject to the authority and guidance of the Conference of the Parties serving as the meeting of the Parties to this Protocol and be supervised by an executive board of the clean development mechanism.
5   Emission reductions resulting from each project activity shall be certified by operational entities to be designated by the Conference of the Parties serving as the meeting of the Parties to this Protocol, on the basis of:
    (a)   voluntary participation approved by each Party involved;
    (b)   real, measurable and long-term benefits related to the mitigation of climate change; and
    (c)   reductions in emissions that are additional to any that would occur in the absence of the certified project activity.
6   The clean development mechanism shall assist in arranging funding of certified project activities as necessary.
7   The Conference of the Parties serving as the meeting of the Parties to this Protocol shall, at its first session, elaborate modalities and procedures with the objective of ensuring transparency, efficiency and accountability through independent auditing and verification of project activities.
8   The Conference of the Parties serving as the meeting of the Parties to this Protocol shall ensure that a share of the proceeds from certified project activities is used to cover administrative expenses as well as to assist developing country Parties that are particularly vulnerable to the adverse effects of climate change to meet the costs of adaptation.
9   Participation under the clean development mechanism, including in activities mentioned in paragraph 3(a) above and acquisition of certified emission reductions, may involve private and/or public entities, and is to be subject to whatever guidance may be provided by the executive board of the clean development mechanism.
10 Certified emission reductions obtained during the period from the year 2000 up to the beginning of the first commitment period can be used to assist in achieving compliance in the first commitment period.

Source: United Nations (1997).

THE CLEAN DEVELOPMENT MECHANISM (CDM)

The Kyoto Protocol adopted by the Conference of the Parties to the Framework Convention on Climate Change (FCCC) in December 1997 established, in addition to Annex I binding commitments, the Clean Development Mechanism (CDM) (see Box 6.3). The purpose of this new mechanism is to assist non-Annex I countries to achieve sustainable development, while contributing to the ultimate objective of the convention, and to assist Annex I countries to meet their emission reduction commitments. This new mechanism enables both the private and the public sectors in Annex I countries to invest in projects undertaken in non-Annex I countries which result in emission reductions and to receive credit for some of these reductions against the investing annex I country's commitment. Only real, quantifiable long-term emissions reductions that would not have taken place otherwise will be credited.

For CDM to become operational, many procedures and modalities need to be worked out, including governance (executive board), rules for certifying emissions reductions or greenhouse gas sinks and units of measurement and equivalence between different reductions of different greenhouse gases. Developing countries would want to ensure that their development priorities are not compromised but advanced. The experience gained from joint implementation projects during the pilot phase will help in the development of this new financing mechanism for both sustainable development and protection of the global climate. Whether it will be developed into a significant source of funding will depend in part on institutional arrangements to minimize transaction costs (including brokerage, monitoring verification and risk management).

Chapter 7

Selecting the Right Instrument

As we have seen, there is a large set of economic instruments from
which to choose when attempting to manage the environment in an
atmosphere of constrained resources. Given the large number of available instruments, criteria for specific instrument selection need to be
established, or if a set of instruments is selected, an assessment must
precede implementation. Furthermore, the adoption of an economic
instrument approach to environmental policy and sustainable development and the specific instruments chosen have institutional and
human resource requirements and financial implications that need to
be addressed. For example, certain instruments such as secure land
titles require cadastral surveys; environmental bonds and self-assessed
charges require environmental auditors; and revolving funds may
require new institutions. The objective of this chapter is to detail the
criteria for instrument evaluation and selection and to assess the
human, institutional and financial requirements. Particular attention is
paid to distributional considerations, dynamic efficiency and political
acceptability.

The chapter concludes with two summary tables. Table 7.2 presents
a qualitative assessment of 18 economic instruments in terms of seven
criteria, ranging from feasibility and effectiveness, through efficiency
and equity, to administrative and institutional practicality. Table 7.3
summarizes the charges typically recommended for different pollutants
and sources.

ASSESSMENT OF INSTRUMENTS

The selection and assessment of instruments is best done by asking and
answering the following nine questions, all conditioned by the special
circumstances of the particular country concerned:

Environmental effectiveness

*Will the instrument achieve the environmental objective within the specified
time span and what degree of certainty can be expected?* If the environmental outcome is somewhat uncertain or experimental (trial and error)
and different instrument levels are needed, how acceptable is deviation

from the set goal? The answer depends to a large extent on the nature of environmental damage in question. The acceptable margin of error is much higher for reversible environmental damages, depletion of substitutable resources or generation of biodegradable waste than for irreversible loss of unsubstitutable assets such as biodiversity and species loss and generation of hazardous waste. Setting benchmarks and milestones and monitoring of progress towards the set targets are required for assessing the environmental effectiveness of instruments. Midstream adjustments in the instrument (eg, charge rate, tax base, etc) may be required.

Cost effectiveness

Will the instrument achieve the environmental objective (or target) at the minimum possible cost to society? Not only are environmental budgets limited, but any savings can be used to achieve other social objectives (eg, equity) or to pursue further environmental improvement. The costs to society of pursuing certain environmental objectives through a particular instrument or set of instruments are not limited to the cost of monitoring and enforcement by the environmental agency. The largest component of the social cost of environmental intervention is the cost of compliance by the industry in terms of output reduction, capital and operating cost of abatement technology and the additional cost of switching to higher-cost inputs, such as natural gas. A second component of the social cost is the distortionary effect of the particular instrument chosen. Most economic instruments, if correctly chosen and set at the right level (eg, Pigouvian taxes set equal to the marginal damage cost), are corrective of existing distortions and hence have a negative distortion cost, or a correction benefit. There are, however, economic instruments such as subsidies which, though statically equivalent to environmental taxes, dynamically (in the long run) encourage entry into the polluting industry, thereby increasing rather than reducing pollution and hence violating the environmental effectiveness criterion above.

Flexibility

Is the instrument flexible enough to adjust to changes in technology, the resource scarcity, and market conditions? For example, in the face of inflation will it maintain its potency or will it be gradually eroded into an ineffective instrument? Indexing to inflation is one way of maintaining the value of the instrument, another is by setting the instrument, for example a charge, in terms of a percentage of the price, rather than at a fixed nominal monetary value. With regard to scarcity, the instrument's value or level must rise with increasing resource or environmental scarcity. For example, while tradable emission permits meet this criterion, as do property rights (their value rises with scarcity),

Table 7.1 *Cost Savings from a Shift of Environmental Policy from Command-and-Control Regulations to Least-cost Instruments (based on US experience)*

Study	Pollutants covered	Geographic area	CAC benchmark	Ratio of CAC cost to least-cost
Atkinson and Lewis	Particulates	St Louis	SIP regulations	6.00[a]
Roach et al	Sulphur dioxide	Four corners in Utah	SIP regulations Colorado, Arizona and New Mexico	4.25
Hahn and Noll	Sulphates standards	Los Angeles	California emission	1.07
Krupnick	Nitrogen dioxide regulations	Baltimore	Proposed RACT	5.96[b]
Seskin et al	Nitrogen dioxide regulations	Chicago	Proposed RACT	14.40
McGartland	Particulates	Baltimore	SIP regulations	4.18
Spofford	Sulphur dioxide	Lower Delaware Valley	Uniform percentage regulations	1.78
	Particulates	Lower Delaware Valley	Uniform percentage regulations	22.00
Harrison	Airport noise	United States	Mandatory retrofit	1.72[c]
Maloney and Yandle	Hydrocarbons	All domestic DuPont plants	Uniform percentage reduction	4.15[d]
Palmer et al	CFC emissions from non-aerosol applications	United States	Proposed standards	1.96

Notes: CAC, command-and-control, the traditional regulatory approach; SIP, state implementation plan; RACT, reasonably available control technologies, a set of standards imposed on existing sources in non-attainment areas.
a Based on a $40\mu g/m^3$ at worst receptor.
b Based on a short-term, one-hour average of 250 $\mu g/m^3$.
c Because it is a benefit-cost study instead of a cost-effectiveness study, the Harrison comparison of command-and-control with the least-cost approach involves different benefit levels. Specifically, the benefit levels associated with the least-cost allocation are only 82 per cent of those associated with the command-and-control allocation. To produce cost estimates based on more comparable benefits, as a first approximation the least-cost allocation was divided by 0.82 and the resulting number was compared with the command-and-control cost.
d Based on 85 per cent reduction of emissions from all sources.

Source: Tietenberg, (1990b).

Box 7.1 Regional Flexibility of Fee Systems in China

Distributional equity and the perceived impact on low-income groups in China significantly affected the levels of user charges and the enforcement of levies and charges on small-scale producers. China has allowed significant regional variation in the discharge fee system, issued temporary short-term permits to firms unable to meet regular permit conditions and allowed local officials to waive the levy fees for unprofitable operations so as not to threaten the viability of vital local enterprises. This involves significant trade-offs and costs in terms of economic efficiency and environmental effectiveness.

The vastness of countries such as China implies enormous regional diversity in natural resource endowment, in assimilative capacity, in geo-climatic conditions and in level of industrialization and development. The severity of environmental problems, the level of exposure, and hence, the consequent damages also vary enormously across regions as does enforcement capability. Flexible economic instruments can much more readily and efficiently accommodate heterogeneity and diversity than uniform environmental standards and mandated technology. Indeed the greater the variability in costs and benefits of environmental management, the greater the cost savings from allowing trading, offsets, credits and other forms of exchange between pollution sources as long as care is taken to avoid pollution hotspots through appropriate selection of airsheds and watersheds within which trades and other exchanges can be allowed.

Source: Panayotou (1995a).

---

command-and-control standards and environmental bonds do not adjust automatically to changing resource scarcities; they need to be deliberately and periodically adjusted. With regard to technology, will the instrument adjust to changes in monitoring, abatement, and production technology or will it soon be made obsolete by new technologies? For example, mandated best available technology, an extensively used command-and-control instrument, does not meet this criterion unless it is deliberately and regularly revised, at great cost (see Table 7.1). Large countries, such as China, need also consider the great variation in levels of development, resource endowment and degree of exposure to damage across regions. In China's case (see Box 7.1), economic instruments in general provide the flexibility that command-and-control instruments do not.

Dynamic efficiency

Does the instrument provide incentives for developing and adopting new environmentally cleaner and economically more efficient technologies? Does it promote development of an environmentally sound infrastructure and economic structure in general? Charges and tradable permits, for example, meet this criterion while effluent standards or mandated technology do not. Perhaps more important for developing countries is the extent to which the instrument provides an incentive for environmentally sound and economically efficient structural change. A dynamically efficient instrument is one that encourages the flow of resources towards activities in which the country has a genuine comparative advantage: towards commodities that can be produced at a domestic resource cost, inclusive of the resource depletion cost and environmental cost, which is lower than the world price. The structural change effects of the instrument are equally important with regard to infrastructure and urban development. For example, low gasoline prices in the United States have resulted in a dispersed pattern of development and land use that make the development of most transit systems unprofitable and the economy dependent on private driving. The ultimate consequence is that high air quality standards are very costly and difficult to accomplish. The lock-in effect of underpricing of energy and uninternalized externalities is reflected both in urban sprawl and in vested interests and political economy which resist change. In contrast, European cities' mass transit systems are profitable because of the high-density land use induced by high gasoline prices.

Equity

Will the costs and benefits of the instrument be equitably distributed? Who gains and who loses? This is a complex question but of critical importance to the successful introduction of economic instruments. Different instruments have different distributional implications. Environmental taxes tend to be regressive compared to regulatory standards. The pollution control costs fall more heavily on low-income groups, especially with product taxes or pollution charges which affect the prices of commodities (such as food, clothes or shelter) on which the poor spend a higher proportion of their income. The benefits of environmental enhancements such as improved water supply, sanitation and reduction of indoor pollution by suspended particle matter (SPM) and lead emissions, tend to be progressive (pro-poor); the poor are more exposed to these pollutants owing to their living and working conditions and they lack the means for preventive or mitigating expenditures. On the other hand, when these benefits are valued in monetary terms, their distribution may in fact be regressive because the poor have a much lower willingness to pay for environmental improvements due to their low income. Thus, ultimately, the distributional impact of economic instruments depends on: (a) how the property rights or pollution permits are allocated; and (b) how the revenues from environmental taxes and charges are spent.

Property rights and trading programmes (pollution permits, development quotas, catch quotas, etc) can lead to large transfers of wealth between socioeconomic groups and locations. As such, they can also act as instruments of social policy or income transfers to improve income distribution. For instance, the poor could be issued secure property rights over open access resources such as land rights and water rights. The regressivity of environmental taxes can be dealt with through differential taxation (lower taxes on necessities). In principle, even tradable pollution permits can be allocated in a way that benefits the poor (see Chapter 3).

The distributional impact of environmental taxes (and other instruments) varies with the level of economic development. For example, in India and China gasoline taxes are likely to be progressive, while in the USA and UK they are regressive.

In controlling global climate change, internationally tradable CO_2 emission permits are emerging as a major source for transferring financial and technological resources from North to South. The distributional impacts of different instruments vary by location and time horizon; they are higher in targeted areas (eg, industrial towns, coal producing areas, etc) and during the transitional period than in other areas and subsequent periods, respectively. Retraining, compensation for impacts, gradual implementation, grandfathering of old (or small) producers and revenue neutrality (commensurate reduction of other taxes) are some ways in which the distributional impact of economic instruments can be compensated for or mitigated.

Ease of introduction

Is the instrument consistent with the country's legislative framework? If new legislation is necessary, how feasible is it? Does the executive branch of government have the administrative capacity to issue the necessary regulations and administer the instruments? What is the administrative opportunity cost given the limited administrative resources in a poor country? This criterion favours instruments that do not require new legislation and can be administered with existing administrative structures, such as the income tax or excise tax collection authorities. For example, in countries with very scarce administrative resources, product taxes, which use the existing tax collection system, are preferable to pollution charges or tradable pollution permits which require new legislation and new collection and enforcement institutions.

Ease of monitoring and enforcement

How difficult or costly will monitoring and enforcement be? This is partly a function of the administrative capacity (discussed above and below) and partly a function of the structure of the industry towards which the instrument aims. Large numbers of scattered, small-scale economic units imply high monitoring and enforcement costs. A country with limited monitoring and enforcement capability will opt for indirect instruments such as product taxes over effluent charges, which are embodied in the prices of inputs and outputs, or other self-enforced instruments such as bonds and deposit-refund systems, which shift the burden (and the cost) of monitoring and enforcement to the polluters.

Community resource management and customary use rights have the great advantage that the monitoring and enforcement costs are decentralized and internalized to communities which enforce them using their own internal organization, kinship relationships and social norms. In terms of the introduction of new instruments, the challenge is to design them so they are self-enforced by drawing lessons from traditional systems. For example, the pollution charge imposed on an individual firm could be made a function of both the firm's own emissions and of the industry's total emissions, or of the airshed's or watershed's ambient quality, thereby providing incentives for the industry to police itself.

Predictability

Does the instrument combine flexibility and predictability? Flexibility is critical for cost minimization, adjustment to varying conditions, locations and changing circumstances, and for gradual implementation. Predictability is critical for dynamic efficiency both in terms of technological innovation and structural change. The effectiveness of any instrument depends critically on the perception of its permanency and direction of change. Only when the industry perceives that a standard, a tax or a charge is in place to stay (that its value will escalate over time towards full-cost pricing rather than be eroded by inflation) will it modify its long-term investment plans to reduce environmental costs. It is the instability and unpredictability of environmental policy rather than the costs of compliance that the industry finds disruptive and ultimately more costly.[1] Therefore, when an instrument is introduced gradually, the compliance or escalation schedule must be pre-announced and adhered to (see Chapter 8, Box 8.2).

Acceptability

Is the instrument understandable by the public, acceptable to the industry and politically sellable? This is perhaps the most difficult criterion to meet and definitely one that puts economic instruments in a disadvantageous position. Unlike the hidden costs of command-and-control regulations, the costs of economic instruments such as product taxes, pollution charges, user fees, environmental bonds and liability systems, are all too transparent. Taxes are generally unpopular and user charges are unwelcome when the service is taken for granted or if it has been available at a subsidized cost for a long time. Underpricing and subsidies become capitalized into property values and their removal is seen as a net reduction in the owner's wealth.

Environmental groups and the general public often resist market creation, such as tradable pollution permits, as a licence to pollute. Polluters resist economic instruments, such as taxes and charges, if they perceive unenforced command-and-control standards as a feasible alternative, or if they see an easier opportunity for regulators' capture in non-economic instrument approaches to environmental management such as the process of negotiation between polluters and regulators practised in the UK. Exploiters of open access resources would generally resist regulations or closure of the commons from fear that they might be the ones that are excluded. Finally, the public is likely to be receptive to allegations that economic instruments for environmental management are just another form of taxation or licence for big polluters to continue to pollute. They are also likely to be receptive to calls for 'environmental justice' in the form of either equal pollution reduction (in absolute or percentage terms) by all sources or uniform emission standards.

Therefore, the promoters of economic instruments have a difficult marketing task. Without making the benefits and costs of the available options (including that of no action) clear to the industry, to the environmental groups and the public, the chances of acceptance and successful implementation are severely limited. Selecting simple and easily understood instruments makes the marketing task easier and the likelihood of acceptance greater. In addition, a number of mitigative and compensatory measures can be introduced to lessen both the transitional and the long-term cost.

One such measure is revenue neutrality: the reduction of other taxes such as income taxes which reduce the incentive for work, or sales taxes and import tariffs which distort consumption decisions, offsetting the revenue gains from the economic instrument.[2] Other mitigation measures include gradual implementation and grandfathering of existing producers. The support of environmental groups and the industry can often be secured through greater communication and participation in the selection and implementation of economic instruments.

INSTITUTIONAL AND HUMAN RESOURCE REQUIREMENTS

Economic instruments as a group tend to have lower institutional and human resource requirements than command-and-control regulations because they operate through incentives rather than through coercion. First, it is far easier to implement an instrument that puts compliance in the best interest of the economic agent than an instrument which forces compliance through command-and-control regulation. Second, economic instruments make maximum use of the superior and privileged information that the polluters and resource users have on their own pollution control and resource conservation cost without the requirement to find out what that information is. This contrasts with the considerable informational demands of command-and-control regulations, which include intimate knowledge by the regulators of the production and pollution control technologies of a multitude of production processes. The informational parsimony of economic or market-based instruments can be compared to the informational advantage of market economies over centrally planned economies.

Nevertheless, the informational requirements of economic instruments are not insignificant, especially when one attempts to introduce them at the optimal level, where the marginal control cost equals the marginal damage cost. This presumes knowledge of pollution control (or conservation) cost functions and environmental damage functions, neither of which are readily available. These informational requirements are considerably reduced if we seek only to attain cost-effectiveness; the environmental objective is set through some other means such as the political process or at scientifically established ecological thresholds, and the economic instrument only attempts to achieve this objective at minimum cost. Experimentation with pilot projects or trial and error would help reveal the needed information for determining the optimal level of the instrument. Since gradual introduction is often preferable, the instrument can first be introduced at a very low level and progressively escalated, gaining information in the process until the optimal level is approximated.

Informational requirements can be reduced further by taking into account the special conditions of the country (see Chapter 7), the industry, the environmental media and the specific pollutant or resource whose control is sought. When the instrument is tailor-made to fit these conditions, the informational and enforcement costs are minimized. An ill-designed economic instrument or one which is alien to the culture of the country and the structure of the industry could have higher informational and enforcement requirements than well-designed command-and-control regulations. For example, effluent charges applied to scattered, small-scale industries in developing countries with a large underground economy have enormous information requirements and little chance of successful implementation. Under these circumstances, product taxes and deposit-refund systems, though indirect instruments, are more effective overall.

While every effort should be made to choose instruments, designs and modes of introduction that minimize the informational and management/enforcement requirements, there is an irreducible minimum level that must be met if environmental policy is to produce results on the ground. Informational and management requirements are translated into institutional and human resource requirements: two resources in high demand and limited supply in developing countries. To minimize institutional demands, maximum use must be made of existing administrative structures such as existing tax collection bureaucracy, industry licensing procedures, the vehicle registration system, the town and country planning department, the government tourist agency and line ministries or departments such as forestry, mining, industry and agriculture. For example, product taxes can be integrated with existing sales, excise tariffs or value-added tax systems and collected by the relevant collection agencies. Betterment charges can be integrated with property taxes and collected by the existing property tax department. Wastewater treatment charges or watershed protection charges can be incorporated into the monthly water bill and collected concurrently. Transferable development rights or land use taxes can be implemented through the land registration department to maximize use of the private land market institutions (eg, real estate firms, land surveyors, property value assessors, etc)

Using existing institutions significantly reduces the need for new institutions and additional human resources though it will not eliminate it entirely. For example, water rights, tradable catch quotas or emission permits require a special registry, which is regularly updated. Issuance of secure land titles requires cadastral surveys and a process for the resolution of conflicting claims, while land use taxes call for land use registry. Performance bonds require a financial institution that will manage and reinvest the funds, pay interest, assess performance and dispose the bond accordingly. Effluent charges require a monitoring and collection system that has relatively high institutional and human resource requirements, because these charges call for specialized knowledge and measurement capabilities. While existing institutions can be restructured or upgraded to handle many of these tasks, additional specialized organizational and human resources need to be added.

Among the new professions required are specialists in environmental impact assessment and valuation (damage or betterment assessment), environmental auditors and inspectors, environmental engineers and economists, financial analysts and environmental tax experts. While people with some of these skills may not be available in developing countries, related skills exist and can be easily retrofitted for the use of economic instruments in environmental management. External training and technical assistance might be needed for some time in certain countries but local expertise would not take long to respond if effective demand exists because related skills are often available.

What about legal institutions, legislation and regulations needed to back economic instruments? Property rights and enforcement of contracts are essential for the efficient operation of markets, on which the effectiveness of economic instruments, also known as market-based instruments, depends. As we have seen, where property rights cannot be defined in physical space, they can be defined in legal space through permits, licences, quotas and the like, which assign right of use. Economic instruments require enabling legislation, or legal framework, not detailed regulation. Environmental charges need to be legislated, unless they qualify as taxes or user charges permissible by executive decision within the existing legal framework. Similarly, performance bonds and transferable development rights need to be legislated and environmental funds need to be legally constituted. However, once economic instruments are in place, they should be more or less self-enforced; otherwise, they have not been properly designed.

The economic instruments approach to environmental management and sustainable development requires regulations to set the rules of the game, not to specify and arbitrate every move. In most real world situations, a command-and-control structure already exists and economic instruments should not seek to replace it overnight, but to support it and make it more flexible and cost effective, making allowances for differences in compliance cost through credits, offsets, trades and other mutually beneficial exchanges.

FINANCIAL AND FISCAL IMPLICATIONS

With the exception of subsidies, tax credits and financial incentives, which are generally not favoured by the economic-instruments approach to environmental management, all other economic instruments have positive financial and fiscal implications.[3] Removal of distortionary subsidies (eg, on fossil fuels, agrochemicals, water, etc) would save substantial amounts of government revenue as well as generate additional taxes in the long run through the enlargement of the tax base following the removal of the distortion. Environmental taxes, by virtue of being non-distortionary and corrective, generate additional government revenues at minimum cost. In fact, estimates by the Norwegian Statistical Office indicate that the costs of raising a tax dollar through conventional taxes is greater than one dollar due to the distortion effect (eg, disincentive for work), while the same dollar could be raised through environmental taxes at a cost of less than one dollar: in fact, at a negative cost due to the correction effect.[4] (See Figure 7.1)

This corrective and revenue generating quality of environmental taxes contrasts sharply with the distortions, zero revenue (except from fines) and considerable expenditures associated with command-and-control regulations. There are, of course, issues as to whether the revenue from environmental taxes should be earmarked and used for environmental investments or go to the treasury to be used for general expenditure, or for the reduction of other taxes (eg, income tax). Revenue generated by user charges or full-cost pricing for wastewater treatment, road access, water use or other public utilities are payments for services rendered and are retained by the utility for cost recovery.

On the other hand, tradable emission permits, tradable catch quotas, transferable development quotas, fishing licences, and other forms of market creation do not automatically generate revenue, unless they are auctioned or sold by the issuing authority, in which case they can generate substantial amounts of revenue. When they are given free of charge, the issuing authority may introduce a capital gains tax on the price of the permit or quota –which is likely to appreciate over time because of rising demand for permits against a fixed supply – to finance the administrative costs of issuing, registering and monitoring the permits. Administrative fees may similarly be imposed for issuance of land titles, water rights and transferable development rights to defray costs. Capital gains from these rights may also be taxed to raise general budget revenues.

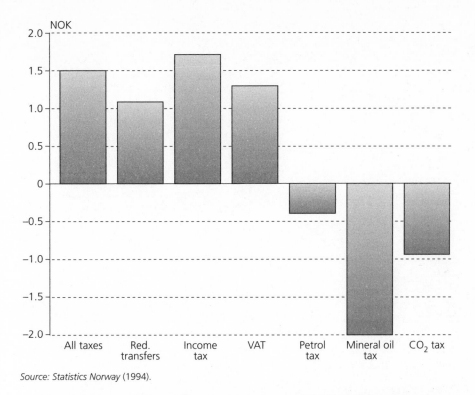

Source: *Statistics Norway* (1994).

Figure 7.1 *Cost of increasing taxes and duties in Norway*

Despite the favourable financial implications of economic instruments over the medium to long run, depending on the instrument, a short-term cash flow problem may be created by the effort to introduce economic instruments such as secure land titles, water rights, fishing licences, and tradable emission permits. The financial deficit may arise from the fact that property rights acquire value (and can be used as collateral for access to financial markets) after they are issued. Since cadastral surveys, resolution of conflicting claims and title issuance and registration take time (3–5 years is not unusual), a cash flow problem is created for the issuing agency which assumes the cost without an immediate means of cost recovery. Given the severe scarcity of domestic financial resources in many developing countries, external financial assistance or borrowing is necessary for the implementation of certain instruments such as property rights. For example, Thailand in the 1980s received a $30 million loan from the World Bank, in conjunction with its structural adjustment programme, specifically for the purpose of cadastral surveys, land registration and titling.

Market creation instruments, such as tradable emission permits or fishing licences, may also face a financial problem because in order to secure acceptance by the industry, the government may allocate, free of charge, permits to all existing firms to cover fully their current emissions (grandfather system). Not only are the costs of establishing the system

Table 7.2 Assessment of Economic Instruments

Mechanisms/ Instruments	Feasibility	Environmental effectiveness	Economic efficiency (static)	Dynamic efficiency	Equity & distribution	Administrative efficiency	Institutional parsimony
Domestic/Sectoral							
Land resources							
Differential land use tax	H	H	H	L	+,−,(*)	L	M
Secure land titles	H	M	H	H	+,−,(*)	H	M
Soil conservation incentives	H	H	M	L	+	M	M
Forest resources							
Long-term Forest concessions	M	M	H	H	+,−,(*)	M	H
Area-based							
forest taxation	H	M	M	H	+	H	H
Tradable reforestation credits	H	H	M	M	+,−,(*)	M	M
Forest mgmt. Bonds	M	H	L	M	+	H	L
Water							
Watershed protection fees	H	H	M	L	+	M	M
Tradable water rights or shares	M	M	H	H	+,−,(*)	M	L
Sustainable agriculture							
Agrochemical taxes	H	M	M	H	+,−,(*)	H	H
Sustainable agricultural premia	M	M	M	H	+,−	L	L
Tradable development Rights	M	H	H	M	+,−,(*)	M	L
Global							
Global warming							
Carbon taxes	L	H	H	H	−	M	L
Air travel tax	H	M	M	L	+	H	H
Tradable CO$_2$ permits	M	H	H	H	+,−,(*)	M	M
Carbon offsets (JI)	H	H	H	H	+,−,(*)	M	M
Biodiversity							
Tradable conservation credits	M	H	H	M	+,−,(*)	M	L
Biospecting concessions	H	M	M	H	+,−,(*)	L	M

Notes: H, High; M, Medium; L, Low; +, Progressive; −, Regressive; (*), depends on allocation arrangements.

Table 7.3 *Pollution Charges Typically Recommended for Different Pollutants and Sources*

Source	Air pollutants				Water pollutants		
	Particulates	SO_x	CO_2	Lead	BOD	P	Metals
Vehicles:							
petrol	n/a	n/a	fuel tax	fuel tax			
diesel	fuel tax	fuel tax	fuel tax	n/a			
Households and small enterprises	fuel tax	fuel tax	fuel tax	n/a	user charge based on water use or flat-rate		n/a
Power and heat utilities	emission charge or/ and limit	fuel tax or/and emission charge	fuel tax	n/a			
Industry: general	(presumptive) emission charges or/and limits		fuel tax	emissions limits (plus charge)			
– connected to collective wastewater treatment plant					user charge (plus pollution surcharge) based on water use; or user charge based on pollutant load		emissions limits (plus charge)
– not connected to collective wastewater treatment plant					effluent charge based on load or presumptive effluent charge based on water use		emissions limits (plus charge)

Source: World Bank (1989)

not recovered, but the government needs substantial additional financial resources to buy back a large number of permits or licences in order to reduce emissions or fishing effort to the desired level. These costs can later be recovered through a capital gains tax on the market value of the permits, which will rise as more licences are withdrawn and as demand for permits rises over time due to economic growth.

In conclusion, the introduction of economic instruments is generally a bankable project and even poor countries should be able to find the financial resources from development or environmental assistance or external borrowing to finance the short-term implementation cost. Alternatively, they can implement a cross-instrument subsidization; for example, the revenues from product charges can be used to finance the introduction of more sophisticated instruments such as tradable emission permits. Table 7.2 summarizes the assessment of 18 economic instruments in terms of the criteria discussed in this chapter.

Ultimately, the most appropriate instrument for a specific case would depend on the type of pollutant (whether hazardous or not, whether uniformly mixing or not, etc), the type of source (whether point or non-point surface) and the country's monitoring charge collection and enforcement capability, among others. Knowledge of both the target pollutant and the context of implementation of the specific case are indispensable to the selection and design of the instrument; unavoidably some tailoring and adaptation to local conditions is needed, including a phase-in period of adjustment. However, some generalization can be given here. Table 7.3 summarizes pollution charges typically recommended for different pollutants and sources.

Chapter 8

Introducing Economic Instruments in Developing Countries

Economic incentives as instruments of environmental management in developing countries have several advantages over command-and-control regulations. First, they can achieve the desired effect at the least possible cost; this is vital to developing countries with limited resources and a dire need to maintain their competitiveness in world markets. Second, economic incentives are easier to enforce; this is important for countries with limited enforcement capability. Third, economic incentives present fewer opportunities for rent-seeking behaviour than do regulations and therefore they are likely to be both more effective and more equitable. Finally, unlike regulations which require bloated bureaucracies and large budgets, economic incentives generate revenues that should be welcomed by countries facing tight budgets and budgetary deficits.

There is a large toolkit of economic instruments that can be used in support (or replacement) of command-and-control regulations. Each instrument has several variants and the potential number of combinations of instruments is practically infinite. Choosing the right instrument or combination of instruments for a particular problem and circumstance makes the difference between efficient and effective intervention that mitigates market failures and a costly distortion that worsens the allocation of resources and reduces social welfare. What works under one set of circumstances may be totally ineffectual under another. Again, the Appendices provide a good overview of what has been tried thus far.

THE APPLICABILITY OF ECONOMIC INSTRUMENTS IN DEVELOPING COUNTRIES

Despite the increasing use of economic instruments by developing countries, their applicability to developing country conditions continues to be questioned by environmental groups, development assistance agencies and developing countries themselves. Indeed, much of the technical assistance received by developing countries is skewed towards the use of command-and-control regulations. The conventional wisdom that economic instruments are of limited applicability to developing countries is based on the argument that their circumstances are radically different from those of developed countries and therefore developed country experience is of limited relevance. The increasing use of economic instruments by developing countries is often dismissed as experimentation by middle-income, newly industrialized economies; experimentation that is of little relevance to low-income agrarian economies. The objectives of this chapter are to examine the special circumstances of developing countries that might affect the applicability of economic instruments, either positively or negatively, and to assess the applicability of particular instruments to specific circumstances, especially those of low-income countries.

By definition, developing countries differ from developed countries by their level or stage of development, as measured by income per capita. This definition of development is by itself unsatisfactory for inter-country comparison, even in the narrow economic sense. Converting income per capita into purchasing power parity alters significantly the 'development' ranking of countries. Further adjustments need to be made for differences in quality of life indicators such as child mortality, life expectancy and literacy, which are not always correlated with income. These adjustments result in further changes in the development ranking of countries.* Even then, resource depletion and environmental degradation are not accounted for and hence the development ranking is biased against countries that practise resource conservation and environmental protection, even after the purchasing power and quality of life adjustments.

With these caveats in mind, we use the conventional definition of developing countries: the non-OECD countries, excluding the transitional economies of Eastern Europe and the former Soviet Union and the high-income, oil-exporting countries such as Brunei, Kuwait, Saudi Arabia and the Gulf States. This definition leaves more than 120 countries ranging from the tiny Pacific Islands to China. The ecological, cultural and political diversity is at least as wide as the differences in size and geography. Therefore, the special circumstances described below are generalizations that apply more to some countries than others, but do constitute distinguishing features of developing countries as a group, from the OECD countries also taken as a group. However, since developing countries are far from a homogeneous group, a further classification into low- and middle-income countries is appropriate. The latter group is defined to include the newly industrializing economies. Correspondingly, the special features of developing countries discussed below apply par excellance to low-income countries and, to a lesser degree, to middle-income countries.

---

* For example, the UNDP's Human Development Index is described and debated in Gormely, Patrick J (1995), 'The Human Development Index in 1994: Impact of Income on Country Rank', *Journal of Economic and Social Measurement*, Winter, 21(4):253–268; Streeten, Paul (1995), 'Human Development: The Debate about the Index', *International Social Science Journal*, March, 47(1):25–36; and Acharyn, Arnab and Howard J Wall (1994), 'An Evaluation of the United Nations' Human Development Index', *Journal of Economic and Social Measurement*, Spring, 20(1):51–66.

Development priorities: growth and distribution

Economic development and poverty alleviation are the top priorities of developing countries, while maintenance of prosperity and quality of life, through economic stability and environmental protection, is the primary concern of developed countries. A 2–3 per cent growth rate, considered an accomplishment among OECD countries, is lamented as a failure among developing economies, which, given 2–3 per cent population growth must grow at least that fast to stand still at what is a very unsatisfactory standard of living. Growth rates of 5–10 per cent are aspired to by all developing countries but achieved by only a few. Still, high growth rates remain a priority even for those developing countries that are experiencing stagnation or even economic decline (eg, sub-Saharan Africa), perhaps more so. As a result, these countries are unlikely to give high priority to environmental protection unless it is seen as an effective means of escaping stagnation and of achieving high rates of economic growth. This has significant implications for the applicability of economic instruments in general and for the right choice of instruments in particular.

First, instruments with applications to natural resource management are of special interest to low-income, resource-based economies while instruments of industrial pollution control are of particular interest to newly industrializing countries. Second, the effect of the instrument on economic growth is of great concern. Instruments that restrict or constrain economic growth conflict with developing country priorities. The instrument must achieve its purpose at the lowest cost possible, and whatever that cost is, it must not be high enough to affect adversely the competitiveness of the country's exports as a whole, even if particular exports might be affected.

More positively, the instrument must help improve the efficiency of resource use, increase productivity, and economize on scarce resources (eg, capital, skills and management). It is also desirable that the instrument promotes the search, development and adoption of more efficient, less wasteful production technologies. Clearly, the development priority of developing countries favours the efficiency, cost-effectiveness and flexibility of economic instruments over the rigidity and cost-insensitivity of command-and-control. Moreover, it has clear implications for the choice of economic instruments and the mode and speed of their introduction. Clearly, secure property rights, efficient taxation of natural resources and gradually phased-in pollution charges are favoured by the high priority that developing countries attach to their growth objectives.

At the same time, poverty alleviation and improved income distribution are also among the top objectives of developing country governments. Therefore, the distributional implications of economic instruments are also of primary concern. It is not sufficient that secure property rights to open access resources are assigned; it also matters who gets them. If the poor, who depend on these resources for survival, are assigned the property rights, both efficiency and distribution improve.

If not, efficiency is gained at the expense of equity. Similarly, the incidence of pollution or product charges may by regressive if they raise the price of goods that account for a higher percentage of poor people's expenditure, or if the environmental improvement so attained benefits mainly the rich. Distributional concerns may disqualify certain instruments, such as bidding for open access resources; favour differential rate structure, such as lower charge rates for basic necessities; or suggest mitigation measures, such as offsetting the regressivity of tax charge incidence by the progressivity of spending charge revenues. Of course, the ultimate choice of the appropriate instrument will also be influenced by other features of developing countries, to which we now turn.

Low willingness to pay for environmental amenities

The lower per capita incomes of developing countries imply higher marginal utility of income and lower willingness to pay for environmental improvements and amenities. Whenever a development opportunity and environmental protection are in conflict (or in a trade-off relationship), the choice between the two would be influenced by existing levels of income, as well as by other factors such as preferences and environmental awareness. All other things being constant, low-income people would assign a relatively higher value to each additional dollar of income (from the development opportunity) than rich people would, because of the higher marginal utility of income at low income levels. At the same time, poor people have a lower willingness to pay for environmental quality or amenities because environmental services are income elastic. In other words, their demand is low at low income levels but rises more than proportionately with income growth. Both these factors result in individuals assigning higher priority to development than environmental protection, unless of course the latter is an input to the former.[1]

Thus, economic instruments set according to estimates of marginal damages or marginal benefits derived from estimates of people's willingness to pay for a benefit (or accept compensation for a damage), better accommodate the significant differences in willingness to pay and marginal valuations of income between developed and developing countries than do command-and-control regulations. This is particularly important at low levels of income, where a small change in prices or a reduction in income can threaten survival. Therefore, the developed country regulations and standards (or level of pollution charges) are not suitable for poor countries and if enforced, can in fact lower welfare and even threaten survival. Developed country environmental standards (not consumption patterns) can only serve as long-term targets or aspirations, in the same way as developed country living standards.[2]

The above argument in no way justifies the transfer of polluting industries or the shipment of hazardous waste from developed to developing countries, a common criticism. In the case of direct foreign investment, environmental standards or charges are a relatively minor factor by comparison to access to new markets and to low-cost labour and material. Moreover, the environmental standards of developed countries are embodied in the capital and technology of the industry that moves to a developing country. Furthermore, the liability laws of the country of origin may apply and exported products must reflect the environmental standards of the trading partners. Shipment of hazardous waste is not justified because of the asymmetry of information regarding its true nature and potential risks between the shipper and receiver and because the receiver (developing country) lacks the knowledge and technology to treat and dispose of the waste safely. Furthermore, because of the low or zero assimilative capacity of the environment for hazardous waste, and the risk of leakage, spill or dumping during transport, hazardous and toxic waste is best handled at its place of origin. In light of the uncertainty and asymmetry of information, treatment and disposal at the source are required for full internalization of the externality and application of the polluter pays principle.

Limited tax revenues

Tax revenues in developing countries are usually severely constrained by a narrow tax base, low incomes and limited tax collecting capacity. As a result of limited revenues and major infrastructural expenditures, developing countries tend to run sizeable budget deficits. Hence, they can ill afford the costs of a large environmental bureaucracy. As a result, their monitoring and enforcement budgets are very limited and their infrastructure for collection, treatment and disposal of waste grossly inadequate. At the same time, they face severe administrative and human resource constraints. Given these constraints, the opportunity cost of resources necessary to implement, monitor and enforce end-of-pipe command-and-control regulations are significantly higher than those in developed countries. The limited experience with administrative regulations and the inadequate information available for setting standards may lead to overly ambitious or unenforceable regulations. In contrast, economic instruments, if properly selected, can have low enforcement costs and generate significant government revenues. In contrast to command-and-control regulations, which often lead to increases in a developing country's already excessive dependence on narrowly based, highly distortionary taxes, economic instruments are corrective taxes that can lower this dependence by serving as alternative sources of revenues.

The choice of specific economic instruments is significant in the light of developing countries' limited administrative and enforcement capability. For example, product taxes that use existing administrative structures may be preferable to emission charges or tradable permits which require new collection mechanisms or additional administrative arrangements. Since product taxes are indirect instruments, they are not as efficient as pollution taxes, which directly attack the externality; the right instrument is determined by the balancing of the administrative cost savings against the efficiency losses. Low-income countries may thus opt for product taxes while middle-income countries may choose pollution charges or tradable permits on account of greater administrative and charge collection capacity. Refundable deposits and performance bonds are also easily administered instruments, but may not be equally suited to the resource endowment of poor countries. The collection and return of residuals and waste is usually a labour-intensive activity, well suited to the labour-surplus conditions of many poor countries. Posting a bond, on the other hand, requires substantial capital, which is usually scarce and costly in developing countries but more available and less costly in middle-income and newly industrializing economies.

Legal, institutional and cultural constraints

Where legal institutions are weak or not well developed, as is the case in many developing countries, instruments that rely on legal action for enforcement are unlikely to be effective. Examples include command-and-control regulations, such as effluent standards or mandated technology, which provide for fines, prosecution, closure and imprisonment in case of non-compliance. Another class of instruments difficult to enforce under these circumstances is legal liability systems, used extensively in the United States. Moreover, because of a long backlog of cases in the courts of most countries, the threat of court action does not act as a deterrent or compliance incentive.

In addition to the weakness of the legal system, many cultures are not given to litigation in the same way that Western culture is. Courts are used as a last resort, which means they are rarely used. Since this is common knowledge, regulations that depend on court action are not complied with. Fines are set at levels that are too low to deter violators given also the low probability of apprehension and conviction. Regulations that are replicas of developed country regulations have little grounding in local realities and culture and are therefore largely unenforceable. In cultures where the institution of private property rights is not sanctioned and contracts are not enforced by courts (eg, parts of sub-Saharan Africa), economic instruments that are based on private property rights or market creation are likely to fail. In these cases, the recognition and protection of customary, communal or tribal rights is preferable to their supplantation by alien institutions of private and state property. Papua New Guinea provides an example of sensitivity and accommodation to institutional weaknesses and cultural traditions and realities (see Box 8.1). Indeed, traditional societies, while having weak legal systems and undeveloped modern institutions, often have time-tested traditional institutions, management systems and customary use rights. These traditional institutions can be strengthened or used as models for the development of new institutions and instru-

---

Box 8.1 Policy Success: Communal Tenure in Papua New Guinea

Unlike most of the developing world, Papua New Guinea has maintained its communal tenure customs while adapting to the requirements of an increasingly market-oriented economy. While the latter requires clear land ownership, Papua New Guinea's experience has shown that converting land from communal to freehold ownership may confuse rather than clarify the rights of ownership. The widespread land degradation encouraged by the insecure tenure, loss of entitlements and open access characteristic of state-owned land elsewhere has been absent from Papua New Guinea.

Most countries have responded to market pressures for clear ownership by imposing a new system of private or state ownership. In contrast, Papua New Guinea's land law builds upon the customs governing its communally held land. The country's Land Ordinance Act calls for local mediators and land courts to base settlements on existing principles of communal ownership. Consequently, 97 per cent of the land remains communal, has been neither surveyed nor registered and is governed by local custom (Cooter, 1990).

This communal tenure seems to provide clearer ownership rights, with all their environmental and market implications, than private ownership. Settlements that convert communal land to freehold are often later disputed, and reversion back to customary ownership is a frequent outcome. Yet unlike state-owned land in other developing countries, communal land in Papua New Guinea is in effect neither unowned nor public. Rather, the bundle of rights deemed 'ownership' in the West does not reside in one party. For example, individual families hold the right to farm plots of land indefinitely, but the right to trade them resides in the clan (Cooter, 1990).

The island's communal systems have long resulted in the sustainable use of its more densely populated highlands. Even with a nine-thousand-year agricultural history, a wet climate, and population growth of at least 2.3 per cent, the highlands remain fertile. The population, which is primarily agricultural, enjoys a per capita income more than twice that of El Salvador, Western Samoa and Nigeria (Cooter, 1990). In marked contrast to much of the developing world, only 6 million of its 46 million hectares of forest land have been converted to other uses (Australian UNESCO Committee, 1976).

The lack of deforestation comes as no surprise since those who control the land have an interest in the sustainable, productive use of the forest. Rather than dealing with a distant government in need of quick revenues and foreign exchange, companies seeking logging rights must negotiate directly with those who have secure tenure and who use the land not only to farm, but also to gather fruit, hunt and collect materials for clothing, buildings and weapons (Panayotou and Ashton, 1992). Because the communal tenure patterns provide an entitlement to all clan members, individuals have little incentive to sacrifice future value for current use.

Source: Panayotou (1993c).

---

ments that fit the local cultures and traditions as well as emerging new realities such as commercialization, new technology, population growth and the like.

Undeveloped capital markets and high discount rates

Natural resource conservation and environmental protection are analogous to investment, in the sense that they involve high current costs in return for a stream of future benefits of higher present value. This creates a cash flow problem, especially for societies with limited cash incomes. This problem can be solved through current borrowing and future repayment, a solution that presupposes well-functioning capital markets. In many developing countries, capital markets are segmented or distorted through interest rate ceilings, credit rationing and capital subsidies among other things. Credit is generally very costly for small borrowers and often unavailable to those with no secure property rights for collateral. Furthermore, low incomes, often barely above survival levels, economic uncertainty and political instability result in very high private discount rates applied to future benefits.

The implications of capital scarcity and high discount rates for the selection of instruments are that the right instrument does not impose a high initial capital cost. Therefore, mandated technology such as water treatment plants, and economic instruments, such as environmental performance bonds or auctioning of pollution permits, are not suitable for countries with undeveloped capital markets and high rates of discount.[3] Where initial capital costs are unavoidable, as in the case of water or energy supply projects, instruments that aim at full-cost pricing must accommodate the capital constraint by amortizing the capital costs into monthly payments integrated with the variable costs (user charges). In the case of natural resources, especially land, assignment of secure property rights is usually an effective mechanism for improving access to capital markets and for lowering the private discount rate for poor farmers. Removal of interest rate ceilings and capital subsidies (investment incentives) for large-scale industries increases the availability and reduces the cost of rural credit, further encouraging long-term investments such as soil conservation and tree planting.

Formative stage of development

In developed countries, the selection of instruments for environmental management is often constrained by the legacy of existing regulations, an entrenched environmental bureaucracy and vested interests created by past and present policies and structures. Furthermore, with mature industries and cities and virtually all infrastructure in place, it is technically difficult and economically costly to introduce radical policy changes or new instruments. Retrofitting industrial plants and urban infrastructure, put in place under a different policy regime, is often very disruptive and costly, necessitating a very slow and gradual process of adjustment with grandfathering of existing industries.

Developing countries, being in the formative stages of their development, have considerably more flexibility than developed countries to introduce new policies and instruments of environmental management. First, without a large environmental bureaucracy and the vested interest created by past regulations, developing countries have nearly a clean slate to introduce new instruments that best fit their own circumstances. Second, the limited fixed plant and infrastructure in place, the higher rates of investment and economic growth and the rapid turnover of capital stock imply lower implementation and compliance costs for new instruments, and greater effectiveness. This assumes, of course, that the instruments are expected to remain in place and escalate over time to internalize environmental costs fully.

Economic instruments have the advantage that they can influence the direction and pattern of development of human settlements and industries without unduly constraining the pace of development. The rapidity with which urban and industrial centres are growing in developing countries provides economic instruments with the opportunity to achieve cost-effective environmental improvements through structural change, an opportunity that flees with every new investment planned and implemented under existing policies.

A related characteristic of developing countries is the large number of scattered, small-scale industries which are difficult to either regulate or tax. Product taxes, refundable deposits and incentives for waste delivery are clearly preferable to effluent standards and charges or to market creation instruments which are costly to monitor and enforce when a large number of small and scattered polluters are involved.[4] Rapidly growing vehicular pollution and traffic congestion, as a result of increasing car ownership, are other characteristics of developing countries that the selected instruments must address cost effectively. Car ownership taxes, differential fuel taxes and road tolls are among such instruments, provided that alternative means of transport (eg, mass transit systems) are available.

ELEMENTS OF A SUCCESSFUL STRATEGY

The level of development and structure of the economy are critical factors (because they determine enforcement needs and capabilities), as are social organization and culture. For example, in a country in an early stage of development with an economy dominated by agriculture, small-scale industry and a large informal sector, regulations such as effluent standards and economic instruments such as effluent charges are likely to be ineffective because they are costly to monitor and enforce. Given the size, scattered distribution and elusive nature of artisanal and small-scale industry, the costs of monitoring are likely to be high relative to the damage caused by the individual polluting activity. Similarly, the administrative costs of collecting charges for such entities are likely to be large relative to the expected revenues. Under such circumstances the right intervention would be indirect instruments, such as product charges and differential taxes, imposed at easily monitored points (ie imports, exports, raw material production, etc). Moreover, economic instruments in developing countries need to be both simpler and more sophisticated than in developed countries. They need to be simpler because developing countries have a limited administrative capacity for tax and charge collection; and more sophisticated because the resource systems and ecology (especially in the tropics) are more complex than in temperate developed countries. A successful selection of instruments has several distinguishing characteristics, reviewed below.

Scale of production

First, a successful set policy intervention is differentiated according to scale of production. In the case of a small number of large industrial conglomerates (as in Korea), emission standards, effluent charges, tradable pollution permits and even mandatory installation of pollution equipment can be effective because monitoring and enforcement are relatively easy. In contrast, a large number of small cottage industries calls for indirect instruments such as input taxes, refundable deposits and waste delivery incentives.

Degree of competition

Second, successful environmental intervention is differentiated according to the degree of competition. Monopolistic or oligopolistic industries do not respond to economic incentives to the degree that competitive firms do because the demand for their product is more inelastic. In the presence of highly concentrated industry, standards and mandated control equipment, which do not depend on market response can be more effective in attaining the desired level of pollution control.

Ownership and control

Third, a successful intervention is differentiated according to ownership and control. An industrial sector dominated by public enterprises facing a soft budget constraint or cost-plus pricing formulas does not respond to pollution charges or to fines for non-compliance, as the experience of Poland (under a command economy) and the former East Germany demonstrate. Both Poland and East Germany had a very sophisticated system of pollution charges which proved totally ineffective because the charges were paid and then recovered from the government budget as part of the cost of production.

Composition of industrial pollution

Fourth, a successful intervention is differentiated according to the composition of industrial pollution. Flexible systems, such as pollution charges/permits or inadequately enforced standards, are inappropriate if the pollution is dominated by waste for which the environment has no assimilative capacity (ie heavy metals, corrosive materials or radioactive wastes). Strict regulations, manifest systems, performance bonds and central collection treatment and disposal facilities are more appropriate in such instances.

Monitoring and enforcement capabilities

Fifth, successful interventions consider explicitly the monitoring and enforcement capabilities and provide for an institutional support system. Where the feasibility of monitoring and enforcement is low and shutdown undesirable, mandatory installation of pollution control equipment may be preferable provided that effective use can also be mandated and monitored. Even then, taxation of inputs and performance bonds might be preferable because they have generally lower monitoring and enforcement costs.

Control region heterogeneity

Sixth, successful intervention accommodates control region heterogeneity (and hence, high information requirements) through the decentralization of authority to local agents and an allowance for locally tailored solutions. The more diverse or heterogeneous the control region, the greater the need for locally tailored policies and instruments which automatically figure-in the local conditions, such as effluent charges set at a percentage of total effluent emission.

Industry acceptance

Seventh, for a policy intervention to be successful, acceptance by the industry must be solicited and obtained. This is often accomplished through a new-source bias or grandfathering system that assures the industry that the objective is not punishment for past pollution but redirection of new investments towards less polluting technologies and industries. Gradual implementation is also necessary in order to allow time for industry adjustment and to preserve competitiveness. These allowances are temporary so as not to institutionalize inefficiency and sustain obsolete technologies (see Box 8.2).

The seven features of a successful policy intervention described above refer to the adaptability of the intervention to prevailing local

Box 8.2 The Pre-announced Gradually Escalated Effluent Charge in Quito, Ecuador

The Municipal Environment Directorate of the city of Quito, Ecuador, in collaboration with Fundacio Natura, a local NGO, have designed a gradual pollution charge system to control industrial effluents. (A similar system is designed for emissions.) Ecuador has national water quality regulations which establish eight different water quality standards depending on intended resource use. The new system is a hybrid between a norm based on these standards and a pure effluent charge. To start with, the discharge norm is set at the level that will ensure the least strict of water quality standards in the city's rivers. Firms which discharge less than the norm would pay no charge; those whose discharge exceed the norm would pay a per unit charge equal to the cost of municipal treatment, which is currently $0.66 per kg. The discharge will be made gradually stricter according to a predetermined and published schedule. Thus, the level of discharge exempt from payment of the charge will be reduced correspondingly in order to attain the next level of water quality. It is expected that after 8–10 years, the discharge norm will reach a level of ambient water quality that would permit the use of water downstream of the city for irrigation, cattle and drinking after primary treatment.

The system works as follows. Industrial firms are required to report their discharge every six months. A six month charge is then assessed as the average daily discharge for the period above the norm, times 125 days times $0.36. If a firm takes measures during the six-month period to further reduce its effluents, it can apply to the Directorate for Reassessment, and if its claim survives scrutiny, a lower charge is applied. While it is too early to assess its performance, the system has many of the features of a successful intervention strategy.

Source: Huber (1997).

conditions (eg, the market structure, scale, the age and ownership of the industry, the composition of the waste flow and the nature of the environmental media or receptor of wastes). The success of the instrument will ultimately be judged by its benefit–cost ratio, or at least cost-effectiveness. Benefits include the present value of avoided costs and the correction of distortions in resource allocation in addition to direct benefits, while costs include induced distortions in resource allocation in addition to the direct cost of enforcement by government and compliance by industry. The objective is not simply to treat and safely dispose of waste but to promote efficiency, to reduce waste, and in general, to induce a change in behaviour more in line with the public interest while allowing flexibility for response and time for adjustment.

For a policy intervention to be truly successful in reducing overall emissions, it must control inter-media substitution through an integrated emission reduction strategy for all media. Mandated use of scrubbers to control SO_2 from power plants should not result in increased water pollution, nor should wastewater treatment result in soil pollution through inappropriate disposal of sludge.

Finally, a successful policy intervention should aim to reduce damage cost or at least environmental risk exposure, rather than the attainment of fixed ambient standards. This means that it takes into account the level of toxicity of pollutants, the pollution damage or risk exposure and the cost of risk reduction for each pollutant.

The most critical first step to introducing economic instruments is to make the principles of eventual full-cost pricing and internalization of external cost acceptable to industry and the public in exchange for recognition of their legitimate concerns and the need for gradual intro-duction and adjustment assistance. Once the principles have been agreed upon, the next step is a gradual phase-in period (usually 5–10 years), which is roughly the time it takes for the average-age capital stock to depreciate. In this manner future investments are generally directed towards a more desirable mix (eg, less energy intensive, less polluting) without penalizing past investments. It is preferable for a country to begin with nominal charges — based on solid principles which earn wide acceptance and support — and work its way to full implementation on a pre-announced schedule, rather than to go for a gamut of regulations which give the illusion of being firmly in command but leave the situation no better overall. Indeed, it may be counter-productive for the country to initiate an overarching, grand regulatory scheme which can not be monitored or enforced. (For an example of gradual implementation of effluent and emissions charges, see Box 8.3).

Another principle which needs to be observed is the minimization of enforcement/monitoring requirements of the system and of the latitude for discretion by regulators. Compliance should be made in the interest of the resource user or the polluter. The regulators should be indifferent as to whether the polluter cleans up or pollutes and pays, wastes or conserves water, cuts or plants trees. If the regulator is not indifferent then the price or charge is too low. The need to minimize regulatory, enforcement and monitoring costs arises from the low enforcement capability in developing countries and the rent-seeking behaviour that high charges and low salaries bring about.

The ideal economic incentive is one which is incorporated into the price of a resource or product; it can be avoided only by avoiding the use of the resource or product. Other instruments that meet this condition are refundable deposits, performance bonds, presumptive charges at clean-up-cost levels, transferable development rights, property and land use taxes and transaction quotas. Hazardous waste management is an example where an imaginative combination of presumptive charges, performance bonds and environmental auditing can be at least as effective as strong preventive measures and a lot more efficient (Panayotou, 1993a).

Hybrid systems of economic incentives and regulations do exist but they should not be confused with a mixture of the two, arising from the unwillingness of regulators to depart from their command-and-control posts. In the hybrid systems the government sets a long-term target (eg, ambient standard, rate of reforestation, water conservation) and market-based instruments are used to achieve the target at minimum cost.

By necessity, regulations and economic incentives are complementary instruments in the sense that a minimum amount of regulation (legal framework) is necessary for economic incentives to be operational. Similarly, without economic incentive, regulations either remain on paper or generate de facto financial flows through side payments. An efficient system is one which sets a broad regulatory framework that is implemented through a well thought out and structured set of economic instruments.

CONCLUSION

Economic instruments as a group are at least as applicable to developing countries as they are to developed countries. The earlier, formative stages of development in which developing countries find themselves make the introduction of new, flexible instruments both easier and more beneficial. However, underdeveloped and inefficient markets and institutional and administrative constraints call for careful selection of specific economic instruments that fit (or are adapted to fit) the country's special circumstances. In addition to the stage of development and associated constraints and opportunities, the country's cultural traditions and social organization are critical factors to consider and build on in selecting and introducing incentive-based instruments for environmental management and sustainable development.

Transitional economies, that is, formerly planned economies that are now in the process of market reforms and industrial restructuring, temporarily experience some of the characteristics of developing countries such as low incomes, limited tax revenues and priority for recovery and growth. In other aspects such as levels of industrialization and education, however, they share features common with developed Western European countries.[5] Transitional economies like Poland and Russia have historically used economic instruments for pollution control: pollution charges. Their effectiveness as incentives, however, was minimal owing to the lack of enterprise autonomy and existence of the soft budget constraints (charges were paid and included in production costs to be covered by state subsidies) as well as the infamous lack of enforcement of what appeared on paper to be very strict standards. This lack of effectiveness notwithstanding, the familiarity of transitional economies with economic instruments and their bitter experience with command-and-controls in the economic sectors help them resist misguided Western advice to replicate Western command-and-control regulations. Many of these countries aspiring to join the European Union (EU) are in the process of adopting EU environmental standards, but appropriately aim to attain them gradually, through pre-announced compliance schedules and with the use of

---

Box 8.3 Implementation Lessons from Transition Country Experience

Analysis of the experience of the transitional economies of Eastern Europe and the Former Soviet Union over the past five years suggests the following ten lessons for implementation of economic instruments in transitional economies. They are equally applicable to developing countries:

1   Simplify systems and focus attention on the most important pollutants.
2   Choose national/regional policy objectives in terms of aggregate emissions levels or aggregate emissions reductions linked to ambient environmental quality goals.
3   Set annual performance standards codified in permits by pollutant and by facility, not by individual source (for example, by stack).
4   Choose a core set of priority air and water pollutants and a two-tiered charge structure which is linked to facility performance limits.
5   Where possible, use abatement costs to guide the choice of charges and the jump between base and penalty rates.
6   Develop cost-effective and non-adversarial approaches to implementation and enforcement.
7   Use penalty charge rates to define levels of liability for accidental discharges and for deliberate evasion.
8   Integrate the system of pollution charges into the general system of income/profits taxation.
9   Charge levels must be clearly indexed for inflation, and such indexing must automatically occur each time period (for example, year, quarter).
10   Creating some form of pollution charge waiver and 'environmental fund' is probably a political necessity in response to distributional concerns associated with charges.

Source: Bluffstone and Larson (1997).

---

economic instruments. Box 8.3 summarizes the lesson from the implementation of economic instruments in transitional economies.

Chapter 9

Developed Country Experience and its Relevance to Developing Countries

The experience of one country does not readily transfer to another. Particularly problematic is the transfer of developed country experience to developing countries because of differences in the stages of development, and in culture, traditions and political and administrative infrastructure, among others. Nevertheless, there are lessons to be learned from other country experience which either transcend these differences or at least could be sifted through for relevant elements. With regard to economic instruments, developed countries have a relatively longer experience which may help developing countries just beginning to experiment with such instruments to avoid earlier errors or to follow more promising routes of experimentation. In this chapter we briefly review developed country experience and examine its applicability to developing country conditions. The main categories of instruments covered in this review are the following: (a) market creation; (b) fiscal instruments; (c) charge systems; and (d) deposit-refund systems.

MARKET CREATION: FROM TRADABLE EMISSION PERMITS IN THE UNITED STATES TO INDIVIDUAL TRADABLE FISHING QUOTAS IN NEW ZEALAND

Tradable emission permits

The major applications of tradable emission permits have been in the USA: (a) trading of emission rights of pollutants regulated under the Clean Air Act; (b) inter-refinery trading of lead credits; and (c) trading of permits for water pollution control. Three additional uses are being initiated or actively considered: (a) acid rain; (b) chlorofluorocarbons (CFCs); and (c) newsprint.

Interestingly, the US trading of emission rights arose from an attempt to implement strict emission regulations, which in many areas could not be met within the set timetable or could be met only at substantial opportunity cost in terms of forgone economic growth. When it was realized that many states could not meet the planned emission reduction, the Environmental Protection Agency (EPA) formulated an offset policy by which new and modified emission sources were allowed in 'non-attainment areas' as long as any additional emissions were offset by reductions in existing sources. This led to the 1986 Emissions Trading Policy Statement, which covers several pollutants such as carbon monoxide, sulphur dioxide, particulates, volatile organic compounds (VOCs) and nitrogen oxides. The US emissions trading programme has several elements. The geographic 'netting' or 'bubble' element allows 'trade' of emission reductions among different sources within a firm, as long as the combined emissions under the 'bubble' are within the allowable limit. The 'offset' element allows firms to trade emission credits between existing and new sources within a firm and among firms, new sources of emissions can be constructed as long as the new emissions are (more than) offset by a reduction of emissions from existing sources. Finally, the 'banking' element allows firms to accumulate and store emission reduction credits for future use or sale.

It is estimated that 5,000–12,000 trades have taken place within firms for the modification or expansion of plants (Hahn and Hester, 1989) and 2500 trades (some between different firms) for the location of plants in 'non-attainment' areas (Dudek and Palmisano, 1988). Large companies such as Amoco, Dupont, USX and 3M have traded emission credits, and a relatively active market for such trades has developed (Stavins, 1991). It is estimated that the US emissions trading programme, despite its many limitations, has saved participating firms between $5 and $12 billion in compliance costs (Stavins, 1991) by affording them greater flexibility in meeting emission limits. These are substantial savings considering that only 1 per cent of potentially tradable emissions was actually traded and that virtually all trading took place within firms rather than between firms where the highest cost savings are likely to be found.

The US Emissions Trading Program has several weaknesses which limit participation and inter-firm trading. First, states are encouraged but not required to allow trading in their implementation of the Clean Air Act. Second, inter-firm trades must be approved by the regulators who are not accustomed to trading practices. Third, there is uncertainty about the programme's future and about the content and nature of rights that are being traded.

Despite these limitations, the Emissions Trading Program fared well in both environmental effectiveness and economic efficiency. According to Rehbinder and Stewart (1985), trading has produced at least as high an ambient air quality as direct regulations and at a much lower cost (as the savings of $5–12 billion reported above suggests). In contrast to 'technology forcing' implied by the strict technology requirements of the Clean Air Act, emissions trading allows plant operators the flexibility to choose the technologies most suitable to their own circumstances, to come up with their own inventive technological solutions, and to go beyond the minimum requirements of the imposed standards to control pollution for profit. In management terms, emissions trading allows the flexibility and acceptability that comes from specifying ends rather than means.

Singapore is using tradable permits for ozone depleting substances, allocating the permits through a sophisticated auction system (World Bank, 1997a). The system has been found to be more cost-effective than traditional technology standards and relatively easy to implement. It has also had the added benefit of raising funds for the government which have been used to 'subsidize recycling services and for the encouragement of alternative technologies' (World Bank, 1997a). An outcome of emissions trading of particular relevance to developing countries is that it allowed the construction of a large number of new plants in highly polluted areas without increasing pollution levels, by buying and retiring older, dirtier and less efficient plants; this outcome would not have been possible with direct regulations. (The substantial data and monitoring requirements of emissions trading and their implication for developing countries will be addressed below.) Developing countries cannot afford to retard their industrialization and economic development through inflexible and costly regulations or mandated technology standards. Emissions trading offers industrial firms the option to avoid meeting stringent emission standards for new plants by reducing emissions in existing plants or purchasing emission credits from other firms which can reduce their emissions at lower costs. On the negative side, the administrative costs of the US emissions trading system have been high because the system evolved from efforts to enforce direct regulations rather than from a clear definition and allocation of pollution rights. The replacement of the requirement for approval of abatement technologies by the requirement for approval of emissions trading transactions did not reduce the involvement of the regulators and the administrative costs. It did, however, shift decisions about the choice of abatement technology and its location from regulators to plant operators.

In developing countries, an emissions trading system would be further limited by the high monitoring of, and transaction costs between, a large number of small firms, many of which are unregistered. Yet there is no reason why an emissions trading system could not be applied to public utilities, multinationals, large local firms and industrial estates, while small sources may be controlled by a system that targets fuel use rather than emissions. The main limitation is that emissions trading does not apply to more than one pollutant simultaneously, unless some equivalence index is developed (OECD, 1991a).

Another environmental market creation was the EPA lead trading programme during 1982–1987. Gasoline refiners were given the flexibility to produce gasoline with a lower or higher lead content than the level mandated by the standard; those with lower-than-standard lead content accumulated lead credits that they could sell or bank for future use while those with higher-than-standard lead content could use past lead credits or purchase them from other firms. About 15 per cent of total lead rights were traded and 35 per cent were banked and traded or used later. The EPA estimates the annual savings from lead trading to be $200 million. This means that the lead standard mandated by direct regulations was attained at a cost that was 20 per cent lower with trading than without trading (EPA, 1985).

There are good reasons why lead trading has been more successful than other emissions trading. First, there was consensus about the objective: the phasing out of lead in gasoline. Second, lead in gasoline can be easily monitored both technically and administratively, involving a relatively small number of refineries. Third, the content of the right that was traded was well defined, the programmes had a known fixed life, and no complex approval process for the trading was required.

Tradable permit programmes have also been used in controlling water pollution in the USA. There are two notable cases: (a) the Wisconsin Fox River water permits for point pollution sources; and (b) the Colorado Dillon Reservoir water permits for non-point pollution sources.

In 1981, the state of Wisconsin issued discharge permits to 14 paper mills and 4 wastewater treatment plants discharging effluents into the Fox River. The permits were issued only for reductions of biochemical oxygen demand (BOD) discharges exceeding the levels required by treatment standards. Trading of permits was allowed in order to give firms more flexibility in controlling and treating their effluents, although trading solely to reduce costs was prohibited (Apogee Research, 1992). Despite estimates of potential cost savings of up to $7 million per year, only one trade has taken place thus far (Smith and Vos, 1997). The reasons are many and varied. First, the oligopolistic structure of the pulp and paper industry and the regulated public utility status of the wastewater treatment plants limit competition. Second, the required justification of the need for permits and the requirement for modification or re-issuance of permits after every transaction create high transaction costs which discourage the trading of permits. Third, the five-year fixed life of the permits and the lack of an established process for reallocation (Hahn and Hester, 1990), create uncertainty about both the value of the permits and the effect of trading on their future allocation as well as questions about the legality of the trades (Smith and Vos, 1997).

Somewhat more promising is the permit trading programme between point and non-point pollution sources at the Dillon Reservoir in Colorado. Under this system point sources are allowed to treat their effluents at less than required (drinking water) standards in exchange for reduction or treatment of non-point pollution sources. In the Dillon Reservoir case, the point sources are publicly owned sewage treatment plants, and the non-point sources are agricultural, recreational, and urban activities. The scope for trading arises from the lower marginal costs of treating discharges from non-point sources to some standard (say from zero to 60 or 70 per cent) compared to treating point discharges to a standard of 95–98 per cent, which requires new purification facilities. The fact that trading in this system is between the waste treatment facilities and the water authorities implies low transaction costs and hence easier implementation. Despite some estimates of cost savings of approximately $1 million a year (Hahn and Stavins, 1991), only one point/non-point source trade and a few non-point source trades have taken place since the programme's inception in 1984 (Smith and Vos, 1997). This dearth of trades can probably be attributed to the requirement of prior government approval (Hahn and Hester, 1990).

The USA has more recently employed a tradable permits system to control acid rain. The SO_2 allowance trading system sets an 8.9 million ton per year national cap on SO_2 emissions from utilities beginning in 2000 to be reached in two phases (Joskow, 1991); 8.9 million SO_2 allowances (each allowance representing a ton of SO_2) were issued and allocated freely to existing sources based on baseline fuel use and a specified emissions rate. (The available allowance for Phase II units is ratcheted down to meet the national cap on SO_2 emissions by the year 2000). To comply with the statute, each existing unit must hold allowances equal to or greater than their emissions during the year. Allowances can be traded within and between utilities as well as banked for future use.

By allowing low-cost abaters to 'over-comply' and sell surplus allowances and high-cost abaters to 'under-comply' and purchase additional allowances to cover their deficit, the system aims to minimize the overall cost of compliance with the national SO_2 cap. New sources must purchase allowances from existing sources. Firms found to produce excess emissions pay a penalty of $2000 per ton and are required to offset their excess the following year. Except for monitoring compliance and a small EPA auction and fixed-price sale (programmes involving less than 3 per cent of Phase II allowances), the EPA's involvement in private market arrangements is minimal. For this very reason the programme is working better than earlier emission trading programmes. Another reason is that monitoring technologies for SO_2 exist and firms are required to install continuous emission monitors. The first phase of emissions reductions was achieved in 1995. During this phase emission limits were assigned to the 263 most SO_2-emissons-intensive generating units at 110 power utility plants. Under Phase II of the programme (beginning 1 January 2000), all fossil fuel power plants will be included.

The SO_2 emissions trading programme worked very well, achieving and exceeding the targeted emissions reductions. More than four million tons of allowances were transferred in 1996 between independent plants. The market resulted in cost savings of about $1 billion annually compared to the cost of the command-and-control regulatory option (Stavins, 1998). The benefits are expected to exceed the cost by a significant margin.

The US Congress is considering a marketable permit system to stimulate the recycling of old newspapers. The bill under consideration requires producers and importers of newsprint to use an increasing percentage of recycled fibres each year and hence a diminishing percentage of virgin pulp. A system of marketable permits or credits would help the individual producers and importers meet the industry-wide percentage of recycled fibre content at a lower cost than uniform percentages. Dinan (1992) has studied the proposed system and concluded that the level of production under a percentage-based permit system would be higher than under a quantity-based system. The cost savings are also potentially high but their realization depends on: (a) level of compliance; (b) competitiveness of the permit market; (c) transactions costs; and (d) the certainty regarding the legitimacy of permits and the future prospects of the market for permits, essential factors in any tradable permit market.

At a somewhat superficial level, tradable emission permits (TEPs) appear to have little applicability to developing countries. First, TEPs involve trading pollution rights in countries where even commodities are not freely traded in undistorted, competitive markets. Second, the system of TEPs seems to require a level of market sophistication and abstraction that does not exist in many developing countries. More damagingly, TEPs seem to have large data and monitoring capability requirements which are very scarce in developing countries.

All of these criticisms are valid if developing countries attempt to copy the US system of TEPs which is clearly overregulated and cumbersome. The concept which is most useful to developing countries is that of earning and trading pollution credits between industries of differential abatement costs. First, because production costs vary more widely between developing country firms than firms in developed countries, the gains from trading pollution credits are likely to be proportionately larger. Second, because the industry in developing countries is undergoing faster growth and structural change and has a wider scope for efficiency improvements than its developed country counterparts, the introduction of TEPs is more likely to lead to efficiency gains and structural changes than to increased cost of production and shifting of economic growth. This is especially true if the system is phased in over a period of 5–10 years. A developing country can begin by introducing TEPs for large domestic and foreign firms as well as public utilities. At a second stage, trades can also be established between point and non-point sources of pollution. By working with local industry associations and experimenting with pilot projects, governments can reduce monitoring and enforcement costs. The application of these elements of the TEP can be found in proposed pollution abatement credit trading for Indonesia (see below) in support of the existing, but unmet, regulatory standards.

Tradable fishing quotas

Like most of the world's fisheries, that of New Zealand suffered from excess fishing efforts and overfishing which threatened the resource. To reduce overfishing, in 1986 the New Zealand government issued tradable catch quotas on all fish harvested, allocated to individual fishermen according to their historical catches (Leith, 1995). Fees were imposed on the recipients of these quotas, and the revenues generated were used to buy back quotas from fishermen who would rather have the money than the right to fish their allocated quota. Fishermen were asked to indicate the price at which they were willing to sell their quotas and leave the industry, the government bought back the quotas from those fishermen who were willing to sell at the lowest price until the desired level of fishing effort reduction was reached. Since the quotas were also tradable between fishermen, they began to be transferred to the most efficient fishermen, ensuring that the aggregate fishing quota was caught at minimum cost. Those who left the fishery by selling their quotas to other fishermen or the government did so voluntarily and were fully compensated. Thus, the scheme accomplished four objectives:

1   protection of the resource;
2   increased efficiency (maximization of fishery rents);
3   fairness; and
4   self-financing (from fees on quotas rather than from the government budget).

For these reasons, the system of individual tradable catch quotas is of particular relevance and applicability to developing countries with heavily overexploited fisheries. They can be combined with fee-financed retraining and relocation programmes to encourage surplus fishermen to sell their quotas and take up alternative occupations. A problem arises when unemployment and underemployment in the rest of the economy are widespread since few fishermen would be willing to sell their catch quotas and exit the fishery if employment alternatives are not available. While under these circumstances a larger than normal level of fishing effort is justified; maximizing rents and distributing them according to pre-assigned resource shares to existing fishermen is preferable to allowing overfishing to continue unchecked.

New Zealand and its system of tradable catch quotas also offers some keen insights and conclusions about other important transitional factors, such as the relationship between the fishermen and the government. One of the key elements of New Zealand's success, although it is not perfect, is the strong communication link between the legislative body and the fishermen, and public participation. The government understood in the beginning that there would be many sceptics regarding this new system. In order to elucidate some of the preliminary enigmas, the administration, through the New Zealand Ministry of Fisheries, set up meetings to consult with the community and industry leaders initially and then with the general public. This enabled the government to educate the public about the transferable catch quotas with ample time to organize feedback sessions. These hearings took place during a three-week span in late 1984 and early 1985. The response by the industry and public was so strong that there were approximately 65 meetings held by the Ministry (Clark, 1994).

The feedback from these consultations aided the government in their process of creating the system and tailoring it to the unique needs of the fishermen in their country. The fishermen expressed their concern for issues which are also commonplace in many developing countries. One such issue was that of initially allotting quotas based on each fisherman's past tax claims. The fishermen in New Zealand, similar to many workers in developing countries, did not always file accurate tax claims and therefore were concerned that this system of allocation would not be an accurate measure. Small-scale fishermen were also concerned that the larger companies would eventually gain control of the industry by acquiring all of the quotas. Through discussions and public panels these two problems were resolved. The initial allotment of quotas was based on the average catch histories from the best two of their previous three years (Clark, 1994). In order to control the monopolizing of the fisheries an amendment was added to the Fisheries Act which limited the total individual catch share (TAC) to 20 per cent. The government also offered an appellate process for those who felt the allocations were unfair.

In order to lower enforcement costs New Zealand changed its system of monitoring. Before transferable quotas were introduced the administration used a system of 'game wardens'(Clark, 1994, p 54) to control fishing; this method has shifted from 'game warden' to 'auditor'(Clark, 1994, p 54). This is because of the new system of paperwork, which both the fishermen and the processing plants are required to complete. After each catch all fishermen are required to fill out various forms documenting the type of fish caught, the region in which they were caught, their fisher identification number and so forth. This system allows the government to cross check the data from the ships with that of the processing plants in a methodical and cost efficient manner. By having each boat and worker registered, the government virtually never, with the exception of poaching and recreational fishing, needs to go to sea in order to pursue violators (Clark, 1994).

There have been significant criticisms levelled at the programme, however. First, the programme has been expensive to police as the individual incentives to cheat on catches increased (Barlow, 1996). Second, it has been difficult to administer, as witnessed by the recent computer glitch that led to the Government rescinding its $10 million offer to 'correct' the computer bungle 'which has potentially short-changed thousands of fish quota holders' (Gamble, 1997). Third, there is 'evidence that Individual Transferable Quotas (ITQs) lead to corporate concentration' in the industry (Leith, 1995, p 100). Perhaps most damaging to the programme are the allegations of significant quota overruns; Leith (1995) notes 1992/93 mackerel quota overruns as high as 500 per cent, with no fines levied. This last problem is said to be due to the built-in catch allowances, which were meant to allow for the difficulties of catching a particular desired fish or catching a mixture. Tightening or removing these allowances could therefore control this overfishing.[1]

Despite these problems, many believe that to this day New Zealand has been the most effective country in imposing this type of system. While there are many factors contributing to this success, one of the most important is the constant interaction between the administration and the industry. This communication enables the two parties to resolve problems in an efficient and fair manner. In the words of Ian Clark (1994, p 57) regarding the situation in New Zealand: 'The administration and the industry both agree that the quota management system is the only sensible management option and that by and large it does work to meet the objectives of conservation, sustainability, and economic efficiency'. Indeed, Roodman (1997, Table 1, p 18) also concluded that the ITQ system in place in New Zealand has reduced overfishing: 'Many stocks appear to be rebuilding. The fishing industry, unlike that of most countries, seems to be stable and profitable despite the lack of subsidies'.

DEPOSIT-REFUND SYSTEMS IN THE USA, EUROPE AND JAPAN

The experience of developed countries indicates that deposit-refund systems are cost-effective instruments for reducing littering and waste disposal costs and for conserving material inputs. In the case of beverage containers, the relative price increase of the product as a result of the deposit may be more important than the absolute level of the deposit, while in the case of scrap cars the latter appears to be important in relation to the scrapping price. Deposit-refund systems are compatible with the polluter pays principle and have high administrative efficiency because they require no monitoring or collection costs, especially when they are operated by the private companies that produce and distribute the products in the first place. According to the World Bank (1997a), Japan is one of the most successful recyclers of solid waste. For example, 92 per cent of beer bottles are recycled: the result of an aggressive deposit-refund scheme whereby beer manufacturers, wholesalers, retailers and consumers each have a monetary incentive to return bottles up the chain to their originator.

Deposit-refund systems on beverage containers combined with product charges on non-reusable containers have also been operating successfully in Finland, Norway and Sweden. The percentage of containers returned is 90 per cent for beer and soft drinks and 70–80 per cent for wine and liquor, while the market share of non-returnable bottles is kept small: less than 5 per cent in Finland (Opschoor and Vos, 1989). Similarly, successful deposit-refund systems for beverage containers operate in many states in the USA. There is evidence to suggest that consumers are responsive to the level of the deposit. For example, in 1983 Sweden introduced a deposit of ECU 0.04 on aluminum beverage cans, which resulted in the return of 60–70 per cent of the cans. In 1987, the government doubled the deposit (which by that time had lost part of its real value to inflation), and in response 80 per cent of the cans were returned.

The success with deposit-refund systems has encouraged several European countries to extend the system to other products such as batteries, car hulks and pesticide residues. Denmark introduced refundable deposits for batteries with a high content of cadmium and mercury to control soil contamination, and several other countries, including the Netherlands, are considering such a move (Opschoor and Vos, 1989). A deposit-refund system for car batteries has been introduced or is being considered in several European countries. US consumers seem particularly sensitive to the amount of effort required to return the bottles or cans. A return rate of approximately 90 per cent is reported in various countries despite 'considerable differences in the price level'. (As cited in Smith and Vos, 1997.)

Norway and Sweden introduced deposit-refund systems for scrap cars in the mid-to-late 1970s to reduce solid waste and visual pollution and to promote the reuse of materials. The system worked well in Norway and poorly in Sweden for a good reason. In Norway the deposit in 1988 was ECU 130 per vehicle, while in Sweden it was only ECU 42. While in both countries a larger amount was refunded when the car was delivered, in Sweden the deposit and the refund were lower than the cost of scrapping. Thus, a much smaller percentage of unused cars was returned in Sweden than in Norway: 90–99 per cent (Opschoor and Vos, 1989).

Lastly, there is an interesting Dutch proposal for extending the deposit-refund concept to various polluting chemicals such as cadmium and mercury. The producer or the importer of the substance would pay the deposit; it would then be passed on to the user of such products and refunded to the final user (or exporter) when the product is disposed of or exported. Producers of products containing polluting chemicals could also be eligible for a refund of any waste of the substance they return or dispose of safely. Thus, the deposit-refund system is gradually expanding from an instrument of limited scope (mainly beverage containers) into a more generic instrument. It can be used at the micro level by industry to limit environmental liability risks (as in the case of hazardous chemicals) and at the macro level by policy makers to transform the current linear production process into a more ecologically sound circular flow.

Deposit-refund systems are of particular relevance to developing countries for several reasons:

1 The high administrative efficiency (self-enforcement) of deposit-refund is a great advantage for countries with administrative constraints and limited enforcement capability.
2 The low opportunity cost of labour in developing countries implies that even small deposits would generate an active collection

market which would have both economic and environment benefits.

3   Because the users of batteries, cars and products with heavy packaging are better off than the waste collectors and scavengers, deposit-refund systems would have positive distributional implications as long as the deposits are not set very high and are extended to a great variety of waste products.

4   Since most toxic and hazardous substances are imported, it might be administratively simple (reduced audit requirements) to impose a deposit at the import point and refund it to the final users or exporters.

FISCAL INSTRUMENTS IN EUROPE

Developed countries, especially in Europe, have a long history of experience with the application of economic instruments in environmental management. This experience has been mixed, but a general lesson is that fiscal instruments, while effective in generating fiscal revenues, are generally ineffective as incentives for changing behaviour unless they are set high enough to alter the relative profitability of inputs, products, technologies and practices, as already mentioned. Countries are often reluctant to set taxes and charges high enough to act as economic incentives because of political reasons, resistance by industry or concerns about competitiveness. Among developed countries, only the Netherlands has come close to charging the marginal damage cost of pollution. France lies at the other extreme: charges have been set at less than a quarter of the level necessary to induce a significant change in behaviour, and 90 per cent of the charge revenue is returned to the industry as subsidies for investment in pollution abatement technology (Opschoor and Vos, 1989).

In this section we briefly review the developed country experience (mainly European) with fiscal instruments focusing on: (a) effluent charges; (b) product charges; (c) tax differentiation; and (d) subsidies.

Effluent charges

Effluent charges have been applied in developed countries to air, water, waste and noise pollution. Air emission charges are rare, having been used in Sweden (see Chapter 4), recently in Poland and the Czech Republic, and in France with rather modest results. The charge was set at ECU 19 per ton of sulphur oxides, which is only 1 per cent of the charge required to meet the European Union directives were they to be attained exclusively through charges. Ninety per cent of the charge revenues is returned to the charge payers as a subsidy for pollution control equipment, and the rest is used to develop new technologies (Opschoor and Vos, 1989). The performance of this system is limited by the infeasibility of the collective treatment of air pollutants and the complexity of monitoring when applied to more than one or two pollutants. This system is clearly unsuitable for developing countries with monitoring difficulties.

Many countries, at least 11 as of January 1997 (Smith and Vos, 1997) — notably France, the Netherlands and Germany — have used effluent charges to control water pollution. France has had such a system since 1969 (Opschoor and Vos, 1989). The effluent charge is levied on all fresh and seawater polluters – both households and industries – and applies to several pollutants such as BOD, chemical oxygen demand (COD), soluble salts, organic ammonia, nitrogen and phosphorus. Industries are charged on a flat rate set by actual measurement. The system is designed to raise revenues rather than to act as an incentive for waste minimization, as the charge rate is set too low to induce a change in the production process. France's success with effluent charges lies in the acceptance of these charges as a way of doing business. The key has been the gradual introduction of these charges at low levels and on a few pollutants and their progressive escalation to higher levels and wider scope (Hahn, 1989). A recent OECD report notes that these charges are increasing sharply, by 146 per cent between 1992 and 1996, with concomitant revenues increasing 'from $0.7 billion per year over 1987–91 to an annual average of $1.6 billion over 1992–1996' (Smith and Vos, 1997, p 40). It is expected that this increase will produce an additional incentive effect, as well as increased revenues.

In Germany, a water pollution charge was implemented in 1981 with an explicit incentive purpose and a close link to direct regulations. Although the nominal charge per unit of discharge was set at ECU 5.75 in 1981 and raised to ECU 19.20 in 1986, the effective charge varies according to the degree of compliance with standards. For example, a 50 per cent discount is applied when minimum effluent standards are met. Although it is difficult to assess the effectiveness of the system separately from that of direct regulation, there is evidence of substantial incentive effects. Ten per cent of the firms complied with the standards in order to benefit from the charge discount; several large firms treated more than the minimum requirements for economic reasons; one-third of the municipalities claimed that the charge system induced them to intensify their water treatment facilities; and the clean technology market grew rapidly (Opschoor and Vos, 1989).

On the other hand, the administrative efficiency is low because over 50 per cent of the revenue is spent on administering the system. The revenue, however, could quadruple with little increase in administrative costs if the charge rate were raised to the optimal level: the average treatment costs. The OECD (Smith and Vos, 1997) reports that the system was to be adjusted in 1989 to increase the discount on the charge to 100 per cent for a discharge of less than half the minimum standard, and to 80 per cent for the application of 'state-of-the-art' techniques for the control of toxic waste.

The Netherlands have a combined effluent user charge system: the Water Boards and firms pay an effluent charge (based on BOD and COD) to the State Water Authority for discharges into state waters;

firms and households pay a user charge to Water Boards for discharges into other waters that are treated by the Water Boards. The overall charge is calculated by the Water Boards in order to balance their budgets for water treatment. The individual polluter's charge is based on both volume and concentration. Large polluters are monitored and charged accordingly; medium-sized firms are charged according to a table of coefficients that vary by type of industry; small firms and households are charged a standard fee (one-person households may apply for a reduction). In addition, there is a system of discharge licensing. The charge system in the Netherlands has been effective not only in raising substantial revenues to finance water quality improvement (about 0.5 per cent of total government revenue in 1990, according to the World Bank (1997a)), but also in its significant incentive impacts, and in inducing behavioural and technological changes in certain industries such as chemicals, food, beverages and tobacco. According to the World Bank (1997a), waste water discharge was reduced by 73 per cent during 1969–1990. Bressers and Schuddeboom (1993) reports that differences in effluent charges account for 50–70 per cent of the variation in pollution abatement among 14 Dutch industrial sectors.

The success of the Dutch system is attributed to the fact that the charge rates have increased considerably over time (from ECU 4.70–17.20 per pollution unit in 1977 to ECU 12.30–34.00 in 1985), generating expectations for further increases. In per capita terms the Dutch charges are eight times those of France and 16 times those of Germany. While it is difficult to separate the effects of the licensing structure from the charge, their administrative costs are also low, ranging from 2 per cent for state charges to 4–9 per cent for others. Despite some disagreements about pollution coefficients and industry complaints about the increase in charge rates, the system is well accepted (Opschoor and Vos, 1989). One area where the Dutch charge system has been less effective and regulations more suitable is the control of heavy metals from diffuse sources. As a result, revenues raised are more than 20 times those in Germany and five times those raised in France (Smith and Vos, 1997).

In conclusion, effluent charges for water pollution (in combination with regulatory standards) have been reasonably effective and acceptable in Europe. Where the charges were set at relatively high rates and escalated over time, there has been a continuing incentive for firms to minimize waste and to abate pollution, most notably in the Netherlands. The charges have also been a major source of revenue for collective water treatment. It is also important to note the need for variability in charges according to source and type of pollutant (ie small vs. large, toxic vs. non-toxic).

Effluent charges for water pollution are quite relevant to developing countries that experience heavy pollution loads in rivers flowing through urban and industrial centres. Of the three country experiences reviewed, the Dutch system is the most relevant, not only because it has been very effective and administratively inexpensive but because it takes monitoring and enforcement difficulties into account, differentiating between large, medium, and small firms and households. Similar concepts to those of the Dutch system were used in formulating the proposed Industrial Environmental Fund for Thailand (Panayotou, 1993a).

Effluent charges for solid waste are rarer than water pollution charges.[2] Belgium imposes a charge of ECU 0.02–2.15 per ton of industrial and municipal waste, depending on the type of waste and its treatment before dumping, while exempting recycled wastes. To encourage recycling, Denmark charges ECU 5.20 per ton of 'harmful' waste dumped. In 1994 Danish taxes on waste disposal were the highest of OECD countries surveyed at ECU 14.4 per ton, rising to approximately ECU 27 per ton for waste delivered to landfill sites and about ECU 22 per ton for waste delivered to incineration plants (Opschoor et al, 1994; OECD, 1995a). Regarding effectiveness, Christensen (1996, p 12) reports 'the waste charge has been the main cause of the increase of the reuse of waste from the construction industry from 12% in 1985 to 82% in 1993'. The Netherlands imposes a progressive charge on surplus manure, which is a major source of acid depositions, eutrophication and soil pollution. The United States levies ECU 1.85 per dry ton of hazardous waste on waste site operations to finance the restoration of the site after closure.

While these charges have been shown to result in reduced waste,[3] the problem with these simple charge systems for waste is that low charges are sometimes not effective, as is the case in Woodstock, Illinois (Anderson et al, 1990). It has also been suggested that 'high charges would encourage evasive behavior and illegal dumping' (Opschoor and Vos, 1989). Therefore, effluent charges for solid waste are not recommended for developing countries unless they are combined with delivery bonds and auditing.[4] User charges on waste disposal are preferable, more common, and their use is recommended for developing countries.

Product Charges

One product charge that has been used by many European Union countries, such as France, Germany and Italy, and is currently used by Finland and Norway, is a charge on lubricant oils. Its effectiveness in terms of waste oil recovered was high in Germany, where the charge was set at ECU 96 per ton, and low in France, where it was set at only ECU 6 per ton (Opschoor and Vos, 1989). The most remarkable product charge is the new Dutch general fuel charge, which replaces five previous charges. Two-thirds of this tax is a surcharge on excise duties applied to mineral oil, and one-third is a levy. Its purpose is to raise revenues – GLd 1.5 billion in 1993 – to finance the environmental programmes of the Ministry of the Environment (OECD, 1995a). The incentive value of the general fuel charge is low, but it is enhanced with rebates for installation of sulphur dioxide abatement technologies. Administrative costs are low, since they are tied to the excise duties on fuels (Opschoor and Vos, 1989).

Some common product charges include charges on batteries, fertilizers and pesticides, non-returnable containers, and oil products. The USA has a general feedstock charge on industries using chemical and other hazardous materials in their production process in order to finance the 'Superfund' for the cleaning up of abandoned hazardous waste sites (OECD, 1995a). The incentive effect of this charge is limited and so is its efficiency, but it is accepted by the industry.

Opschoor and Vos (1989) concluded that product charges lack a strong incentive impact. The reduction of waste accomplished is because consumption of the product has been discouraged, not because the producers have an incentive to minimize or treat waste. Thus, only prevention through sufficiently high product charges to discourage consumption and/or encourage reuse and recycling of reusable and recyclable material would result in environmental improvement. In contrast, the revenue-raising impacts of these charges is considerable, especially when the demand for the product is price inelastic.[5] Since the administrative efficiency is also high, despite their drawbacks, product charges have particular relevance to developing countries. The low monitoring and enforcement capabilities of developing countries present difficulties for many other economic and regulatory instruments.

Tax differentiation

Tax differentiation has been used mainly in Europe to reduce transport-related emissions by: (a) speeding up the shift from leaded to unleaded petrol; and (b) encouraging clean car sales (Opschoor and Vos, 1989).[6] As with other charge forms, tax differentials have an incentive effect only to the extent that they are sufficiently large to alter behaviour. In Europe, leaded and lead-free petrol differentials (including VAT), range between ECU 41.41 per 1000 litres in Spain to ECU 102.66 per 1000 litres in Denmark (Kogels, 1995). Table 9.1 shows the level of differential taxes and relative market share of unleaded fuel in selected OECD countries. Evidence from Germany shows that a tax differential of ECU 0.034 per litre has resulted in an increase of the market share of leaded petrol from 11 per cent in 1986 to 28 per cent in 1987 and to 88 per cent by 1992 (Opschoor and Vos, 1989; Opschoor et al, 1994). Subsequent reduction of the tax differential to ECU 0.029 in 1987 and ECU 0.024 in 1988 reduces its effectiveness as an incentive.

It must be noted, however, that European countries have used tax differentiation as a transitional policy to speed up the implementation of direct regulation of air pollution from vehicles. In terms of transport-related emissions, the general level of petrol taxes (and hence the general level of petrol prices) is at least as important as gas tax differentials. For example, the USA has traditionally maintained low gas taxes

Table 9.1 *Differential Excise Taxes and Market Share of Unleaded Petrol in Selected Countries*

	Differential excises + VAT (ECU/1000 l)	Market share unleaded gasoline (estimate %)
Denmark	102.66	70
Norway	95.05	55
Austria	93.82	65
Belgium	86.43	70
Finland	83.18	70
Luxembourg	82.58	85
Sweden	74.54	60
Netherlands	73.75	65
United Kingdom	71.17	45
Portugal	70.88	15
Greece	69.51	15
France	66.18	35
Germany	58.50	85
Switzerland	48.80	65
Italy	43.92	15
Ireland	41.70	30
Spain	41.41	10
Average in 1992		50
Average in 1988		28
Average in 1986		0

Source: Kogels (1995, Table 2, p 67).

and domestic oil prices below world price levels while Europe and Japan have practised the reverse. This has resulted in significant differences in energy efficiency. The World Bank (1997a) gives estimates of energy productivity, as defined by gross domestic product (GDP) per kilogram of energy, in 1994, as 9.6 for Japan, 6.1 for Germany and 3.2 for the USA.

Several European countries introduced tax differentiation in 1985 and 1986 as an instrument for the promotion of cleaner cars to meet existing or forthcoming regulations. Buyers of 'cleaner' cars were given a tax advantage paid by buyers of 'dirtier' cars. Tax differentiation was based on pollution characteristics, size of vehicle and/or year of purchase. Evidence from several countries indicates considerable effectiveness of tax differentials as instruments for speeding up the implementation of regulations. In 1986 only 56 per cent of new cars in Germany met stringent emission standards; in 1987 90 per cent of new cars met these regulations and qualified for tax advantages. Similar results are reported for Sweden and the Netherlands (Opschoor and Vos, 1989).

Two other variants of tax differentiation proposed in the Netherlands warrant mentioning here because of their potential applicability to developing countries: (a) a differential VAT (value added tax) between environmentally friendly and unfriendly products; and (b) a reduction in the annual road tax on cars and an increase in the indirect tax on car fuels (Opschoor and Vos, 1989). The latter resulted in a tax differential between light and heavy car users and discouraged driving in general. This tax differential is thought to have three related benefits: reduction of energy use, of pollution, and of congestion. The disadvantages are that foreign tourists driving through the Netherlands face higher costs and residents of border areas buy fuel abroad.

The side-effects noted in the case of the Netherlands are of less importance in developing countries. Also, the long-run price elasticity of fuel consumption is likely to be higher in developing countries, and hence indirect taxes on car fuels are likely to discourage car use more than they do in developed countries. Thailand has recently implemented differential leaded and lead-free petrol taxation with encouraging results, although according to O'Connor (1994), this tax differential is actually made up of a subsidy on unleaded petrol which makes it relatively less expensive rather than a charge on the leaded petrol.

Subsidies

Most OECD countries, with the exception of the UK and Australia, have provided some financial assistance for environmental investments to the private sector in the form of grants, soft loans or tax allowances. Table 9.2 provides a quick summary of these subsidies. The main objectives of such subsidies are:

1   to speed up the enforcement of direct regulations;
2   to assist firms, especially small ones, which face cash flow problems or financial difficulties caused by capital investments required by compliance to new regulations; and
3   to support the research, development and introduction of pollution control equipment and cleaner technologies.

Subsidies are financed from charges, revolving funds and the general budget. The use of user charges to finance collective pollution control and treatment facilities is not considered a subsidy; only the part of the expenditures not covered by user charge revenues is considered a (hidden) subsidy. We have estimated that environmental subsidies in Europe range between 5 and 20 per cent of total environmental investments.

In France, most environmental subsidies are closely linked to charge systems: polluters pay for their emissions, but as much as 90 per cent of the revenue is returned to them as refunds for environmental investment and other improvements that they make. About 10 per cent goes to finance research and development of new technologies. Subsidies financed from the general budget are found mainly in industrial and household waste collection and treatment.

Table 9.2 *Main Types of Environmental Subsidies for Private Investments in OECD Countries (Based on Past and Present Practices)*

	Grants	Soft loans	Accelerated depreciation	Tax reduction	Tax deductible funds	Earmarked taxes
Austria		✔				
Denmark	✔					
Finland		✔	✔	✔		
France	✔		✔			✔
Germany		✔	✔			✔
Japan		✔	✔	✔		
Netherlands	✔				✔	✔
Norway	✔	✔	✔	✔		
Sweden	✔					✔
USA		✔	✔	✔	✔	

Source: Opschoor and Vos, (1989).

In Germany, subsidies are financed mainly from the general budget with the aim of assisting small firms during the transition period and speeding up implementation of new environmental regulations. Revolving funds provide an additional source of financing. Subsidies are given in the form of soft loans to polluters facing strict environmental standards who are being held fully accountable for their environmental costs. There is conflicting evidence as to the environmental effectiveness and economic efficiency of these subsidies. While the responsible Federal Ministry claims 100 per cent success in emission reduction, others argue that 'subsidies have no incentive impact ... but may only give rise to "windfall profits"' (Opschoor and Vos, 1989). The function of subsidies in speeding up the enforcement of regulations is also disputed. The economic efficiency of subsidies — that is, their contribution to optimal pollution reduction — is also reported to be low, not only because of the windfall profits they give rise to but also because subsidies are not tied to specific environmental outcomes; non-environmental criteria play a role as well. Finally, subsidies are a violation of the polluter pays principle to the extent that part of the environmental costs are not borne by the polluters; however, OECD accepted that subsidies to target groups facing difficulties, especially during well-defined transitional periods, are not in conflict with the principle.

The United States has limited experience with environmental subsidies, which are applied mainly in waste treatment and noise abatement. The government subsidy to investment in wastewater treatment facilities was initiated in 1956 and has varied over time between 30 and 75 per cent (Opschoor and Vos, 1989). The US experience indicates the following:

1   With the exception of a few financially strapped communities,

---

Box 9.1 Lessons from Developed Country Experience with Environmental Subsidies

The developed country experience with environmental subsidies suggests the following lessons for developing countries:[7]

1   The use of subsidies should be minimized, targeted and of limited duration during the transitional phase.
2   Subsidies should not be escalated but rather phased down over time to create incentives for accelerated rather than delayed compliance.
3   Subsidies should not be tied to a particular technology or investment but to specific environmental outcomes (improvements).
4   For subsidies to be compatible with the polluter pays principle they should be financed from charges on polluters and given in connection with specific environmental improvements; partial refunding of charges may help secure the industry's cooperation and willingness to pay the charges.
5   Subsidies from the general budget may be justified for cleaning accumulated hazardous waste prior to the introduction of control policies, for abatement of non-point pollution or waste generated by large numbers of small and dispersed units, and for support of research and development of new pollution abatement and cleaner production technologies.

---

subsidies were not indispensable to the waste water treatment programmes.
2   The variation in the level of subsidies over time induced a postponement of investment and of compliance with regulations in expectation of higher subsidies.
3   The high subsidy share of investment costs has induced capital-intensive treatment plants with excess capacity (Opschoor and Vos, 1989).

The lessons learned from developed country experience with subsidies are summarized in Box 9.1. Environmental subsidies are relevant to developing countries because their industry is dominated by a large number of small, unregistered, dispersed and fugitive firms that cannot be easily regulated and monitored; nor can effluent charges be collected at reasonable administrative costs. Indirect instruments such as product charges, differential taxes, refundable deposits and subsidized collection and treatment of residual waste are superior instruments under these circumstances. Similarly, user charges may not fully cover the costs of sanitation and solid waste collection services, making subsidies unavoidable. Every effort, however, should be made to finance such subsidies from surcharges on related public utilities and property taxes approximating as much as possible the polluter pays and beneficiary pays principles.

Finally, in developing countries with little experience in pollution charges, subsidies in the form of refunded charges for environmental

---

Box 9.2 Worldwatch Institute's Six Principles of Good Subsidy Policy

1　Subsidies may be warranted if they make markets work more efficiently, for example, by overcoming barriers to the commercialization of new technologies, or by favouring environmentally benign technologies over ones with hidden costs.
2　Subsidies may be warranted if they advance societal values other than economic efficiency, such as slowing the disintegration of company towns or feeding the poor.
3　Subsidies should be effective.
4　Subsidies should be efficient: they should directly and exclusively target intended beneficiaries.
5　Subsidies should be the least-cost means of achieving their purpose.
6　All costs, including environmental costs, should be counted when weighing the worth of subsidies. This entails sometimes difficult judgments about how to compare different kinds of harms and benefits.

Source: Worldwatch Institute, published in Roodman (1996, p 15).

---

improvements might be indispensable for obtaining the agreement of the industry to the introduction of such charges. The great danger with subsidies in developing (as in developed) countries is that they become institutionalized in public policy and capitalized in the value of economic assets (such as land), resulting in windfall profits or capital gains with little influence on behaviour towards more environmentally benign activities and practices. Again, it should be stressed that developing countries should test these instruments through pilot projects to assess implementation difficulties and improve the application prior to mass administration.

The Worldwatch Institute's Six Principles of Good Subsidy Policy is reproduced in Box 9.2 as a checklist for policy makers when choosing this particular instrument, along with the lessons outlined in Box 9.1.

CHARGE SYSTEMS IN EUROPE AND THE UNITED STATES

User charges

User charges are applied to the collection and treatment of municipal solid waste and wastewater in the public sewage systems. Virtually all developed countries apply a form of user charges for wastewater. Some, such as Belgium and Denmark, levy flat user charges on households and pollution load-based fees on industry. Others, such as France and Germany, apply the same rate, based on water use and wastewater volume, to households and firms, respectively (Opschoor and Vos, 1989). Most countries, however, target both firms and households. The most common form of user charge on households is a flat rate. A few countries such as Canada, Sweden and the USA, supplement the flat rate with a water use charge, while others, such as France and the UK, charge according to water use only (ie no basic flat rate). In a few countries, such as Finland and the USA, user charges for firms are based partially on a flat rate and partially according to pollution load. Only Denmark and Germany levy a user charge according to the volume of wastewater discharged (Opschoor and Vos, 1989). In some countries, such as Sweden, there is cross-subsidization of households (which pay a low charge) by firms (which pay a high charge). Because in most countries the charge is not on water pollution strength, industries that reduce their water use and hence their wastewater may simply be raising the pollution load. To avert this problem the USA has introduced a water-pollution-strength charge, but because of high monitoring costs it is applied only to large dischargers (Opschoor and Vos, 1989).

User charges for solid waste collection services also exist in virtually every developed country, but only a few provide incentives for waste minimization and recycling. A flat rate charge is usually used for households and a waste-volume-based charge for firms (Opschoor and Vos, 1989). In Finland, a joint private–public sector chemical waste treatment firm offers its services for hazardous waste treatment at a user charge based on the volume and type of waste and transport distance (OECD, 1995a). In the past, France has had the only system that provided incentives for waste minimization: a household waste collection charge that is based on the actual volume of waste that households and firms offer for collection and the unit service costs. Currently, volume-based charges are in operation in Germany, Iceland, Italy and the Netherlands, among others (OECD, 1995a). In Denmark, owing to problems with invoicing and with the charge base, this system is being increasingly replaced by a household waste collection tax based on property value.

In the case of user charges there is a clear trade-off between incentive impact and administrative efficiency. User charge systems are generally acceptable and effective, but as structured provide little incentive for waste minimization and recycling. User charges, however, can be made to provide such incentives if they are based on the quantity and quality of waste for large polluters and if they rely on a simpler system (eg, waste collection taxes) for small firms and households. Despite the unimaginative use of user charges in developed countries, the scope of user charges for solid waste collection and other public services is considerable.

Access charges (road pricing)

The traditional response to traffic congestion has been the building of more roads. An ever increasing demand for road infrastructure combined with budgeting pressures has stimulated interest in demand management in general and in road pricing in particular. The costs of building new highways are increasingly recovered from revenues collected from road tolls, a form of user charge that serves both as a cost recovery instrument and as a traffic regulator. A major problem with toll highways, however, has been the need for drivers to stop and pay the toll, thus slowing down traffic and negating some of the congestion reduction benefits of the system. In response to this problem, automatic toll and entry fee systems have been introduced in Denver, Colorado; Cambridge, England; and Bergen, Oslo and Trondheim, Norway (Hau, 1992).

Here we will briefly review the automatic toll system in Colorado. Toll highway E-470, the first high-tech toll highway in the USA, was opened in July 1991. Unlike conventional tolls, E-470 allows cars to drive through at full speed. The toll booth automatically charges a toll to the driver's credit card by picking up electronic signals from the ID card displayed on the car. According to Hau (1992), this toll system has the capacity to alter the charge based on the level of congestion (ie to charge higher tolls during rush hours) and thus to regulate and smooth out the flow of traffic. Knowing that a higher toll is charged during rush hours, drivers tend to take alternative routes or to start earlier/later for work. Drivers with inflexible schedules or urgent business are then able to use an uncongested highway during rush hours by simply paying a higher toll or using car pools.

The benefits from such a system are many. First, congestion costs in terms of loss of time and fuel are reduced, thus motorists benefit. Second, pollution is reduced because of higher speeds, less time on the road and fewer cars running (as a result of car pooling). Third, the government raises revenue for maintenance and expansion of road infrastructure. The main objections to the system have to do with the concerns that people's movements are thus monitored in violation of individual freedoms. Hong Kong has considered an automatic road toll system and rejected it on these grounds (Hau, 1992). However, this objection has now been addressed through a technological innovation that automatically deducts charges from the balance on each vehicle's ID card account without recording time, location and vehicle. An alternative solution is to give a choice to motorists by providing separately manned tollbooths for those who prefer not to use the electronic toll system, just as they are provided today for those who do not have exact change.

Road pricing in general, and the electronic toll system in particular, should be applicable in any country regardless of the level of development. Since car owners in developing countries belong to the elite and the upper middle class, a road pricing system would not only be efficient but also distributionally progressive. This is especially true if the revenue from tolls is used to subsidize an efficient mass transit system that is less polluting and more affordable to low income groups.

Table 9.3 Evaluated Taxes, their Functions and Effectiveness

Instrument	Environmental function	Environmental effects	Incentive effects[a]
Fiscal environmental taxes			
Sulphur tax (Sweden)	To increase penetration of low-S fuels and adoption of S-abatement measures	Reduction of 6000 tons of S corresponding to 6% reduction of total S emissions;[b] reduction of S content of oil by 40% on average; 1/4 of tax payers reduced S emissions by 70% on average	Average abatement costs were about SEK 10, lower than the tax rate of SEK 40 therefore strong incentive effect
CO_2 tax (Sweden)	To reduce CO_2 emissions	Hard to evaluate due to short period of operation; possible shift in fuels and increased competitiveness of combined heat and power plant	Unknown
CO_2 tax (Sweden)	To reduce CO_2 emissions	CO_2 emissions dropped by 3–4% in 1991–1993 from a rising trend	Price of heating oil increased 15% and price of petrol increased 10%; otherwise unknown
Tax on domestic flights (Sweden)	To reduce emissions by nationally operated air transport	Unknown, but most likely very small	Unknown
Waste charge (Denmark)	To reduce waste generation and increase recycling and reuse	Reused fraction of demolition wasted increased from 12% to 82%; contributed to an increase in reuse and recycling rate of 20–30% between 1985 and 1993.	Tax rate doubles average cost of waste dumping and increases cost of incineration by 70% on average; otherwise unknown
Incentive charges			
Tax differentiation on leaded petrol (Sweden)	To increase penetration of unleaded petrol	Emissions of lead dropped by about 80% between 1988 and 1993	Tax differential exceeds additional production costs of unleaded petrol
Tax differentiation for diesel (Sweden)	To increase penetration of low-pollution diesel fuels	75% reduction of S emissions by diesel cars; 95% in cities; reduced emissions of particles, smoke, NO_x, hydrocarbons and PAC expected but not quantified	Tax differential higher than additional production of costs of classes I and II.
Toxic waste charge	To reduce the amount of	Reduction of toxic waste production of	Tax rate increased average dumping

(Germany) toxic waste		20–45% between 1991 and 1993	and incineration costs by at least 5–15%; rate doubled in 1993 increasing this cost to 10–30%; otherwise unknown
NOx charge (Sweden)	To speed up reduction of NO$_x$ emissions from large combustion plants	Main cause of the reduction by 9000 tons in 1992 (35% of liable emissions)	Charge rate of SEK 40 exceeds average abatement costs of SEK 10
Fertilizer charge (Sweden)	To reduce the demand for fertilizer	N down by 25%; P down by 65% between 1980 and 1992; charge was one of the factors	Unknown
Water pollution charge (France)	To simulate adoption of in-plant wastewater treatment measures and building of treatment plants	Modest	Charge rate considerably lower than average pollution abatement costs
Water pollution charge (Germay)	To support adoption of water pollution abatement in permit application process	Early announcement contributed to stepping up construction of wastewater treatment capacity	Original relation between charge rate and marginal abatement damage costs were not implemented
Cost-covering charges: user charges			
Water pollution charge (Netherlands; non-State)	To finance wastewater treatment plants	Water pollution (BOD) down to 5% of households and to 4 million ie from industry	Average charge slightly lower than average pollution abatement costs
Household waste charge (Netherlands)	To promote a fair distribution of waste management costs over users	10–20% less household waste supply in 'pay-per-bag' villages	Unknown
Cost-covering charges: earmarked charges			
Battery charges (Sweden)	To cover costs of collection and disposal and of information	Collection of lead-batteries 95%; decreasing share of small Hg and NiCd batteries	Charge renders recycling of Pb-batteries feasible
Aircraft noise charge (Netherlands)	To finance insulation and redevelopment programmes around airports	Insulation of buildings around airport areas	Very low

Notes:

a Incentives for producers and consumers.

b Not all sulphur emissions are taxed in this way. The percentage reduction of the lower, taxed emissions of sulphur is much higher, but a figure is not available.

Source: European Environment Agency (1996).

CONCLUSION

Developed countries, even those that think of themselves as free market economies, have relied on command-and-control regulations for the protection of the environment. It is only recently that there has been a trend towards increased use of market-based incentives to achieve environmental objectives. This shift, which is still in its early, largely experimental phase, has been prompted by four factors:

1   the lacklustre performance of regulations in achieving the objectives of environmental management;
2   the high costs of administration, monitoring and enforcement with regulations as well as the high cost of compliance to regulations;
3   the need to raise revenues to pay for these costs as well as the costs of residual clean up, which have been substantial; and
4   growing evidence that market-based incentives might accomplish the same benefits at lower costs.

In a 1989 OECD survey of economic instruments used for environmental protection, at least 14 OECD countries employed between 1 and 20 such instruments, with Germany, Sweden and the Netherlands in the lead. (See Appendix 1 for a summary.) A total of 151 instruments were in operation, approximately one-half of which were charges and one-third subsidies, with a variety of other instruments such as deposit-refund systems, market creation and enforcement incentives making up the balance. In a 1997 survey by the OECD, this total was over 320 (OECD, 1997). It must be noted, however, that there are hardly any cases of economic incentives actually replacing regulations; they have been introduced in parallel, supplementary to regulation, with the primary aim of collecting revenues rather than altering behaviour in favour of environmentally less destructive activities and practices. The trend, however, is towards increased reliance on economic incentives as instruments of behaviour modification. There has also been a trend towards increased use of instruments such as charges, market creation, deposit-refund systems and decreased use of subsidies. Table 9.3 summarizes a recent assessment of environmental taxes and charges in the European Union in terms of function, incentive effects and environmental effectiveness.

The developed country experience with economic incentives is mixed but encouraging and replete with lessons for developing countries. One should not look for economic instruments that have succeeded in developed countries in order to transfer them wholesale to developing countries, rather for lessons that would help avoid the pitfalls that lie ahead. Ultimately, it is a combination of lessons from developed (and developing) country experience and accommodation of local conditions and realities which will indicate which economic instrument might be applicable and in what form. A number of developing countries have already experimented with economic incentives that support regulatory standards, and their experience is of particular relevance to other developing countries contemplating the use of economic incentives. In the following chapter we review developing countries' experience with economic instruments.

Chapter 10
Developing Country and Transitional Economy Experience

Contrary to conventional wisdom, economic instruments are neither foreign to non-Western cultures nor new to developing countries. Traditional societies, especially in developing countries, have a wealth of economic instrument-like incentive-building systems such as customary use rights, communal management systems and customs that provide incentives for efficient use and management of natural resources. These range from water rights in India, to communal forests and land rights in Papua New Guinea (Panayotou, 1993c), to customary fishing rights in Brazil, Sri Lanka and the Ivory Coast.

These systems, far from being outdated, contain valuable lessons and essential elements for the design of effective modern systems of managing natural resources in developing countries. Customary communal rights over resources is a dynamic balance between the diseconomies of collective management and the gains from internalization of externalities. While many of these traditional systems did not withstand the test of time and others are undergoing intense pressures from population growth, new markets and modern technologies, they nevertheless constitute prototypes of management systems that are attuned with the local cultures and provide insights into the design of modern systems of natural resource management in non-Western societies.

Similarly, the developing country experience is not limited to customary use rights for communal resources. Private water rights in India provide incentives for efficient management of increasingly scarce water resources, and concessions for private supply of water in the Ivory Coast have increased access and collection rates (World Bank, 1997a). Concession bidding, forest fees, timber taxes and environmental bonds are employed in West and Central Africa to promote sustainable forest management. As early as the mid-1970s Malaysia introduced a system of effluent charges for its palm oil and rubber industries, and Singapore, still a developing country at the time, instituted marginal cost pricing of access to the city centre to combat traffic congestion (Watson and Holland, 1978). More recently, China introduced industrial discharge permits and emission charges that double or triple when the allowable discharge standard is exceeded. Turkey has effectively used relocation incentives for urban-based industry. Chile has instituted both tradable emission permits and tradable water rights, and Puerto Rico used transferable development rights for coastal conservation. Costa Rica introduced biodiversity prospecting rights and tradable reforestation tax credits and is currently experimenting with internationally tradable development rights and carbon offsets. Virtually all Eastern European countries introduced pollution charges, and some of them (Poland, Czech Republic, Lithuania and Kazakhstan) are in the process of experimenting with tradable emission permits for industrial pollutants.[1] The rapidly accumulating experience of these countries in the use of economic instruments is of particular relevance to other developing or transitional economies contemplating the introduction of a more market-based approach to environmental management. In this chapter we review developing country applications of economic instruments in a number of sectors.[2]

FISHERIES MANAGEMENT: THE EXPERIENCES OF BRAZIL, THE IVORY COAST AND SRI LANKA WITH CUSTOMARY FISHING RIGHTS

Efforts to regulate fishing and prevent overfishing have ranged from quantitative controls (such as catch quotas) to area controls (such as closed areas and seasons) to economic instruments (such as taxes on catch or effort and fishing licensing schemes).[3] Traditional fishing communities in a number of developing countries have solved the problem of overfishing through customary territorial rights, which combine economic incentives and internally imposed quantitative controls sanctioned by the community's social organization.

Resource allocation through territorial rights — such as leasehold arrangements, franchises, or allocations of ownership over an area or a stock — aims at creating the appropriate environment for self-management through the establishment of private or community 'ownership' over common property resources. The 'owners' of the resource, having an interest in its current and future productivity, would be inclined to control fishing effort in order to maximize the net benefits from the resource in much the same way as farmers regulate their farming activities to maximize the returns from their land. For such a system to be workable, however, those allocated rights to the resource should not only be in a position to deny access to others, but they should also clearly perceive that their actions have a direct and pronounced effect on the state and productivity of their portion of the resource (and hence on their future profits).

The above conditions are certainly met in the case of sedentary or slightly mobile resources, such as seaweed and oyster and clam beds, and in the case of resources within well-defined geographical areas such as tidal lands, swamps, self-contained bays, lagoons and river estuaries. Even with more mobile resources (like crustaceans) and open areas (like coastal waters) there is a possibility of dividing up the resource as long as the fish displacements and migrations between portions are not sufficient to obscure the connection between the owner's current actions and his/her future profits. The revival and rejuvenation of traditional community rights over coastal resources offer perhaps the best possible management option for scattered, remote and fluid small-scale fisheries.

There are several examples of territorial rights in traditional fisheries in countries as diverse as Brazil, the Ivory Coast and Sri Lanka. Canoe fishermen operating in a river estuary in Valencia, *Eastern Brazil*, succeeded through a rather complex system of zoning and timing based on the lunar-tide cycle, in controlling internal population pressures and setting limits on the intensity of fishing through access limitations, establishing fishing as a reliable long-term occupation (Cordell, 1980). Although the resource moved with the tide, the fishermen were able to map out its distribution in time and space and establish 'temporary territorial rights which (could be) converted into long-standing territorial claims' (Cordell, 1980). Competition between different fishing methods was eliminated through the zoning which had matched fishing methods and fishing grounds according to the effect of the tide cycle on their efficiency. This had a 'boat-spacing' effect. Competition within the same type of gear was reduced through the selection of fishing spots (which had both a spatial and a temporal dimension) by individual captains on the basis of their knowledge of the tide movements and the fishing grounds. Although it was not unlikely for two or more captains to select the same fishing spot, the first to reach the spot had a temporary territorial claim. In the absence of clear-cut prior claims, lots were drawn. What prevented a common-property type of race for the premium fishing spots was a community ethic by which captains would anticipate and avoid competitive encounters in deciding where to fish each day. This resulted in a situation where a limited number of captains owned 'chunks of the lunar-tide fishing space', exercised deliberate control over the 'opportunity structure of fishing', and passed their skills to a limited number of apprentices. Thus, the fishermen on their own were able to stabilize their production system, set limits on the intensity of fishing and resolve inter-gear conflicts through a system of temporary territorial claims (Cordell, 1980).

Sri Lankan coastal fisheries have a history of traditional property rights in the form of rights of access and closed communities. In earlier times, beach seine owners controlled the access to coastal waters and had associated fishing rights which, along with other property, were subject to bilateral inheritance (by descent or marriage). Although at the start each beach seine owner had his own beach for which he had exclusive rights to operate, each of his children had only a fraction, not of his beach, but of his right to fish off the beach along with his brothers and brothers-in-law. While there was no limit to the number of nets that anyone holding rights to access could have constructed, the fishermen on a given beach, being a single kinship group, refrained from constructing additional nets unless they could bring in a catch whose value would have been higher than the cost of the net. That is, they acted as a single economic unit.

Sri Lankan coastal fishing villages are generally 'closed' communities in the sense that persons from outside the village are not allowed access to the fishing grounds of the community. Outsiders are not allowed to anchor or beach fishing boats along the shoreline of the community, and labour is not recruited from outside the village. These restrictions on entry help to explain why Sri Lankan coastal fishermen, unlike many other small-scale fishermen in Asia, earn incomes appreciably above their opportunity costs (Fernando, 1982).

Another example of the stark contrast between the situation of a fishery under open access and that of a fishery with traditional fishing rights is provided by the case of two lagoon fisheries in the *Ivory Coast* (S M Garcia, pers. comm.). In Lagoon Ebrie near Abidjan, traditional customary rights of fishermen operating fixed gears broke down following the introduction of mobile gears, such as purse seines, by outsiders (mainly town investors). The Ebrie fishery is now overcapitalized and heavily overexploited in both the biological and the economic sense, as evidenced by the small size of fish caught and the relatively low incomes of fishermen.

In contrast, the rather isolated fishery of Lagoon Tagba, over 100 kilometres from Abidjan, is still controlled by a limited number of chiefs (fishing team leaders) who have knowledge of the biological features of the resource and are enforcing traditional regulations on mesh size and on fishing in spawning areas. Though several tribes operate on the lagoon, the limited migration of catfish (the main species exploited) permits each community to manage its own portion of the lagoon. In the late 1960s a severe conflict arose between fishermen from neighbouring countries and local fishermen when the outsiders attempted to introduce purse-seine fishing to the lagoon. The latter managed to capture the purse-seine nets, but they did not use them themselves. Instead, they piled them up as a warning against similar attempts in the future. With so jealously guarded territorial rights, it is no wonder that local fishermen are reported to enjoy relatively high incomes and no surplus labour is evident. The fishermen also claim that the size of fish caught has not changed much in living memory (S M Garcia, pers. comm.).

FOREST MANAGEMENT: FROM TENURIAL INCENTIVES IN SOUTHEAST ASIA TO ECONOMIC INCENTIVES IN WEST AND CENTRAL AFRICA

Most countries have responded to market pressure for secure ownership of resources by imposing a new system of private or state ownership, disregarding customary community-based use rights to forest resources by the state. This deprived communities of any incentive to practise forest protection and sustainable forest management and led to encroachment and unsustainable harvesting practices (Panayotou and Ashton, 1992).

Papua New Guinea is one of a few countries which have formally recognized customary community rights over land and forest resources, as described in detail in Box 9.2. As much as 97 per cent of the land remains communal; it has been neither surveyed nor registered, and is governed by local custom (Cooter, 1990). This communal tenure seems to provide clearer ownership rights, with all their environmental and market implications, than private ownership; settlements that convert communal land to freehold are often later disputed, with reversion back to customary ownership a frequent outcome. Yet, unlike the reality of state-owned land in other developing countries, communal land in Papua New Guinea is neither unowned nor public. Rather, the bundle of rights deemed as 'ownership' in the West does not reside in one party. For example, individual families hold the right to farm plots of land indefinitely, but the right to trade them resides with the clan (Cooter, 1990).

In marked contrast to much of the developing world, only 6 million of Papua New Guinea's 46 million hectares of forest land have been converted to other uses (Australian UNESCO Committee, 1976). This should come as no surprise since those who control the land have an interest in the sustainable, productive use of its forest. Evidence reveals that even if these inhabitants are poor, their reliance on the land prevents its misuse. In support of this claim geographer Sheldon Annis, who has performed extensive research on poor land owners in Central America, concludes that:

> *'Such poor, but not impoverished, farmers typically manage resources with great care, even elegance. They optimize the use of every microscopic scrap of resource – every ridge of soil, every tree, every channel of water, and every angle of sunlight. They protect what they must depend on for their families' future'.*
> (Annis, 1992, p 11)

Rather than dealing with a distant government in need of quick revenues and foreign exchange, companies seeking logging rights must negotiate directly with those who have secure tenure and who use the land not only to farm, but to gather fruit, hunt, and collect materials for clothing, buildings and weapons (Australian UNESCO Committee, 1976; Harvard Institute for International Development, 1988). Because the communal tenure patterns provide an entitlement to all clan members, individuals have little incentive to sacrifice future value for current use.

Two conclusions may be derived from the Papua New Guinea experience with communal forest tenure:

1   Basing land law upon customary communal tenure patterns can be a viable adaptation to the requirements of a market economy.
2   Communal tenure may prevent deforestation more effectively than either state or private ownership if it provides an entitlement and secure tenure to a group that benefits from a forest's sustainable use.

In an effort to reverse past policies, the Philippines have recently granted 25-year communal forest leases through a Community Forest Stewardship Agreement between communities and the Forest Management Bureau. The lease is renewable for an additional 25-year period. While 25-year contracts are less than the optimal limitless contracts, this is a step in the right direction. The community undertakes the responsibility to protect the remaining forest area in exchange for legalization of the community's occupation and use of the area and government assistance in keeping migrants out of the communal area. Fifteen agreements covering an area of 44,221 ha were reported by the end of 1990. While it is too early to evaluate the programme, benefits are reported in the form of: (a) sustainable use of land and forests within the leased area, and (b) reduction of encroachment by migrant farmers (Lynch, 1991). Despite the relative success of the programme, the Philippine Government until recently was not prepared to increase the incentives for sustainable forest management by recognizing full ownership to ancestral lands.

In a 1991 paper, Somanathan reports the apparent problem of forest degradation in the central Himalayan region. The author traces the history of ownership and land use rights in this region, tying the tragic degradation to the misuse and lack of communal authority over the land (Somanathan, 1991). In this region of the Himalaya, forests, which at one point in time were rich with oak trees, are now barely regenerating with pine trees as a result of unregulated degradation. Where the oak trees were holding earth and water sufficiently to prevent erosion, the pine trees provide poor soil protection. Oak trees also provide fuel and useful resins while pine 'burns dirty' and is of little other use. In this case the government did not properly assure the peasants that they had the right to the land in the distant future. The land was at times open to many beneficiaries who were concerned with getting their share of the land's riches, thereby accelerating its destruction. Without property rights, the peasants had no incentive to protect the land (Somanathan, 1991). Somanathan proposed that the best solution to the problem would be to give the local peasants the right to the land, giving each one an equal share in the products from the property. Allotting property rights to local peasants who rely on the land for their livelihood was seen as an efficient solution. Not only are the peasants able to protect the land, but their proximity also enables them to witness any negative impacts affecting the land, and take protective measures.

Logging concessions in tropical forests are usually awarded through a long administrative process, following negotiations with logging companies, or in an arbitrary fashion that invites corruption. The concession area is typically too large to be protected and managed efficiently and the duration of the conversion is typically too short to encourage careful harvesting and regeneration for a second crop.[4] Forest fees and taxes are generally too low to capture timber rents and to internalize the negative externalities of logging. When forest taxation provides any incentive at all, it is a perverse one; for example, logging taxes are based on the quantity of merchantable timber removed (rather than on the timber on the site), thus encouraging high grading and damage to the remaining trees. The concessionaire is not given an economic incentive, rather, forest management and regeneration are prescribed through regulations, such as minimum diameter, maximum allowable cut, selective cutting, and replanting requirements which are rarely monitored or enforced.

In recent years, a number of West and Central African countries have begun introducing economic incentives for improved forest management. In the *Congo* in newly opened areas for logging and in areas where existing concessions are cancelled or returned, concessions are allocated by bidding. Bidders submit a bid per cubic metre for the annual volume available for cutting (Grut et al, 1991). The *Ivory Coast* has also introduced bidding for new logging concessions and *Ghana* has agreed to do the same (World Bank, 1988). The Ivory Coast government in early 1991 auctioned log export rights: 30 out of 40 registered bidders participated, 20 were successful and the average sale price was 25 per cent higher than the administratively set price. When there is sufficient competition, bidding ensures: (a) that concessions go to the most efficient and productive operation; and (b) that the government or community that owns the resource extracts the maximum amount of revenues (rents). The bidding price also provides a market based indicator for adjusting forest fees to their correct levels – even for concessions that cannot be allocated by bidding.

The system could be improved further through the following steps:

1   Replacing logging concessions with forest management concessions.
2   Using sealed tender.
3   Including technical competence among the allocation criteria.
4   Entrusting the bidding procedure to an independent auctioneer.
5   Opening the concession bid to local communities and NGOs as well as local and international firms.
6   Auctioning the concessions in small but manageable units and making them transferable.
7   Making concessions sufficiently long to internalize the value of the next crop, with a review every five years to ensure satisfactory performance (Grut et al, 1991).

Economic incentives may also be introduced to support the regulation and management of concessions. For example, prepayment of forest fees or deposit of refundable performance bonds may help avoid logging damage and encourage regeneration. An interesting performance or compliance incentive is the 'interim concession license' (Lettre d'Intention) introduced in *Zaire* in 1984 to weed out speculators acquiring large concessions without making the necessary investments in forest inventory and efficient harvesting and processing. The interim licence requires the satisfactory completion of 20 elements (specified in the application file) before it can be converted into a full concession licence. If the concessionaire does not make the necessary investments within three years, the interim licence is cancelled. Since the applicants are required to pay in advance for inventories of their prospective concession areas, they are more likely to take their responsibilities seriously.

Another innovative incentive is the 'deforestation tax' levied on land clearing in public forests by the *Central African Republic*. It ranges from US$170 to US$500 per ha, depending on the type of public forest land (Grut et al, 1991). To the extent that the deforestation tax reflects the forgone non-timber values from logging, it acts as an economic incentive to reduce deforestation (Grut et al, 1991).

Many countries have attempted to impose a deforestation tax on the assessed value of the property. Too often, however, the assessments of the property value are based solely on the timber value and therefore have an inadequate economic incentive to deter destruction. In most cases the timber value of a forest sells short many additional assets which are commonly found on the land.

Significant evidence was found in the Upper-Napo region of Ecuador that the potential value of timber products and cattle raising in three tropical forest areas in Amazonian Ecuador, which resembles the terrain of many other Latin American countries, yields a net present value (NPV) less than the NPV of harvesting the land for non-timber forest products (NTFPs) (Grimes et al, 1993). Included in these NPV estimates were the harvesting, extraction and transportation costs of the NTFPs, along with the market values of these goods. These non-timber goods included seven fruits, three medicinal barks and one resin (Grimes et al, 1993). A few other NTFPs were omitted from the study by the research team in order to alleviate location bias as much as possible. The study concludes that there is a growing market for non-timber uses of a tropical forest, which in most cases cause less damage to the forest than would deforestation or cattle raising. In order to establish the value of a deforestation tax fairly, the governing authority of the property should be aware of the additional uses and values of the land, which are usually less obvious but more profitable (Grimes et al, 1993).

WATER RESOURCE MANAGEMENT: FROM WATER PRICING IN CHINA TO WATER RIGHTS IN CHILE

From India to Morocco to Botswana, free or heavily subsidized irrigation water obstructs market signals, encouraging farmers to use the resource beyond its economic (or agricultural) optimum and stifling incentives to invest in improvements and maintenance of existing dams which are often plagued by poor drainage and inefficient distribution systems. In Bangladesh, Nepal and Thailand, total costs were at least 1000 per cent of revenues collected (Panayotou, 1993a).

Cheap water often becomes a substitute for other inputs. Over-irrigation by farmers nearest to the water source leads to waterlogging, salinization and alkalization. Meanwhile, those less conveniently located are forced to rely on sporadic and sparse water supply. A study of Pakistan's irrigation systems found that 73 per cent of farmers surveyed complained of insufficient water supplies, while farmers close to the water source of the same system were overwatering (World Resources Institute, 1987). The consequences are reduced crop yields, loss of irrigated lands and increased salt load of return flows and aquifers. Downstream effects include the erosion and siltation of estuaries and deltas.

Water subsidies encourage farmers to treat water as an abundant resource when it is, in fact, scarce. With no water rights, and no effective water user associations or other mechanisms to allocate water efficiently, water scarcity does not register. Indeed, water charges do not reflect the increasing opportunity cost due to increasing scarcity. As long as farmers do not bear the true cost of water, they will be unlikely to appreciate its scarcity or the problems that arise with overuse and until they receive clear market signals indicating otherwise, they will continue to use water wastefully. Beyond the less apparent economic costs, there is an absence of effective financial cost recovery mechanisms. Even at low maintenance levels the revenues collected by water users cover only a fraction of operation and maintenance costs. For example, revenues cover 20 per cent of costs in *Bangladesh*, 27 per cent in *Thailand* and 60 per cent in *Nepal* (Rogers, 1985). If capital costs are included, water charges often cover only 10–20 per cent of costs. It is ironic that capitalist economies such as those of Pakistan and Thailand do not fully price irrigation water, while the centrally planned socialist economy of China does.

In July 1985, the People's Republic of China took an important first step towards promoting greater efficiency in irrigation water usage. The Chinese government instituted agricultural policy reforms that invested a greater degree of financial and managerial autonomy in provincial water management agencies. The policy emphasized 'water as a commodity rather than a gift of nature and clearly attributed wasteful consumption and the imbalance between supply and demand to irrationally low water charges'(Ross, 1988). As a result, irrigation water is priced more closely to its actual cost, and problems associated with overuse and inefficient distribution have diminished. Irrigation service fees are charged at levels to cover operation, maintenance and amortization of capital costs. Beginning in 1980 the government switched from financing systems with grants to providing loans. The move provided an extra incentive for water management agencies to collect higher water fees. In general, water charges are determined by what the water actually costs for different uses. For example, charges may vary according to season, and in very dry areas progressive water pricing schemes have been adopted to reflect scarcity.

In Hungxian County, for example, farmers reported a more reliable water supply and were willing to pay more for the guaranteed supply (Asian Development Bank, 1986). Management is often further decentralized when a local agency purchases water wholesale and sells it in bulk to smaller water user associations responsible for distribution to farmers. These smaller groups strengthen the bond between the water user and the supplier who must recover costs.

Farmers have begun to irrigate their crops more efficiently, and water use per hectare has declined. Decentralized management has led to more efficient distribution through practices such as distributing water according to land area, levying water charges on a volumetric basis rather than charging a flat rate and preparing distribution plans in advance. Crop production has improved, with China producing twice as much as similarly irrigated crops in India (Rogers, 1985).

Chile has both a system of tradable water rights and a full-cost pricing policy towards water (Hartje et al, 1994). Like most other countries in the world, Chile considers water a national resource, yet individuals are granted perpetual, irreversible and freely tradable water use rights independent of land ownership and use. Water use rights are defined for a fixed quantity per unit of time and are awarded following application by a potential user. The Director General of Water (DGA) grants the water right provided that: (a) the new water right does not impair existing rights; and (b) the ecological requirement of minimum flow has not yet been reached by previous right allocations. Water use rights are granted free of charge and recorded in a national register; the granting authority reserves the right to restrict water consumption in times of water shortage.

Downstream owners of water rights have a right to a percentage share of the river flow but no protection against reductions of downstream flows due to increases in upstream use. While owners of consumptive rights (eg, irrigation) have no specified obligation with regard to quality or quantity of return flows, owners of non-consumptive rights (eg, hydropower and recreation) are required to return the same quantity and quality of water. Water users' associations under the control of DGA organize the distribution of water according to existing property rights. The water users' associations are also responsible for maintaining the irrigation infrastructure (Hartje et al, 1994).

Water rights are freely tradable and the market for water rights is quite active. Seasonal water rentals are particularly frequent within the agricultural sector. Farmers also sell or lease water rights to water supply utilities who often find such purchases a significantly less costly source than the development of new sources of supply for urban and industrial use. Individual negotiations determine the price of each transaction.

The tradable water rights system in Chile has both advantages and limitations. On the positive side, growing water scarcity is accommodated through demand management (conservation, improved efficiency and higher prices) rather than through rationing or the expansion of the water supply, with its consequent environmental impacts. Water users receive a price signal indicating the true opportunity cost of water and are thereby encouraged to conserve the resource. Water flows from low-value to high-value use with consequent significant reduction in over-irrigation, a major cause of waterlogging and salinization.

On the negative side, unregulated water markets may fail to internalize externalities such as minimum flow requirements, water quality changes, return flows and watershed protection which requires integrated watershed/river basin management. To deal with these externalities, a number of proposals are being considered including:

1   charges for new water rights;
2   a five year limitation or an annual charge for unused water rights (varying according to regional water scarcities);
3   guarantee of an ecological minimum water flow by the DGA; and
4   the establishment of watershed management corporations to resolve intersectoral water use conflicts, water quality management and watershed protection. Each of these functions is expected to be self-financing through water charges.

Chile also applies the principles of marginal cost pricing and full-cost recovery (including a return to invested capital) in the provision of water supply and sewage collection in urban areas.

> *'The tariffs are based on the marginal cost of additional supply if new investments are necessary and on the marginal cost of the optimized, entire system, based on replacement costs if the existing capacity is sufficient for the foreseeable demand'* (Hartje et al, 1994).

The tariffs are divided into fixed charges (for connection) and variable charges based on the volume of water consumed and wastewater collected. The full-cost recovery system was implemented gradually over a 4-year period and was expected to reach its full targeted level in 1994. Tariffs vary by region depending on the marginal costs of supply in each region: while in Santiago the tariff is US$0.32 per m^3, in the South it is twice as high and in the North, four times as high (Hartje et al, 1994). To cushion the impact on low-income consumers and reduce the regressivity of tariff charges, the government has introduced a personal subsidy system targeted at about a quarter of the users (those with the lowest incomes) at a cost equal to about 2.5 per cent of the total revenues of the water utilities.

CONTROLLING INDUSTRIAL EFFLUENTS: THE MALAYSIAN EFFLUENT CHARGE SYSTEM

As far back as 20 years ago, the *Malaysian* Environmental Quality Act of 1974 included provisions for using economic incentives and disincentives in the form of effluent charges in support, rather than replacement, of regulatory controls on discharges. The act requires that all dischargers pay a fee to obtain a licence to discharge waste into public water bodies. Because the licence fee varies with the level of waste discharged, it is effectively a discharge fee. The fee varies according to one or more of the following factors:

1   the class of the premises;
2   the location of such premises;
3   the quantity of waste discharged;
4   the pollutant or class of pollutants discharged; and
5   the existing level of pollution.

In 1977, the discharge fees provided by the Act were combined with discharge standards into an incentive-supported regulatory regime for controlling pollution from palm oil mills. The standards were announced in advance, spurring firms to make early capital investments in treatment facilities. The first discharge fees were collected in 1978. With the standards becoming more stringent over time and the discharge fees becoming larger with the quantity of waste discharged, the results were dramatic. Despite a 50 per cent increase in the number of palm oil mills between 1978 and 1982 and a steady increase in palm oil production, the total biochemical oxygen demand (BOD) load released in public water bodies dropped steadily from 222 tons per day in 1978 to 58 tons in 1980, 19 tons in 1982 and 5 tons in 1984 (Ong et al, 1987). According to Ong et al (1987, p 39):

> 'The charging of high effluent-related fees as well as granting incentives by way of waiver of fees for research had the effect of expediting the pace of research, and notable successes have been achieved in palm oil mill effluent treatment technology. Malaysia can justly claim credit to have developed its own technology to treat palm oil waste and protect its environment.'

The Malaysian combination of economic charges and standards worked as follows. In the first year (1978) of implementation of the system, the standard was set at 5000 mg BOD per l and was not mandatory, in recognition of the initial difficulties that would be faced by the industry. The effluent related licence fee was set at US$3 per ton of BOD discharged up to the standard. In the following year, the BOD standard was made stricter (2000 mg/l) and mandatory and progressive effluent charges were imposed to provide an incentive for the establishment of waste treatment facilities. If the BOD concentration exceeded the prescribed standard, a surcharge was imposed equal to US$100 per ton above the standard. This is equivalent to a non-compliance fine or a compliance incentive. The rates were set such that the annual fees for untreated discharge exceeded, at a minimum, the capital costs for building treatment facilities based on cost estimates for the anaerobic lagoon treatment facility. This already departs from the theoretically correct effluent charge, which should equal the marginal environmental damage, not the costs of installing a discharge treatment facility. Nevertheless, the system performed fairly well in managing pollution problems in the palm oil industry as long as the charges maintained their real value and were fully collected. By 1984, when the effluent standard was tightened further to 100 mg/l, the BOD load discharge by the palm oil industry was down to only 4 tons per day out of 1640 tons of BOD generated per day. A similar system was adopted for the control of pollution by the rubber industry, apparently with equal success. By 1984, most rubber factories were discharging BOD under 100 mg/l and the total BOD load discharged was down to 5 tons per day out of a total load of 200 tons generated per day.

The combined effluent standard-charge system, however, was more effective than efficient. First, the charge was not set on the basis of marginal environmental damage costs, as the economic theory of externalities requires for optimal pollution control, but based on the cost of capital investment in treatment facilities. The apparent objective was the construction of waste treatment facilities rather than the control of pollution to optimal levels. This assertion is also supported by the fact that the basic effluent charge is no longer enforced, but the surcharge for effluents above the standard is enforced.

A second problem with the Malaysian effluent standard-charge system, with regard to efficiency, is the imposition of the charge on BOD load rather than volume of discharge. This misplacement would clearly provide a perverse incentive for some firms to dilute their effluent to avoid the charge, without actually reducing the total BOD load entering the river. Evidence for this is lacking but some developed countries, such as the Netherlands, base their effluent charges on a combination of effluent volume and BOD concentration which discourages dilution (Opschoor et al, 1994).

A third problem with the Malaysian system is the implicit incentive for intermedia substitution. While both a basic charge and a surcharge are levied on discharges on land, the basis for the charge is volume, not concentration, while the basis for the surcharge is BOD load above the standard. While this is an effort to address the weakness with the BOD-only-based charge system for disposal in water bodies (identified above), it results in a higher discharge level for land disposal and encourages a shift of disposal from land to water. Again, the fee structure did not reflect marginal environmental damage from disposal in different media, but was an attempt to offset the higher cost of waste treatment for discharge into watercourses.

Vincent and Ali (1997) analyse in detail the economic efficiency (cost-effectiveness) of the Malaysian effluent standard and charge system, using an economic model of cost minimizing abatement and disposal behaviour by palm oil mills. The authors then compare this result with alternative policies, such as command-and-control only (aggregate BOD standard allocated among mills according to output) and emissions trading between mills.

This was a pioneer system for a developing country, and despite its inefficiencies, it did not result in loss of competitiveness for the Malay palm oil industry. According to Rahim (1991), Malaysia's palm oil export sector:

> *'lost only 5% of the value of output as a result of environmental regulations from 1982–1986 that reduced allowable BOD discharges by 90%. The CPO [crude palm oil] sector lost even less — only about 1% of the value of production ... despite the highly competitive nature of world oil markets* (cited in Vincent, 1993; p24).'

In contrast, Rahim (1991) found large losses among the primary input producers, the oil palm plantation sector, which bears over two-thirds of the total welfare losses of the industry.

The Malaysian combined effluent standard-charge system is still in effect but has apparently lost part of its original rationale – to promote waste treatment facilities – and its potency. With treatment facilities becoming a licensing requirement and standard feature of palm oil mills, the basic charge is no longer enforced. The surcharge for effluents above the standard is still enforced but it is so low (having lost much of its real value to inflation) that it no longer acts as a compliance incentive. Some mills find it more advantageous to pay the surcharge than treat their effluent sufficiently to meet the standard.

There is no disputing the environmental success of the system. 'In 1975, the BOD load discharged by CPO mills was equivalent to the BOD load in the raw sewage of 12 million people ... By 1985, however, the population-equivalent BOD load fell to only 80 thousand people.' (Vincent and Ali, 1997, p 320.) This decrease is even more remarkable when one considers that at the same time, 'CPO mills more than doubled and the industry's output of crude palm oil more than tripled.' (Vincent and Ali, 1997.) However, it is extremely difficult, if not impossible, to disaggregate the effect of the charge from the effect of the standards, making it a less compelling testament to the potential environmental effectiveness of economic instruments.

In conclusion, despite its weaknesses – and to some extent because of them – the Malaysian mixed regulation-incentive system holds valuable lessons for developing countries that are contemplating the introduction of economic instruments in support of their environmental regulations. Neighbouring Indonesia has recently been considering the introduction of economic incentives to increase compliance to its industrial environmental standards. The Malaysian experience should be helpful both in this general context as well as in the specific case of pollution from the palm oil industry. Sections of rivers in North

Sumatra are reported to be anaerobic because of heavy BOD loads from palm oil mills (some of the them state owned) despite stringent discharge standards. An effluent charge system with improvements drawn from the experience of Malaysia is certain to increase compliance of privately owned palm oil mills.

As for state-owned firms, the Polish experience discussed below indicates that economic charges have little impact on the behaviour of state enterprises for a couple of reasons. First, the profit motive does not operate to minimize costs. Second, the soft budget constraint of such enterprises allows the shift of charge payments to the state budget. Under these circumstances, privatization may be necessary for economic charges to work.

THE CHINESE POLLUTION LEVY SYSTEM: AN ASSESSMENT OF ITS PERFORMANCE IN CHONGQING MUNICIPALITY

Chongqing is in the southwest part of Sichuan province and, prior to its recent jurisdictional expansion and designation as a national municipality, had a population of 15 million in its urban centre and outlying counties. There are 800 large engineering, chemical and electrical industries in the municipality, and 1500 in the counties, with a combined total output value of 15 billion yuan. Another 90,000 townships and village enterprises (TVEs) contribute 13 billion yuan of industrial output. With annual SO_2 emissions of 781,000 tons (1992 resulting in annual mean concentrations (1992) of 390 μg/m^3 (compared to a maximum permitted level of 200 μg/m^3) and discharges of 650 million tons of wastewater (1992), half of it untreated, Chongqing is one of China's most polluted cities. The economic damages from acid rain – a result of burning each year 16 million tons of coal with 3–5 per cent sulphur content – have been conservatively estimated to exceed 500 million yuan in 1990 (Chongqing Research Institute of Environmental Sciences, 1992). A World Bank supported case study of Chongqing's environmental regulations provides the best documented assessment of the effectiveness of China's pollution control system (Zhong et al, 1994). The assessment focuses on four out of the eight programmes (or instruments) of China's environmental policy: effluent and emission standards; the pollution levy or discharge fee system; the 'three simultaneous' policy; and the discharge permit system. Here, we will summarize the levy system.

The pollution charge (levy) system

The study found that the revenues collected (in current years) from pollution charges in Chongqing rose from 8.4 million yuan in 1982 to

30.1 million yuan in 1992. But when expressed in constant yuan, the levy revenues rose until 1988 only and then began to fall as they failed to keep up with inflation (Table 10.1). Indeed when expressed in payments-per-factory, (real) charges fell since 1988 and possibly earlier; in 1992 pollution charges per factory were less than half of their 1986 level. While this drop could be due to increased compliance, and in some cases it is, the overall compliance figures and the rising number of companies that pay charges suggest diminished enforcement and erosion by inflation as the main reasons for the decline. An alternative hypothesis consistent with the data would be that wastewater enforcement is spreading to more medium and small enterprises but enforcement on large state enterprises is weakening because of exemptions granted due to their inefficiency and low profitability. The bulk of the collected pollution charges (over 60 per cent) comes from water pollution, followed by air pollution (20 per cent), noise (13 per cent), and solid waste (2 per cent). As many as 89 per cent of the state and city enterprises paid pollution charges, but less than 2 per cent of TVEs paid any charges; while TVEs account for 22 per cent of the industrial output, they pay under 8 per cent of the pollution charges collected.

Revenues from pollution charges (80 per cent) provided the second largest source of funds for environmental investments after the 7 per cent investment mandate of the 'three simultaneous' policy. The balance of 20 per cent of pollution charges plus 100 per cent of the fines from the 'four small pieces' provided the operating expenses for the local Environmental Protection Bureaus (EPB).

A very positive feature of the Chongqing findings is the substantial leveraging of the pollution-charge-financed investment subsidy through the addition of the enterprises' own funds: to be eligible for an environmental subsidy, enterprises are required to demonstrate ability and willingness to co-finance 50 per cent of the investment. Where the system does not perform well is in the use of sound investment criteria in allocating scarce investment funds. Indeed, the study reports that 2744 new treatment facilities were completed in the municipality during 1986–1990, increasing the treatment capacity for air pollution by 22.5 billion cubic metres per year and for water pollution by 130 million tons per year. Even so, non-compliance charges dropped only by 8 million yuan; this implies significant underutilization of installed pollution abatement capacity.

The study by Zhong et al (1994) identified a number of weaknesses and perverse incentives in Chongqing's system which result in diminished effectiveness:

1   The low and falling real value of charges does not induce compliance.
2   The dependence of local EPB on charge revenues is compromising their interest in law enforcement.
3   The link between payment of pollution charges and the environmental subsidy (rebated charges) further discourages compliance.

Table 10.1 *Compliance Rates, Discharge Fee Payments and Environmental Investments in Chongqing Municipality, 1981–1993*

Year	Compliance with effluent standards (% of enterprises)	Industrial wastewater treated (% of total)	Wastewater charges		Number of enterprises paying discharge fee	Discharge fees per enterprise (1986 yuan)	Air pollution emissions	
			Treated industrial wastewater meeting standard (%)	Discharge fees (million 1986 yuan)			Environmental investment as % of total investment	Annual mean concentration of SO_2 (µg/m^3)
1981–1984							6.49	
1985								
1986		58.9		25.3	2002	12,647		
1987		66.9					6.25	
1988		68.1		28.6	2531	11,304		0.36
1989		73.1						
1990	43.5	71.4	50.9	24.8	2732	9078		
1991	50.0	66.7	32.2				4.80	
1992	53.2	–	–					
1993	58.1	60.1	36.0	20.1	3766	5332		0.39

Note: The current Yuan figures on discharge fees reported in this source were converted into 1986 yuan by using an average inflation rate 5.8 per cent during 1980–1991 and 8.1 per cent during 1992.

Source: Zhong et al (1994).

4   The frequent exemptions of inefficient state enterprises subsidizes inefficiency.
5   TVEs, the fastest growing sector in Chongqing (95 per cent growth rate in the first half of 1994 compared with 18 per cent for the industry as a whole) remain unregulated and unreachable by the high transaction costs (Panayotou, 1998).

CONTROLLING INDUSTRIAL EMISSIONS: THE POLISH PILOT PROJECT IN TRADABLE EMISSION PERMITS

A tradable industrial emissions demonstration project started recently in Poland (Dudek et al, 1992). The project seeks to show that the economic instruments that have been successful in the USA also offer a significant potential for pollution abatement for economies in transition. These countries, which are heavily polluted but striving to attain sustainable growth, face economic and environmental investment costs in excess of annual GNP. If demonstration projects can provide evidence that economic instruments are both environmentally and economically effective, they may help to overcome the institutional, social and political obstacles to the adoption of economic approaches to environmental management and the implementation of economic instruments.

The demonstration project, which began in March 1991 and was implemented in Chorzow, Poland in July 1991, is expected to involve at least six large enterprises and a number of small district heating plants. To date, two enterprises have participated: Steel Mill Kosciuszko (one of Poland's 'Top 80' polluters) and the Power Plant Chorzow. These firms are heavy polluters and need new equipment before they will be able to comply with environmental regulations. Replacing the old equipment could take as long as six years. In the meantime the current regulatory system offers no alternative to current extreme environmental damages and likely plant closure with the loss of municipal heating and electricity supply.

A tradable emissions programme is recommended, using a combination of bubble policy and a revolving fund. The regional administrator would issue an emissions permit for the Power Plant, which would use a combination of control technology and emissions reduction credits to achieve the ambient standard. The Power Plant would obtain these credits through financial support of the Steel Mill, which would reduce pollution by accelerating changes. The system would bring gradual improvement in the city's air quality without disrupting its utilities' operations.

Because the region is extremely degraded, it was felt that some external support was needed. An external subsidy (from regional environmental funds) was provided to the Steel Mill to facilitate restructuring. The subsidy was intended to establish the revolving fund, which would benefit the participating polluters who reduce emissions.

The demonstration project has already shown some promise. Despite legal and social problems, educational efforts have resulted in acceptance of the experiment by potential participants. It is believed that there are also many opportunities for successful replication of the project, both in Poland and in other economies in transition. Hopefully, the success of demonstration projects will promote greater acceptance of economic approaches to environmental management.

DECONGESTION OF URBAN SETTLEMENTS: ROAD PRICING IN SINGAPORE AND AUCTIONING OF STREET USER RIGHTS FOR URBAN BUSES IN CHILE

Road transport imposes a variety of external costs on society not directly paid by the beneficiaries (that is, the road users), namely:

1   wear and tear on the road infrastructure necessitating more frequent maintenance;
2   road congestion necessitating expansion and upgrading of the road system;
3   air emissions that are detrimental to health, property and nature;
4   noise pollution and associated vibrations which affect sleep, mental health, quality of life and property values; and
5   road accidents which damage vehicles, incur medical costs, and cause loss of output as well as pain, grief and suffering.

Not all of these external costs are conventionally thought of as environmental costs, but virtually all have environmental implications. For example, road congestion increases air and noise pollution per kilometre travelled and necessitates road expansion which encroaches on nature and open space. Similarly, increased frequency of road accidents not only lowers economic output and quality of life but also compels expansion or modification of infrastructure which has environmental costs in addition to economic costs.

Like many cities, Singapore has suffered from the environmental effects of a growing car-driving population: congestion resulting in longer travel times for cars and public transport alike, air pollution, wear and tear on roads and a lower quality of life for those living and working in heavily congested areas. Because car drivers do not naturally bear the substantial costs they impose on society, charging for urban road use is theoretically appealing. The success of Singapore's Area Licensing Scheme demonstrates its practical appeal as well.

In 1975, private cars represented half of Singapore's 280,000 registered vehicles and were owned at a rate of 1 per 16 people. In an attempt to reduce central city traffic by 25–30 per cent during peak hours, the city implemented a scheme that charged drivers for using roads in the city centre during these hours (Watson and Holland,

1978). Specifically, the city aimed to: (a) reduce car use within certain areas during particular times; (b) provide those no longer driving into the inner city with attractive travel alternatives; (c) enact a scheme that was easy to implement and enforce; and (d) leave economic activity unaffected. The area-pricing scheme required vehicles travelling through the city centre at peak hours to purchase a daily or monthly licence, raised daytime parking fees within this area, and instituted a park-and-ride service to facilitate easy non-car commuting. Buses, cycles and cars with four or more passengers were exempted from the licensing requirements.

The programme had the following effects. Above all, it achieved a traffic reduction of 73 per cent in the restricted zone during peak hours (Watson and Holland, 1978). In addition, business seemed largely unaffected, and although the park-and-ride option was not heavily utilized, the city found the overall scheme easy to implement and enforce. Car pools increased from 10 to 40 per cent of all traffic. Of car-owning commuters travelling into the zone, 13 per cent switched to public transit, and about the same percentage changed their commuting time to pre-peak hours. For those who did not change their habits to avoid the zone during peak hours, the monthly average commuting cost rose from US$64 to US$95. More significantly, all but one-tenth of 'through zone' commuters changed their route or departure time to avoid licensing fees. Travel speeds increased by 10 per cent on incoming roads and by 20 per cent on zone roads.

There were additional environmental benefits. Although other pollutants were difficult to measure, the level of carbon monoxide declined significantly during the hours the scheme was in effect. Central city residents and shoppers reported greater ease and safety in getting around, less fumes and generally happier living and shopping conditions (Watson and Holland, 1978). Generally, all affected groups concurred that the impact on Singapore was positive, with motorists being the only ones to perceive themselves as worse off, though not badly so. Their perceptions were accurate since they were, in fact, shouldering more of the social costs of their car use.

With an initial return on investment of 77 per cent (which rose to 95 per cent with an increase in licence fees), the scheme achieved its goals without undue budgetary costs. Less quantifiable, but more significant may be the long-run benefits, specifically the road construction or future congestion that may be avoided due to changed habits and attitudes towards public transit and car use (Watson and Holland, 1978).

In another part of the world, Santiago, Chile suffered from a similar congestion and pollution problem in the late 1980s, but for a different reason. Ten years earlier, the Santiago urban public bus system was completely deregulated and made a free access system. This resulted in rapid expansion of the bus fleet to 13,000 buses, 40 per cent above the optimum (rent maximizing) level (Hartje et al, 1994). Congestion resulted both from the excessive number of buses and the lack of coordination of bus stops. Transport-related emissions grew as a result of the large number of buses and taxis scouting the city streets for passengers, the very low speed and the lack of minimum quality standards. Despite the formation of an operators' organization, the 'Consejo Superior del Transport', which was able to raise prices, excess congestion continued as most buses were depreciated and continued to operate with low occupancy as long as they covered their operating costs (Hartje et al, 1994).

To relieve congestion in the streets of central Santiago, a new law was passed in 1991 to enable the Ministry of Transportation to establish regulations regarding minimum air and service quality and access to congested roads. A number of innovations were introduced under this law. First, buses and taxicabs older than 18 years were bought by the government for their scrap value and retired. By 1994, as much as one-third of the fleet was to be retired. Second, a registry for public transport vehicles was established, and entry was limited to new vehicles. Third, service quality and air emission standards were introduced. Fourth, the rights of access by buses and taxis to roads congested by these vehicles were auctioned. To ensure compliance and reduce enforcement costs, only incorporated companies were allowed to bid, thus providing a strong incentive for incorporation of small operations into companies or cooperatives. The selection criteria included quality of proposed service, air emission characteristics, and frequency on specific lines to ensure that the pollution reduction came from frequency reduction not from change in spatial structure of lines (Hartje et al, 1994).

The system had a number of beneficial outcomes. Overcapacity was reduced by 30 per cent, the occupancy rate of buses increased, congestion was relieved and air pollution reduced at least proportionately (specific figures are not yet available). Increased speed of service offset both the reduced frequency of service and the increased waiting time. A negative side-effect of the auction system has been the relocation of small operations to adjacent streets and residential areas, somewhat diluting the effectiveness of the auction (Figueroa, 1993). In response, the government is planning to extend the auction system to a wider area. There is also a proposal for a similar system for private cars, including a road pricing system.

Like the Singapore congestion pricing system, the Santiago auction system may not be applicable everywhere, but the innovative ideas it contains could help in the design of a system for cities, like Manila for example, with similar congestion and pollution problems and a large private fleet of mass transport.

COMMUNITY PRESSURES AS INSTRUMENTS OF CHANGE: THE CASE OF THAILAND

Statistical analysis of a survey of 500 firms in 10 provinces in the greater Bangkok Region revealed that despite very weak enforcement of formal environmental regulations, as many as 60 per cent of the sampled firms have formulated environmental plans or carried out internal environmental audits. When asked to rate the factors that influence their decisions to improve their environmental behaviour, firms rated community and neighbourhood pressures above potential lawsuits and pressures from industry associations, customers abroad and the news media, and almost at a par with government regulations, economic incentives and pressure from shareholders. Only pressures from customers at home and from employees were ranked as more important than community pressures. Moreover, it was found that pressures from groups outside the management (especially community groups) had a significant effect upon the likelihood of an enforcement action by regulation (Panayotou et al, 1997). Hettige et al (1996) found similar results with regard to community pressures in countries as diverse as Indonesia and Bangladesh. The level of education and income per capita explained much of the variation between communities in the level of pressure they exert on the industry in their territory to control its pollution. Informal regulation by communities tends to be stronger when pollution levels are higher and affect more people of higher education and income level. This finding underlines the importance of human development in environmental management. Perhaps regulators should focus more of their efforts on empowering communities to negotiate effectively with the industry, especially where poverty, low education level and lack of information and organization translate into weak bargaining power.

INFORMATIONAL REGULATION: THE INDONESIAN EXPERIENCE

The best known informational regulation in a developing country is the public disclosure programme in Indonesia. In the face of a 10 per cent annual growth of manufacturing, a weak enforcement of formal regulation and mounting pollution damages, Indonesia's National Pollution Control Agency (BAPEDAL) introduced a programme for rating and publicly disclosing the environmental performance of factories. The expectation was that pressure from public disclosure will provide low-cost substitutes for formal enforcement of regulations. The Programme for Pollution Control, Evaluation and Rating (or PROPER), announced in June 1995, assigned a colour rating to each polluter based on BAPEDAL's evaluation of its environmental performance, from black (worst) to gold (best). Factories which meet national environmental standards are assigned a blue rating while factories with pollution control efforts that fall short of the standard are assigned a red rating. Factories with emissions control well above the standard receive a green rating, while outstanding performers receive a gold rating. During the pilot phase, 187 plants were rated but only five green plants were publicly announced. All the plants which were rated red and black, a

A. Data Verification

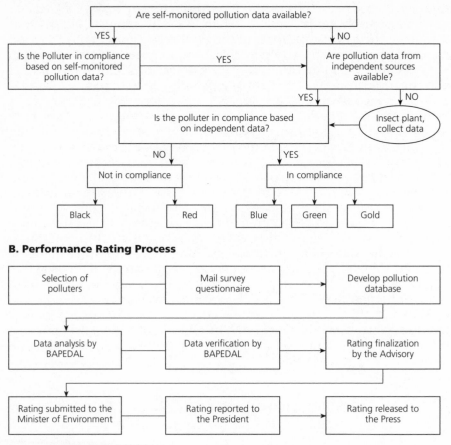

B. Performance Rating Process

Source: Afsah and Vincent (1997).

Figure 10.1 *The Indonesia Programme for Pollution Control Evaluation and Rating (PROPER)*

total of 121, were privately notified and given six months to improve their performance. By the time of full disclosure, December 1995, half the plants rated earlier as black succeeded in upgrading their status, so did a large proportion of the red-rated plants. The number of plants in full compliance (blue) rose by nearly one-fifth from 61 to 72. Most notably, one of the facilities given a green ranking six months earlier was downgraded in response to protests by the community living in the vicinity of the facility. Domestic private firms fared the worst, foreign firms the best and state enterprises in between. The multinationals' strong performance was largely due to scale economies due to their size and only in small part to their export orientation (see Figure 10.1).

While it is too early to evaluate the programme, the preliminary results suggest that industrial polluters respond to informational regulation. Why? For two reasons: (a) public disclosure empowers local communities which use the government-certified performance ratings to negotiate pollution control agreements with factories in their vicinity; and (b) public disclosure works through the market as an incentive regulation through reputational effects and by penalizing bad behaviour and rewarding performance. At the same time, it improves the regulator's information and enlists the help of superior performers in identifying poor performers. Yet the scheme is not without its critics, who are concerned whether it is extendable from the few large factories to the many small ones; whether the scheme will continue to be effective when its novelty wears off; and, whether its higher effectiveness in better-off, more educated communities will encourage relocation of polluting industries to poorer/weaker communities. An attempt to extend the scheme to the Philippines was less successful largely because of inadequate local commitment and participation.

Chapter 11
Conclusion: Policy Lessons and Recommendations

Policy makers charged with environmental management are generally faced with a difficult task to start with because environmental interventions are usually perceived not as productive activities, but as breaks in economic activity. The task is even harder in developing and transitional economies in which environmental concerns are not only low on the list of priorities, but they are also perceived as drags on the development and restructuring efforts, because they compete for scarce resources and weigh down on the economy at its critical take-off stage.

This perception arises partly from a failure to recognize the linkages between environmental protection and the efficiency and sustainability of the development and restructuring process and partly from the dominant type of policy instruments used to implement environmental management. Command-and-control regulations are almost by definition additional constraints which are not welcome in a developing or transitional economy context in which there are already too many constraints (capital, foreign exchange, government budget, technology and institutions) and too few instruments to pursue a multiplicity of objectives. These reasons, along with the inherently limited enforcement capability within these economies, account for the slow and rather reluctant progress of environmental management in all but a limited group of mostly developing countries.

Two rather recent developments, the concept of sustainable development and of economic or market-based instruments, have fundamentally changed the landscape of environmental management in terms of both objectives and instruments. From being a luxury of primary concern to wealthy countries, environmental protection has become one of the foundations of efficient and sustainable development; from being caught in an inevitable trade-off with economic growth, environmental management has become a source of growth, at least in the long run. The perception of the environment has changed from one of economic liability to one of a potential economic asset.

While the concept of sustainable development has clearly enhanced the expected benefits of environmental management from those of an amenity to those of necessity, it did little by itself to lower their costs. Increased benefits of an essential nature do justify more effort in protecting the environment even in poor countries, but a high and sharply rising supply price quickly eats up the newly discovered benefits. The continued use of rigid command-and-control regulations, which are insensitive to compliance cost differences between pollution sources and fail to provide incentives for continued environmental improvement and technological innovation, is not consistent with the positive view of environmental management in the context of sustainable development.

Enter economic or market-based instruments with the promise of flexibility, cost-effectiveness, and dynamic efficiency: all critical factors in development and restructuring efforts. Not only is more environmental management justified on account of lower costs, but also the new incentive structure created improves resource allocation and promotes technological innovation. The premise of economic instruments is that environmental degradation and unsustainable development are behavioural responses to perverse market signals created by the failure to price fully natural resources and environmental assets and their products and services. The economic instruments approach to environmental management aims to correct the incentive structure by phasing out subsidies and other policy distortions and internalizing externalities and other social costs. Since full-cost pricing is essential to both efficient environmental management and sustainable economic development and since the two are interrelated, the use of economic instruments to effect full-cost pricing operationalizes the concept of efficient and sustainable development.

There is a large set of economic instruments to choose from and the choice is neither trivial nor immaterial to the objectives of efficient environmental management and sustainable economic development. First, there is the choice of the right instrument or rather, the right combination of instruments that would best fit the specific conditions of the industry and country in question. Second, there is the choice of the level at which each instrument should be set to either ensure optimal environmental management or at least, attainment of stated environmental objectives at the minimum possible cost. Third, there is the choice of the pace of implementation or compliance schedule to minimize disruption and to ensure public support. Fourth, there is the choice of related or parallel policies necessary to address side-effects such as the regressivity of certain instruments (eg, product taxes).

To inform this choice we reviewed the experience of selected developed and developing countries with a variety of economic instruments, including environmental taxes, emission charges, product charges, tradable permits, refundable deposits and environmental bonds, among others. We concluded that while there is increasing interest in and use of economic instruments, the objective is more to raise financial resources than to change behaviour or institute full-cost pricing. Pollution charges are usually set too low to induce a major change in behaviour, much less to attain an optimal level of pollution. Yet, this experience is suggestive of the potential gains from an incentive-based approach to environmental management. In addition to reviewing past experience, we examined the applicability of economic instruments to the special circumstances of developing countries and modalities and strategy for their successful introduction.

In the short-to-medium run, the best prospects for economic instruments in developing countries are first as sources of revenues and second as supports or supplements of command-and-control regulations. Economic charges may be introduced as enforcement incentives, tradable permits and credits as instruments to increase compliance with effluent or emission standards, and transferable development rights as supports of zoning regulations. The outright replacement of command-and-control regulations by economic instruments does not appear feasible at this time, and even if it were, it would be too disruptive. Economic instruments need to prove themselves before they can be trusted to attain society's environmental objectives, yet governments appear unwilling to set these instruments at levels that have an incentive effect on behaviour. Nevertheless, it would be substantial progress if economic instruments were to be introduced even as a source of flexibility and financing in conjunction with existing standards. By influencing investor expectations, a pre-announced schedule of escalation over time would create the right incentives long before the instrument attains its full force.

In the long run, the prospects for using economic instruments in developing countries (as in developed and transitional economies) are virtually unlimited. They can be the fastest and least costly (and possibly the only) vehicle to sustainable development. Whether the concern is about excessive rates of deforestation and biodiversity loss, soil erosion and water shortages, CO_2 emissions, or unsustainable consumption patterns, the source of the problem is underpricing and free riding externalities. To the extent that economic instruments prove to be effective means of internalizing environmental and depletion costs and instituting full-cost pricing, they hold the key to environmental management and sustainable development. Proximate causes such as poverty, population growth and overconsumption by the wealthy North would lose their potency without the nourishment from institutional, policy and market failures.

Economic instruments such as environmental taxes, effluent charges and tradable emission permits are generally more cost-effective than effluent and emission standards or mandated technology in attaining a given level of environmental quality. Economic instruments significantly lower compliance costs on industry because they allow polluters the freedom to choose their response in order to minimize their cost of compliance: they can pay the charges, reduce or treat their waste, change their input combination, reduce their output, change their production technology, or move to a different location. For example, while with regulations every firm must meet the same standard or reduce its emissions by the same amount as every other firm regardless of cost, with tradable emission permits high cost pollution abaters are allowed to under comply and *in exchange* pay low cost pollution abaters to over comply on their behalf in order to achieve the same overall ambient quality level. The savings could be substantial for both the industry and the government. Moreover, while regulations generate no revenues and require large budgets and bloated bureaucracies to manage and enforce them, economic instruments, if properly designed, could both save in enforcement costs and generate substantial revenues for environmental investments.

Thus, a move towards increased use of economic instruments for environmental management in either support of or replacement of command-and-control regulations should be regarded as an indirect mechanism for financing Agenda 21. Both growth and environmental protection are advanced in a cost effective manner, budgetary resources are saved and new sources of revenue established for investing in sustainable development.

Unfortunately, the trend is for developing countries to copy the command-and-control regulations and rigid environmental standards of developed countries even as developed countries are trying to escape from them. Of course, for economic instruments such as charges and taxes to be effective, they must be set at sufficiently high levels to reflect marginal damage and to induce a change in behaviour; they also must be protected against inflation and political manipulation. While overnight replacement of rigid regulations by economic instruments is unlikely, it would mark substantial progress towards the objectives of Agenda 21 if economic instruments are introduced as a source of flexibility, incentives and financing in conjunction with existing standards. The experience of Malaysia with effluent charges, of Singapore with congestion fees, of Poland with a pilot tradable permit scheme, and of Turkey with industrial relocation incentives, offer grounds for optimism.

The experience of developing countries and more recently of transitional economies suggests a number of lessons and recommendations for securing effective long-term financing of environmentally sustainable development, with which we will conclude:

1   *Rely more on the country's own economic growth and resource mobilization to finance the alleviation of domestic environmental problems than on foreign assistance.* International aid may help in institutional capacity building and occasionally play a catalytic role in domestic resource mobilization, but it is never an adequate or sustainable source of funding for what are recurrent and systemic problems. It is with regard to global environmental problems (global warming, ozone depletion, biodiversity loss) and obligations that arise from international environmental agreements that transitional and developing economies should more aggressively pursue international financial transfers through joint implementation, debt-swaps, GEF grants and the like.
2   *Set realistic and attainable environmental goals which correspond to the country's socioeconomic conditions and national priorities and use economic instruments to achieve those goals.* Over-ambitious targets, excessively strict environmental standards and detailed environmental action plans not matched by commensurate enforcement

capability and funding tend to discredit environmental policy and the credibility of the state as environmental investor. The resulting public disillusionment further erodes the public's already low willingness to pay for environmental investments. It is only by setting and meeting realistic standards and targets that the environmental authorities can earn the public's confidence and the credit-worthiness to access the necessary funds, whether through user charges, municipal bonds or capital markets.

3   *Opt for incentive-based rather than command-and-control-based environ-mental improvements.* Since a good part of needed environmental investment is end-of-pipe clean up and since supply expansions of public utilities are the result of a perverse incentive structure implicit in the pricing and taxation system, it is no wonder that environmental investments are generally perceived not to pay and not to be bankable. Removal of perverse incentives, internalization of environmental costs and implementation of the polluter and user pays principles (even gradually) would reduce the investment needs and expand the available financial resources. Incentive-based systems, such as environmental taxes, pollution charges, user fees, tradable emission permits, deposit-refund systems and environ-mental bonds, discourage wasteful and polluting behaviour, minimize the cost of compliance and generate funds for public investments in environmental protection. The existing charge and fine systems in most countries are revenue raising devices rather than incentive systems.

4   *Encourage private capital inflow, in general, and direct foreign invest-ment, in particular, to relax the financial constraint on all investments (including environmental investments) and to access the best available environmental technology.* What discourages investors most is not strict environmental standards or high pollution charges, but: (a) unpredictable and ever-changing environmental policy; (b) exemp-tions of domestic firms or other competitors through variable and inconsistent enforcement; and (c) uncapped liabilities for past contamination.[1] Contrary to conventional wisdom that low environmental standards are needed to attract foreign investments, multinationals prefer to establish facilities consistent with environ-mental standards at home for two reasons: (a) the plant design and equipment they import employ the latest least-polluting technol-ogy; and (b) their environmental performance in one country affects their image and operations worldwide.

5   *Clarify the potential investors' liability for past contamination to reduce barriers to foreign investment and privatization of state enterprises.* Indemnifying the new owners of privatized state enterprises against clean-up costs or other inherited liabilities arising from past pollution is a win–win solution to effective financing of environ-mentally sustainable development: it raises the sale price of the enterprise by more than the cost of clean up (Panayotou et al, 1994); it encourages private investment and inflow of foreign

capital; and it increases the access to less polluting technology. Indemnification would also establish a dividing line between past and future pollution for which the new owners would be held responsible according to the polluter pays principle. It also allows the government to prioritize clean ups according to expected social benefits and opportunity costs of the funds, thereby making a more effective use of limited resources.

6   *Shift more of the financial responsibility for environmental protection to: (a) the private sector through privatization, and the introduction of environmental bonds, deposit-refund systems, impact fees, betterment charges and clear liability laws; and (b) local communities and munici- palities through decentralization of decision making and resource mobilization, especially the authority to set priorities and to issue debt to finance local environmental improvements within broadly defined national guidelines.* At the same time, national environmental policy makers should seek a more active role in the privatization, the pricing and taxation policy and the investment approval process. Likewise, economic and financial decision makers should involve environmental policy makers in such discussions. Assessing and addressing the environmental consequences of investment projects (especially infrastructural) is generally a more effective means of protecting the environment than undertaking clean up or mitigative environmental investments.

7   *Seek to shape expectations of the future environment pricing policy and regulatory framework in order to influence the design of new facilities at relatively low cost rather than to retrofit existing facilities at high cost.* The preoccupation with the potentially high costs of (the not always necessary) clean up of past contamination and the misguided efforts to retrofit older facilities to comply fully with ex post standards has diverted attention from the once in a lifetime opportunity to shape the future during the formative stages of the emerging new economy. Industrial plants that are being designed and infrastructure that is being developed today, under an uncer- tain policy environment, will determine environmental sustainability and the costs of improving it for decades to come.

8   *Promote a more open discussion and informed debate of environmental issues, of the environment/growth trade-offs, and of policy alternatives (including the costs of inaction) to attract public participation in priority setting and to enlist public support for the chosen priorities.* Understanding and appreciating the benefit of environmental policies and investments and the opportunity costs involved is key to willingness to pay either directly through user fees, or indirectly, through taxation and regulation, and thus key to financial sustain- ability. Given the low public demand and weak political support for environmental investments, the top investment priority ought to be the availability of information and the fostering of public debate, rather than the construction of waste treatment facilities.

9   *Prioritize environmental objectives, policies and investments through vigorous cost-benefit analysis and broadly based public participation to*

make the most of limited available resources and generate new resources.
Estimation of benefits and comparison with opportunity costs,
until recently a luxury for wealthy western economies which can
afford a great deal of waste, is a basic necessity for developing and
transitional economies with meagre resources and colossal needs.
There can be no justification for environmental investments
involving substantial opportunity costs in terms of forgone
economic growth when win–win policies and no-regret investments – such as those that increase energy efficiency and reduce
wasteful water use – remain unexploited. Beyond win–win policies,
low-cost, high-return environmental protection investments must
be pursued ahead of investments and regulations that involve
difficult environment-economy trade-offs.

10 *Leverage limited public funds to mobilize additional financial resources
from the private sector and external sources to alleviate short-term financial constraints while all the necessary reforms for the development of
local capital markets are put into place and take effect.* Leveraging can
take the form of sovereign guarantees, risk sharing, revolving funds
and the like. Existing environmental funds do engage in leveraging, but only as one of many objectives or as a by-product of
financing limits and co-financing requirements. Limited public
funds would go further in promoting sustainable development if
subsidies, grants and soft loans are replaced by leverage-maximiz-
ing instruments.

In conclusion, economic instruments, in their broadest sense, are
powerful and virtually indispensable tools in any sustainable development strategy, because they uniquely combine both motivating and
financing functions which are complementary and mutually reinforc-
ing. Alternatives such as command-and-control regulations which
attempt to force (rather than motivate) a change of behaviour and use
up (rather than generate) financial resources are unenforceable or
unaffordable or both. Similarly, financing instruments which mobilize
funds but do not motivate a change in behaviour are patently wasteful.
It is only when incentive systems and financing mechanisms are
integrated, as they are in economic instruments, broadly defined, that
environmental protection and economic development are reconciled
and advanced concurrently, which is the very essence of sustainable
development.

Applications of Economic Instruments in Developed Countries

Country	Type	Period	Direct instruments	Indirect instruments
General				
Canada	SB	na		Accelerated depreciation for pollution control investments on plants commissioned before 1974[1]
France, Germany	SB	na		Accelerated depreciation for pollution control equipment[2]
Japan	SB	na		Special depreciation for 25% of pollution control equipment investment[3]
Netherlands	SB	na		3–15% investment tax credit for any environmental protection investment
Netherlands	SB	na		Grants and Loans to assist R&D projects[4]
Land and Soils				
Netherlands	C/RS	na	Manure surplus charge on excessive phosphorus	
Sweden, Norway, Finland	C/RS	1989–		Product charges on fertilizers and pesticides
USA	SB	1945–	Subsidy for soil conservation to farmers	
USA, France	TB	na	Rural transferable development rights trading (in USA: Pinelands/NJ, Burlington/NJ, Montgomery/ MD)[5]	
Water Resources				
USA	SB	1970–	Sewage treatment plant construction (to municipalities)	

USA, California	TP	1991–		Water banking and exchange of water rights[6]
Australia	TP	na		Water rights markets and auctions for new irrigation water[7]
New Zealand	TP	1967–		Tradable water rights system
USA (Wisconsin)	TP	1981–	Permits for BOD loads to the Fox River	
France	SB	na	Subsidized loans to industry to reduce water pollution	
Portugal	C/RS	na	Water pollution charges	
Germany	C/RS	1960–	Pollution effluent charge[8]	
Netherlands	C/RS	1969–	Pollution effluent charge	
Italy, France	C/RS	1976–	Pollution effluent charge (firms)	
UK	C/RS	1981–	Pollution effluent charge	
New Zealand, Iceland	TP	na	Transferable fishing quotas[9]	

Toxic Chemicals and Hazardous Waste

USA	C/RS	1983–	Waste effluent charge to waste site operators	
Belgium	C/RS	1981	Waste effluent charge to firms	
Denmark	C/RS	1987	Waste effluent charge to firms and households	
Sweden, Norway	C/RS			Product charges on batteries
Italy	C/RS			Product charge on plastic bags
Germany, Italy	C/RS			Product charge on lubricant oils
Netherlands	SB			Subsidy to industry for R&D and installation of pollution control equipment

Congestion and Air Pollution

Japan	C/RS	na	Air and noise pollution charges	
Greece	C/RS	na	Air pollution charges	
Italy	C/RS	1989–	Airport noise charge	
Netherlands, UK	C/RS	na	Noise pollution charges	
Sweden	C/RS	na	SO_2 and NO_2 emission charges	
Switzerland	C/RS	na	Noise and air pollution charges	
Most OECD	C/RS	1980–		Tax differentiation lead-free petrol
Norway	C/RS	1986		Cordon pricing in the Bergen and Oslo Toll Rings[10]

Country	Type	Year		
USA, Norway	C/RS	1987–		Passive electronic road pricing[11]
Sweden	C/RS	1992–		Electronic and manual zone fees in Active electronic road pricing (ERP) in Randstad area (experiment until 1995)[12]
United Kingdom	C/RS	1993–		Active ERP in Cambridge[13]
USA	C/RS	1994–		Passive electronic road pricing in Orange County Route 91, California[14]
USA	TP	1982–1987	Lead trading between refineries to reduce lead content of petrol	
USA	TP	1976–	Air quality control area bubbles (trading)	
USA	TP	1979–	Air quality control area bubbles (trading between sources in area)	
USA	TP	1992	SO_2 emission permit trading	
USA (Los Angeles)	TP	1992–	Ozone precursor (NO_x, VOC, SO_x) permit trading (RECLAIM)[15]	

Human Settlements

Country	Type	Year		
Sweden, Norway	C/RS			Product charge on beverage containers
Turkey	C/RS	na	Solid waste charge	
Germany	C/RS	1969–		Product tax on virgin oils for financing of subsidies for safe disposal/recycling
USA, France	C/RS	na	Landfill tax (NJ, PA, France)[16]	
USA (New York) France, Switzerland	TP	1970s		Landmark tradable development rights[17]
Italy	SB	na	Recycling of old wastes	
Most OECD Countries	DR	na	Deposit refund on specific beverage containers and bottles	
Denmark	DR	na	Deposit on mercury and cadmium batteries	
Norway, Sweden	DR	1976–	Deposit refund on scrap cars	
USA	other	1969		Incentive zoning in New York City, San Francisco, Anchorage, Cincinnati and Miami[18]

Global Climate

Country	Type	Year		
USA	TP	1988–	CFC reductions trading	

USA, Denmark	C/RS	1989–		Excise tax on ozone-depleting chemicals[19]
Sweden	C/RS	1991–	Carbon Tax (SKR0.25 per kg)	
Denmark	C/RS	1992–	Carbon Tax	

Note: C/RS, Charge or removed subsidy; TP, Tradable Permit; DR, Deposit-refund system; SB, Subsidy; EI, Enforcement incentive.

Applications of Economic Instruments in Transitional Economies

Country	Type	Period	Direct instruments	Indirect instruments
General				
Poland	SB	na		Tax credit for 30% of investments in environmental protection, if project completed within 5 years
Poland	SB	na		Subsidized credit (50% of interest) for investments in pollution abatement
Russia	C/RS	1990–	System of emission, effluent and solid waste fees based on zero-threshold step function or assessment[1]	
Water Resources				
Czechoslovakia, Hungary, Poland	C/RS	na	Pollution effluent charges	
Toxic Chemicals and Hazardous Waste				
Poland	C/RS	na	Charge on dumping and storage of non-recyclable industrial waste	
Human Settlements				
Poland	C/RS	na	User charge for collection and treatment of municipal solid waste	

Note: C/RS, Charge or removed subsidy; TP, Tradable Permit; DR, Deposit-refund system; SB, Subsidy; EI, Enforcement incentive.

Applications of Economic Instruments in Newly Industrialized Economies and Middle-Income Countries

Country	Type	Period	Direct instruments	Indirect instruments
General				
South Korea	SB	na		10% of investment tax credit (3% for imported equipment) for pollution control equipment[1]
South Korea	SB	na		Accelerated depreciation (50% for domestic, 30% for imported) for new technologies[2]
Taiwan	SB	na		Accelerated depreciation and investment tax credit 5–20% depending on type of asset
Water Resources				
Brazil	C/RS	1978–	Effluent charges in Sao Paulo[3]	
Malaysia	C/RS	1978–	Rubber and palm oil mill effluent charges cum water quality standards[4]	
Congestion and Air Pollution				
Singapore	C/RS	1975–		Central zone car licensing fee
Hong Kong	C/RS	1983–		Passive electronic road pricing and area licensing scheme[5]
Mexico	C/RS	na		50% increase in petrol prices (implicit emission tax)[6]

Human Settlements

Egypt, Syria, Lebanon	DR	na	Deposit refund on glass, carbonated beverage containers

Note: C/RS, Charge or removed subsidy; TP, Tradable Permit; DR, Deposit-refund system; SB, Subsidy; EI, Enforcement incentive.

Applications of Economic Instruments in Developing Countries

Country	Type	Period	Direct instruments	Indirect instruments
Land and Soils				
Indonesia	C/RS	1985–		Removal of pesticide subsidies
Forests				
Cameroon	C/RS	na	Fixed and variable taxes on land area and amount of timber harvested	
Water Resources				
India	C/RS	na	Mix of water tariffs, pollution charges and fiscal incentives in Jamshedpur[1]	
India	TP	na		Groundwater markets in Punjab, Uttar Pradesh and Haryana[2]
PR of China	C/RS	1985–		Decentralization of authority to local water management agencies
Congestion and Air Pollution				
PR of China	TP	1985	Pollution discharge permit system, Beijing[3]	
PR of China	C/RS	1985–	Emission fee and fine collection system, Beijing[4]	
Human Settlements				
India	DRS	na	Deposit refund on glass, carbonated beverage containers	
Forests				
Global (proposed)			System of tradable forest protection and management obligations[5]	

Toxic Chemicals and Hazardous Waste

Thailand	Posting of performance bonds based on projected levels of hazardous wastes[6]

Note: C/RS, Charge or removed subsidy; TP, Tradable Permit; DR, Deposit-refund system; SB, Subsidy; EI, Enforcement incentive.

Sources: This matrix was compiled from a variety of sources listed in the references with the assistance of Martin Wolfrum.

Notes

CHAPTER 1

1   See Jorgenson and Wilcoxen (1990) for an estimate of the cost of environmental regulation to the US economy, in terms of forgone economic growth.

CHAPTER 2

1   We don't say 'all' because full-cost pricing is a necessary but not always a sufficient condition for sustainability, when the latter is understood to encompass intergenerational equity.
2   Elasticity of demand is defined as the percentage change in quantity demanded of a commodity due to a 1 per cent change in the price of the commodity. Similarly, the elasticity of supply is the percentage change in quantity supplied due to a 1 per cent change in the price of the commodity.
3   The less elastic of the two will pay more of the 'costs' of a price increase due to a tax or fee or even a technology standard.
4   The classic example is the Bhopal disaster in India where a wealthy, multinational corporation destroyed the lives of thousands of poor Indian workers.

CHAPTER 3

1   Named after Ronald Coase, the Nobel laureate who theorized that a free market would resolve externality problems as long as property rights are well defined and transaction costs low, regardless of who owns the property rights, the polluter or the affected party.
2   After A C Pigou, who proposed taxing externalities as a means of inter-nalizing them, with the tax rate equal to the marginal damage cost where the latter equals the marginal control costs.
3   Table 3.1 and its description are drawn from Panayotou (1996).
4   Fleeting or transitory resources such as offshore fisheries that cross property and even national boundaries; similarly, common pools of oil and ground water.
5   For a thorough discussion of how the number of permits to be issued is chosen, see Callan and Thomas (1996), Chapter 5.
6   For a more complete discussion of New Zealand's ITQ programme, see Chapter 9.

7   See Appendix 1 for developed country specifics, Appendix 3 for newly industrialized country specifics.
8   See also Roodman (1997) Table 4: 'Tax Shifts from Work and Investment to Environmental Damage' page 47, for examples of such moves in selected European countries and the UK.
9   For a further discussion of appropriate alternatives see Panayotou et al, 1994.
10   For discussion of systems in operation in OECD countries, see Opschoor and Vos (1989) and Smith and Vos (1997).

CHAPTER 4

1   Assuming the extractive industry is not capital intensive.
2   More examples are discussed in Chapter 9.
3   As discussed in the introduction, however, this is not usually the case. Rather, it is often politically difficult to effect taxes or charges which influence behaviour; they are used instead as instruments to raise funds. The role of these instruments as revenue raisers is discussed more thoroughly in Chapter 5.
4   See Hettige et al (1996) and Pargal and Wheeler (1996).
5   For further information on informal regulation, see References.

CHAPTER 5

1   See also Gandhi et al (1997, Table 10: '"Order-of-Magnitude" estimates of domestic financing available for sustainable development'.
2   See Hartwick and Olewiler (1986) and Vincent et al (1997).
3   For further discussion of these cases, see Panayotou (1993a).
4   For a more thorough discussion of various types of privatization schemes, see Laffont and Tirole (1993, Chapter 17). For privatization and environment, see Hansen (1994).
5   See also Knight et al (1996).
6   For further discussion of military expenditure reduction with a specific look at gains in sub-Saharan Africa, see Gandhi et al (1997).
7   For an excellent discussion of the assignment of property rights, see Coase (1960).
8   See also Panayotou (1995a).
9   For a further discussion of World Bank Group funding of environmental projects, see World Bank, 1995.

CHAPTER 6

1   Based on a model developed in the World Bank, Shah and Larsen (1992) estimated the potential revenue from a carbon tax of $10 per ton of carbon on fossil fuels by country. The estimates of tax revenues in major countries are listed in this table.
2   Shah and Larsen concluded that at the global level the revenue poten-

tial of the carbon tax could be as large as $55 billion (an average of 0.31 per cent of GDP) in the first year of its operation. Their results also show that the importance of the tax revenues in the government budget varies from country to country. For some countries, like China and Poland, such revenues would be as high as 2 per cent of GDP and would be sufficient to wipe out the central government's budgetary deficit. On average, low-income countries could raise revenues exceeding 1 per cent of GDP and over 5 per cent of government revenue. For the OECD countries, comparable figures would be 0.2 per cent of GDP and 1 per cent of government revenue.

3   For a technical description of a joint implementation model and bargaining scenarios, see Babu and Saha (1996).
4   In the presence of transactions costs, which are likely to be substantial in North–South carbon trade, for transactions to take place the cost differential in carbon reduction or sequestration must be large enough to cover transaction costs, including risk and still allow for share benefit between the joint implementors.

CHAPTER 7

1   For a thorough discussion of this issue, see Panayotou and Vincent (1997).
2   See also Goulder (1995).
3   Pigouvian subsidies are an exception in that they may be the preferred instrument for the internalization of positive externalities and they do require fiscal or financial resources to implement. They could, however, be financed by 'symmetric' Pigouvian taxes as in the case where revenues from deforestation or logging taxes are used to finance reforestation incentives.
4   See Goulder (1995) on the special conditions under which a 'double dividend' may exist.

CHAPTER 8

1   The relationship between level of development and demand for environmental amenities underlies the Environmental Kuznets Curve which relates the state of the environment to the level of economic development (See Grossman and Krueger (1995) and Panayotou (1993b, 1995c, and 1997a).
2   For further discussion of the applications of economic instruments, with case studies, see Panayotou (1995a) and OECD (1994c).
3   This conclusion does not preclude the use of these economic instruments for large-scale producers, both domestic and foreign.
4   This conclusion does not preclude the use of tradable pollution permits to abate non-point source pollution, as long as there are a few large polluters who share the same watershed or airshed.
5   This is less true of Central Asian Republics, which share the conditions of developing countries.

CHAPTER 9

1 See also Smith and Vos (1997) for a further discussion of potential reasons for these problems with ITQs and changes made in the application of the system.
2 For a description of waste disposal and management fees in OECD countries, including charge rates and revenues raised in local currency, see OECD (1995) Table 11.
3 For waste charge effectiveness assessments, see Anderson et al (1990), Resource Futures International (1993), Repetto et al (1992), Hong et al (1993), and Fullerton and Kinnaman (1994).
4 See, for example, the proposed Industrial Environmental Fund for Thailand, Panayotou (1993a).
5 For a list of environmental tax revenues in OECD countries, see OECD (1995a), Table 6: 'Revenues from one-off taxes on sale or initial registration and annual or recurrent taxes of private motor vehicles'.
6 For more examples of OECD countries using differential taxes for leaded and unleaded petrol, see Opschoor et al (1994, Table 3.11) and Kogels (1995, Tables 1, 2 and 3).
7 These lessons can be compared to Box 9.2 the Worldwatch Institute's Six Principles for Good Subsidy Policy, but should be thought of mainly as guides in transferring the experience of subsidies from developed to developing countries.

CHAPTER 10

1 See Smith and Vos (1997, Table 1) and Stavins and Zylicz (1995).
2 For a discussion of the use of economic instruments in transition economies in particular, see Klarer (1994) and Bluffstone and Larson (1997).
3 For a more complete discussion of the economics of fishery management, see Hartwick and Olewiler (1986).
4 See also Panayotou and Ashton (1992) for a more detailed discussion of logging concessions.

CHAPTER 11

1 See Panayotou and Vincent (1997) for a more thorough discussion of the effects on industry of environmental regulations.

APPENDIX 1

1 Jenkins and Lamech (1992, p 488 f).
2 Jenkins and Lamech (1992, p 487 f).
3 Jenkins and Lamech (1992, p 484).
4 Jenkins and Lamech (1992, p 488f).

5   Stewart (1992, p 556), Kayden (1992), Peters (1990).
6   Bhatia et al (1993, p 107 f).
7   Bhatia et al (1993, p 110 f), Dudley (1992).
8   Jenkins and Lamech (1992, p 529).
9   Arnason (1989), Henry (1990).
10 Hau (1992).
11 Hau (1992, 33f).
12 Hau (1992, 51).
13 Hau (1992, 55f).
14 Hau (1992, 50).
15 Dwyer (1993).
16 Economist (1993, Survey p 12).
17 Kayden (1992).
18 Kayden (1992), Svirsky (1970), Getzels and Jaffee (1991).
19 Jenkins and Lamech (1992, p 529).

APPENDIX 2

1   Palmisano and Haddad (1992).

APPENDIX 3

1   Jenkins and Lamech (1992).
2   Jenkins and Lamech (1992).
3   Bhatia et al (1993, p 85 f).
4   Rahim and Vincent (1994).
5   Hau (1992, 44 f).
6   Eskeland (1993, 30).

APPENDIX 4

1   Bhatia et al (1993, p 73–76).
2   Bhatia et al (1993), p 111 f).
3   Brandon and Ramankutty (1993, p 75).
4   Krupnick and Sebastian (1990, p 9 f).
5   Sedjo et al (1991, p 13 f).
6   Brandon and Ramankutty (1993, p 76).

References

Afsah, S, B Laplante and N Makarim (1995) 'Program-Based Pollution Control Management: The Indonesian PROKASIH Program', *Policy Research Working Paper 1602*, World Bank, Washington, DC

Afsah, S and J Vincent (1997), 'Putting Pressure on Polluters: Indonesia's PROPER Program', A Case Study for the Harvard Institute for International Development 1997 Asia Environmental Economics Policy Seminar

Anderson, G D and B Fiedor (1997) 'Environmental Charges in Poland', in R Bluffstone and B A Larson (eds) *Controlling Pollution in Transition Economies: Theories and Methods*, Edward Elgar, Lyme, USA

Anderson, R C, L A Hoffman and M Rusin (1990) 'The Use of Economic Incentive Mechanisms in Environmental Management', *Research Paper 51*, American Petroleum Institute, Washington, DC

Annis, S, (ed) (1992) *Poverty, Natural Resources, and Public Policy in Central America*, Transaction Publishers for the Overseas Development Council, New Brunswick, NJ

Apogee Research (1992) *Incentive Analysis for Clean Water Act Reauthorization: Point-Source/Non-Point Source Trading for Nutrient Discharge Reductions*, Apogee Research, Incorporated for US Environmental Protection Agency, Washington, DC

Arnason, R (1989) *Iceland's Experience with Vessel Quotas*, University of Iceland, Reykjavik

Asian Development Bank (ADB) and International Irrigation Management Institute (1986) *Irrigation Service Fees: Proceedings of the Regional Seminar on Irrigation Service Fees*, ADB, Manila

Australian UNESCO Committee for Man and the Biosphere (1976) *Ecological Effects of Increasing Human Activities on Tropical and Sub-Tropical Forest Ecosystems*, Australian Government Publishing Services, Canberra

Babu, P G and Bibhas Saha (1996) 'Efficient Emission Reduction through Joint Implementation' pp 445–64, *Environment and Development Economics* 1(4)

Bhatia, R, R Cestti and J Winpenny (1993) *Water Conservation and Reallocation*, World Bank, Washington, DC

Bluffstone, R and B Larson, eds (1997) 'Implementing Pollution Permit and Charge Systems in Transition Economies: A Possible Blueprint', *Controlling Pollution in Transition Economies: Theories and Methods*, Edward Elgar, Lyme, USA

Brandon, C and R Ramankutty (1993) 'Toward an Environmental Strategy for Asia', *Discussion Paper 224*, World Bank, Washington, DC

Callan, S and J Thomas (1996) *Environmental Economics and Management: Theory, Policy, and Applications*, Richard D Irwin Publications, Boston, MA

Chongqing Research Institute of Environmental Sciences (CRIES) (1992) Study on the environmental impact by acid deposition in Chongqing municipality and the related countermeasures', Unpublished report CRIES, Chongqing, China

Christensen, H (1996) 'Danish Experience with Waste Charges', Danish Environmental Protection Agency, in *Environmental Taxes and Charges: National Experiences and Plans, Papers from the Dublin Workshop*, European Foundation for the Improvement of Living and Working Conditions, Dublin, Ireland

Clark, I (1994) 'Fishery Management in New Zealand', in Eduardo A Loayza, (ed) *Managing Fishery Resources,* World Bank Discussion Papers: Fisheries Series 217, World Bank, Washington, DC

Coase, R H (1960) 'The Problem of Social Cost', *Journal of Law and Economics*, 3 October, pp 1–44

Cooter, R D (1990) *Inventing Property: Economic Theories of the Origins of the Market Property Applied to Papua New Guinea*, University of California, Berkeley, Mimeo

Cordell, J C (1980) 'Carrying Capacity Analysis of Fixed Territorial Fishing', in A Spoehr (ed) *Maritime Adaptions: Essays on Contemporary Fishing Communities*, University of Pittsburgh Press, Pittsburgh

Dasgupta, S, B Laplante and N Mamingi (1997) 'Pollution and Capital Markets in Developing Countries' Development Research Group, World Bank, Washington, DC

Dillenbeek, M (1994) 'National environmental funds: a new mechanism for conservation finance', *National Environmental Funds* 4:2

Dinan, T (1992) 'Solid Waste: Incentives that Could Lighten the Load', *EPA Journal* 18

Dudek and Palmisano (1988) 'Emissions Trading: Why Is This Thoroughbred Hobbled?' *Columbia Journal of Environmental Law* 13:217–56

Dudek, D J, Z Kulczynski and T Zylich (1992) 'Implementing Tradable Pollution Rights in Poland', Paper presented at the *Third Annual Conference of the European Association of Environmental and Resource Economists*, Cracow

Dudley, N J (1992) 'Water Allocation by Markets, Common Property and Capacity Sharing: Companions or Competitors?' *Natural Resources Journal* 32:757–78

Dunlap, R E, G H Gallup and A M Gallup (1993) *Health of the Planet*, Gallup International Institute, Princeton, New Jersey

Dwyer, J P (1993) 'The Use of Market Incentives in Controlling Air Pollution: California's Marketable Permits Program', *Ecology Law Quarterly* 20(57):103–17

The Economist (1993) 'Creating Incentives', Survey (Waste Management) 29 May pp 58–9

Environmental Defense Fund (1994) *EDF News Release*, 17 November

EPA (1985) *Costs and Benefits of Reducing Leads in Gasoline: Final Regulatory Impact Analysis* VIII–31, Environmental Protection Agency, Washington, DC

Eskeland, G S (1993) 'A Presumptive Pigouvian Tax on Gasoline', *Policy Research Working Papers, WPS 1076*, World Bank, Washington, DC

European Environment Agency (1996) 'Environmental Taxes: Implementation and Environmental Effectiveness', *Environmental Issues Series No 1*, European Environment Agency, Copenhagen

Feder, G, T Onchan and C Hongladarom (1986) 'Land Ownership, Security, Farm Productivity, and Land Policies in Rural Thailand', *Research Project RPO 673–33* World Bank, Washington, DC

Federal Ministry of the Environment (eds) (1993) 'Zehn Jahre Katalysator (Ten Years of Catalytic Converts)' *Umwelt (BMU)* 10:402–403 (Also http://iisd.ca/greenbud/catconv.htm

Fernando, S et al (1982) 'Cost and Profitability of Small-Scale Fishing Operations in Sri Lanka', in T Panayotou (ed) *Small-Scale Fisheries in Asia: Socio-Economic Analysis and Policy*, International Development Research Center, Ottawa

Figueroa, O (1993) 'Transportation and the Environment in Santiago de Chile', *The Urban Age* 2(1):11–20

Fullerton, D and Kinnaman, T C (1994) 'Household Demand for Garbage and Recycling Collection with the Start of a Price Per Bag', *NBER Working Paper No 4670*, National Bureau of Economic Research, Cambridge, MA

Gamble, W (1997), 'New Zealand: Fish Quota Bungle Comp May Not Go to Victims,' New Zealand Herald, May 2

Gandhi, V P, D Gray, and R McMonan (1997) 'A Comprehensive Approach to Domestic Resource Mobilization for Sustainable Development', in J Holst, P Kondal, and J Vincent (eds) *Finance for Sustainable Development: The Road Ahead*, United Nations, New York, pp 169–219

Getzels, J and M Jaffee (1991) '1988 Zoning Bonuses in Central Cities 21', *Planning Advisory Service Report No 410*, American Planning Association, Chicago

Goulder, Lawrence H (1995) 'Environmental Taxation and the Double Dividend: a Reader's Guide', *International Tax and Public Finance*, Kluwer Academic, 2:157–183

Grimes, A et al (1993) *Value the Rain Forest: The Economic Value of Non-Timber Forest Products in Ecuador*, Yale University Press, New Haven, CT

Grossman, G and A Krueger (1995) 'Economic Growth and the Environment', *Quarterly Journal of Economics* (May): 353–77

Grut, M, J A Gray, N Egli (1991) 'Forest Pricing and Concession Policies: Managing the High Forests of West and Central Africa', *World Bank Technical Paper 143*, World Bank, Washington, DC

Hahn, R W (1989) 'Economic Prescriptions for Environmental Problems: How the Patient Followed the Doctor's Orders', *Journal of Economic Perspectives*, 3(2):95–114

Hahn, R W and G L Hester (1989) 'Marketable Permits: Lessons for Theory and Practice', *Ecology Law Quarterly* 16:361f

Hahn, R W and G L Hester (1990) 'Where Did All the Markets Go? An Analysis of EPA's Emissions Trading Program', *Yale Journal of Regulation* 7:109–53

Hahn, R W, and R N Stavins (1991) 'Incentive-based Environmental Regulation: A New Era from an Old Idea?' *Ecology Law Quarterly* 18:1–42

Hammer, J and S Shetty (1995) *East Asia's Environmental Principles and Priorities for Action*, World Bank Discussion Paper 287, World Bank, Washington, DC

Hansen, S (1994) 'Privatization: A Panacea for Sustainable Development?' in Gene Owens (ed) *Financing Environmentally Sound Development*, Asian Development Bank, Manila

Hartje V, K Gauer, and A Urquiza (1994) 'The Use of Economic Instruments in the Environmental Policy of Chile', *Proceedings of the International Conference on Market-Based Instruments of Environmental Management in Developing Countries, Berlin, 5–9 June 1994*, German Foundation for International Development, Berlin, pp 61–80

Hartwick, J and N Olewiler (1986) 'The Economics of Natural Resource Use', in *The Economics of the Fishery: an Introduction*, HarperCollins Publishing, New York, Chapter 8

Harvard Institute for International Development (HIID) (1988) 'Thailand Management of Natural Resources for Sustainable Development: Market Failures, Policy Distortions and Policy Options', HIID, Cambridge, MA

Hau, T D (1992) 'Congestion Charging Mechanisms for Roads', *Policy Research Working Papers, WPS 1071*, World Bank, Washington, DC

Henry, C (1990) 'Microeconomics and Public Decision Making when Geography Matters', *European Economic Review* 34:249–71

Herber, B P (1997) 'Innovative Financial Mechanisms for Sustainable Development: Overcoming the Political Obstacles to International Taxation', in *Financial Issues of Agenda 21, Fourth Expert Group Meeting, 8–10 January 1997, Santiago, Chile*, United Nations, New York

Hettige, H, M Huq, S Pargal, and D Wheeler (1996) 'Determinants of Pollution Abatement in Developing Countries: Evidence from South and Southeast Asia', *World Development*, 24(12):1891–1895

Hong, S, R M Adams, and H A Love (1993) 'An Economic Analysis of Household Recycling and Solid Wastes: The Case of Portland, Oregon', *Journal of Environmental Economics and Management* 25:136–146

Huber, M R (1997) 'The Quito Effluent Charge: Private and Public Sector Collaboration for Pollution Management in Latin America', *Theme Brief 1: The Role of Economic Instruments, A World Bank Electronic Workshop*, World Bank, Washington, DC

IFC (1992) *Investing in the Environment*, International Finance Corporation, Washington, DC

International Institute for Sustainable Development (1994) *Making Budgets Green: Leading Practices in Taxation and Subsidy Reform*, International Institute for Sustainable Development, 115D, Winnipeg, Canada

Jenkins, G and R Lamech (1992) 'Fiscal Policies to Control Pollution', *Bulletin for International Fiscal Documentation* 46:483–502

Jorgenson, D and Wilcoxen (1990) 'Environmental Regulation and Economic Growth', *Rand Journal of Economics* 21(2):314–40

Joshua, F (1996) 'Design and Implementation of Pilot Systems for Greenhouse Gas Emissions Trading: Lessons from UNCTAD's GHC Research and Development Project', Paper presented at the *Conference on Controlling Carbon and Sulphur: International Investment and Trading Initiatives, the Royal Institute of International Affairs*, December 5–6, London

Joskow, P L (1991) 'Implementing the Tradable Allowance System for Acid-Rain Control', Paper presented at the John F Kennedy School of Government, Harvard University, Cambridge, MA

Kayden, J S (1992) 'Market-Based Regulatory Approaches: A Comparative Discussion of Environmental and Land Use Techniques in the United States', *Boston College Environmental Affairs Law Review* 19(3):565–80

Klarer, J (ed) (1994) *Use of Economic Instruments for Environmental Policy in Central and Eastern Europe: Case Studies of Bulgaria, The Czech Republic, Hungary, Poland, Romania, The Slovak Republic, and Slovenia*, Regional Environmental Center for Central and Eastern Europe, Budapest

Knight, M, N Loayza, and D Villanueva (1996) 'The Peace Dividend: Military Spending Cuts and Economic Growth ' *IMF Staff Papers* 43(1), pp 1–37

Kogels, H (1995) 'Rate Differentials as Instrument for Environmental Policy', *Environmental Taxes and Charges: Proceedings of a Seminar held in Florence, Italy, 1993 during the 47th Congress of the International Fiscal Association*, Kluwer Law International and International Fiscal Association, The Hague, the Netherlands

Kozeltsev, M and A Markandya (1997) 'Pollution Charges in Russia: The Experience of 1990–1995', in Randall Bluffstone and Bruce A Larson (eds) *Controlling Pollution in Transition Economies: Theories and Methods*, Edward Elgar, Lyme, USA

Krupnick, A J and I Sebastian (1990) 'Issues in Urban Air Pollution: Review of the Beijing Case', *Environment Working Paper No 31*, World Bank, Washington, DC

Laffont, J J and J Tirole (1993) *A Theory of Incentives in Procurement and Regulation*, MIT Press, Cambridge, MA

Leith, D (1995) 'Closed Competition: Fish Quotas in New Zealand', *The Ecologist*, 25(2/3):97–104

Lovei, M (1995a) 'Environmental Financing: The Experience of OECD Countries and Implications for Transition Economies', in *Environmental Funds in Economies in Transition*, Organization for Economic Cooperation and Development, Paris

Lynch, O (1991) 'Community-Based Tenurial Strategies for Promoting Forest Conservation Development in South and Southeast Asia', Unpublished paper, World Resources Institute, Washington, DC

Margolis, J, G Trivedi and S Farrow (1995) 'Developing an Areawide Emission Trading Bubble for the City of Almaty, Republic of Kazakhstan', A Feasibility Assessment prepared for the Harvard Institute of International Development by Dames and Moore, Almaty, Kazakhstan

Markandya, A (1994) 'Financing Sustainable Development: Agenda 21', Harvard Institute for International Development, Harvard University, Cambridge, MA

Moor, A P G (1997) 'Key Issues in Subsidy Policies and Strategies for Reform', in *Financial Issues of Agenda 21, Fourth Expert Group Meeting, 8–10 January 1997, Santiago, Chile*, United Nations, New York

O'Connor, David (1994) 'The Use of Economic Instruments in Environmental Management: The East Asia Experience', in *Applying Economic Instruments to Environmental Policies in OECD and Dynamic Non-Member Countries*, OECD, Paris

OECD (1996b), *Environmental Performance in OECD Countries: Progress in the 1990's*, OECD, Paris

OECD (1991a) *Environmental Policy: How to Apply Economic Instruments,* OECD, Paris

OECD (1991b) *Renewable Natural Resources: Economic Incentives for Improved Management,* OECD, Paris

OECD (1994c) *Applying Economic Instruments to Environmental Policies in OECD and Dynamic Non-member Countries,* OECD, Paris

OECD (1995a) *Environmental Taxes in OECD Countries,* OECD, Paris

OECD (1995b) *Promoting Cleaner Production in Developing Countries: The Role of Development Cooperation,* OECD, Paris

OECD (1997) *Evaluating Economic Instruments,* OECD, Paris

Palmisiano, J and B Haddad (1992) 'The USSR's Experience with Economic Incentive Approaches to Pollution Control', *Comparative Economic Studies* 34(2):50–62

Panayotou, T (1991) 'Environment and Development in Asia', Asian Development Bank, Manila

Panayotou, T (1993a) 'An Innovative Economic Instrument for Hazardous Waste Management: The Case of the Thailand Industrial Environment Fund', *Greener Management International* 2:21–27

Panayotou, T (1993b) 'Empirical Tests and Policy Analysis of Environmental Degradation at Different Stages of Economic Development', *Working Paper WP238*, Technology and Employment Programme, International Labour Office, Geneva

Panayotou, T (1993c) *Green Markets: The Economics of Sustainable Development,* ICS Press for the International Center for Economic Growth, San Francisco

Panayotou, T (1994a) 'Financing Mechanisms for Agenda 21', Prepared for the United Nations Development Programme Meeting, Kuala Lumpur, Malaysia, February

Panayotou, T (1994b) 'Conservation of Biodiversity and Economic Development: The Concept of Transferable Development Rights', *Environmental and Resource Economics* 4:91–110

Panayotou, T (1995a) 'The Application of Economic Instruments in Environmental Policies in Brazil, China, and Korea: A Synthesis Report', Prepared for a joint OECD/UNEP Workshop, 28 February–1 March, 1995 at UNEP HQ in Nairobi

Panayotou, T (1995b) 'Effective Financing of Environmentally Sustainable Development in Eastern Europe and Central Asia', *Environmental Discussion Paper No 10*, Harvard Institute for International Development, International Environment Program, Cambridge, MA

Panayotou, T (1995c) 'Environmental Degradation at Different Stages of Economic Development', in Iftikhar Ahmed and Jacobus A Doeleman (eds) *Beyond Rio (The Environmental Crisis and Sustainable Livelihoods in the Third World)* International Labour Organization, Macmillan Press, London

Panayotou, T (1995d) 'Financing Mechanisms for Environmental Investments and Sustainable Development', prepared for the UNEP Consultative Expert Group Meeting on the Use and Application of Economic Policy Instruments for Environmental Management and Sustainable Development, Nairobi, December, 1994

Panayotou, T (1995e) 'Innovative Economic and Fiscal Instruments', prepared for the Conference on Servicing Innovative Financing of

Environmentally Sustainable Development Jointly organized by the Earth Council and World Bank, Washington, DC, 2–3 October

Panayotou, T (1996) 'Matrix of Policy Options and Financial Instruments', prepared for the *Third Expert Group Meeting on Financial Issues of Agenda 21, 6–8 February, 1996, Manila, Philippines*, United Nations, New York

Panayotou, T (1997a) 'Demystifying the Environmental Kuznets Curve', *Environmental and Development Economics* 2(4):465–484

Panayotou, T (1997b) 'Role of the Private Sector in Sustainable Infrastructure Development', in *Bridges to Sustainability: Business and Government Working Together for a Better Environment*, Yale/UNDP Program on Public–Private Partnerships, Yale University, New Haven, Connecticut

Panayotou, T (1997c) 'Taking Stock of Trends in Sustainable Development Financing Since Rio', *Finance for Sustainable Development: The Road Ahead Proceedings of the Fourth Group Meeting on Financial Issues of Agenda 21, Santiago, Chile*, United Nations, New York

Panayotou, T (1997d) 'Win–Win Finance', *Our Planet 9(1) The United Nations Development Programme Magazine for Environmentally Sustainable Development*, United Nations, New York

Panayotou, T (1998) 'The Effectiveness and Efficiency of Environmental Policy in China', in *Energizing China: Reconciling Environmental Protection and Economic Growth*, Harvard University Committee on the Environment, Harvard University Press, Cambridge, MA

Panayotou, T and P Ashton (1992) *Not by Timber Alone: Economy and Ecology for Sustaining Tropical Forests*, Island Press, Washington, DC

Panayotou, T, G Hadjipieris, and D Costa (1991), 'Recommendations and Program of Supporting Measures (Phase 2)', Enalion Environmental Management Centre, Nicosia

Panayotou, T and J Vincent (1997) 'Environmental Regulation and Competitiveness', in K Schwab and J Sachs (eds) *The Global Competitiveness Report,* World Economic Forum, Geneva, Switzerland

Panayotou, T and C Zinnes (1993) 'Incentive Structure and Regulation Dynamics in Industrial Ecology', *Development Discussion Paper No 454*, Harvard Institute for International Development, Cambridge, MA

Panayotou, T, R Bluffstone and V Balaban (1994) 'Lemons and Liabilities: Privatization, Foreign Investment, and Environmental Liability in Central and Eastern Europe', *Environmental Impact Assessment Review* 14:157–168

Pargal, S, and D Wheeler (1996) 'Informal Regulation of Industrial Pollution in Developing Countries: Evidence from Indonesia', *Journal of Political Economy* 104(6):1314–1318

Pearce, D (1997) 'Replicating Innovative National Financing Mechanisms for Sustainable Development', in *Financial Issues of Agenda 21, Fourth Expert Group Meeting, 8–10 January 1997, Santiago, Chile*, United Nations, New York

Peters, J E (1990) 'Saving Farmland: How Well Have We Done?' *Planning* 13, September

Rahim, K A (1991) 'Internalization of Externalities: Who Bears the Cost of Pollution Control?' *The Environmentalist* 11(1):19–25

Rahim, K A and J R Vincent (1994) 'Pollution Control in Malaysia', Mimeo

Rehbinder, E and R Stewart (1985) *Environmental Protection Policy,*

De Gruyter, Berlin

Repetto, R (1988) 'Economic Policy Reform for Natural Resource Conservation', *Environment Department Working Paper No 4*, World Bank, Washington, DC

Repetto, R, R C Dower, R Jenkins, and J Geoghegan (1992) *Green Fees: How a tax shift can work for the environment and for the economy*, World Resources Institute, Washington, DC

Resource Futures International (1993) 'The CRD User Pay Waste Management Initiative', Mimeo

Rogers, P (1985) 'Fresh Water', in Robert Repetto (ed) *The Global Possible: Resources, Development and the New Century*, Yale University Press, New Haven

Roodman, D M (1996) 'Paying the Piper: Subsidies, Politics, and the Environment', *Worldwatch Paper 133*, Worldwatch Institute, Washington, DC

Roodman, D M (1997) 'Getting the Signals Right: Tax Reform to Protect the Environment and the Economy', *Worldwatch Paper*, Worldwatch Institute, Washington, DC

Ross, L (1988) *Environmental Policy in China,* Indiana University Press, Bloomington

Ruzicka, P R I and H Speechly (1994) 'Performance Guarantee Bonds for Commercial Management of Natural Forests – Early Experience from the Phillippines', *Commonwealth Forest Review*, 73(2):106–112

Sedjo, R A, M Bowes and C Wiseman (1991) 'Toward a Worldwide System of Tradable Forest Protection and Management Obligations', *Resources for the Future Discussion Paper ENR 91–16*, Washington, DC

Shah, A and B Larsen (1992) 'Carbon Taxes, the Greenhouse Effect, and Developing Countries', *Policy Research Paper No 095*, World Bank, Washington, DC

Shin, E (1994) 'Economic Instruments for Environmental Protection in Korea', prepared for Environment Directorate, OECD, Paris

Smith, S and H B Vos (1997) *Evaluating Economic Instruments for Environmental Policy*, OECD, Paris

Somanathan, E (1991) 'Deforestation, Property Rights and Incentives in Central Himalaya', *Economic and Political Weekly* PE-37 – PE-46, 26 January

Statistics Norway (1994) *Natural Resources and Environment 1993*, Statistics Norway, Oslo

Stavins, R N (1991) 'Incentives for Action: Designing Market-Based Environmental Strategies', Project 88 – Round II A Public Policy Study sponsored by Senator Timothy Wirth, Colorado, and Senator John Heinz, Pennsylvania Washington, DC

Stavins, R N and B W Whitehead (1992) 'Market-Based Incentives for Environmental Protection', *Environment* 34:7–11

Stavins, R N and Whitehead, B W (1996) 'The Next Generation of Market-Based Environmental Policies', in Daniel Esty and Marian Chertow (eds) *Environmental Reform: The Next Generation Project*, Yale Center for Environmental Law and Policy, New Haven

Stavins, R N and T Zylicz (1995) 'Environmental Policy in a Transition Economy: Designing Tradable Permits for Poland', *Environmental*

Discussion Paper No 9, Harvard Institute for International Development C4EP Project, January

Stavins, R N (1998), 'Market-based Environmental Policies,' John F Kennedy School of Government, Faculty Research Paper Working Series; R98-03, Cambridge, MA

Steele, P and D Pearce (1996) 'Promoting Private Sector Financing for Sustainable Development in the Asia Pacific Region', *Sustainable Development Finance: Opportunities and Obstacles. Proceedings of the Third Expert Group Meeting on Financial Issues of Agenda 21, 6–8 February 1996, Manila, Philippines*, United Nations, New York

Stepanek, Z (1997) 'Integration of Pollution Charge Systems with Strict Performance Standards: The Experience of the Czech Republic', in R Bluffstone and B A Larson (eds) *Controlling Pollution in Transition Economies: Theories and Methods*, Edward Elgar, Lyme, USA

Stewart, R B (1992) 'Models for Environmental Regulation: Central Planning Versus Market-Based Approaches', *Boston College Environmental Affairs Law Review* 19(3):547–62

Svirsky, P S (1970) 'San Francisco: The Downtown Development Bonus System', in N Marcus and M W Groves (eds) *The New Zoning: Legal, Administrative, and Economic Concepts and Techniques*, pp 139–145, Praeger Publishers, New York

Swedish Ministry of the Environment (1991) *Economic Instruments in Sweden with Emphasis on the Energy Sector*, Stockholm, Swedish Ministry of the Environment

Sykes, L (1997) 'The Power to Choose', *New Scientist* 155(2098) September

Thomas, V, N Kishor and T Belt (1997) 'Drawing on the Power of Knowledge for the Environment', presented at *Organizing Knowledge for Environmentally Sustainable Development*, Washington, DC, 9 October

Tietenberg, T H (1990b) 'Economic Instruments for Environmental Regulation', *Oxford Review of Economic Policy* 6(1):17–33

Tietenberg, T H (1993) 'Market-Based Mechanisms for Controlling Pollution: Lessons from the US' in T Sterner (ed) *Economic Policies for Sustainable Development*, Kluwer, Dordrecht

United Nations (1992) *Conference on Environment and Development: Earth Summit 1992.* The UN Conference on Environment and Development, Rio de Janeiro, Brazil, Regency Press, London

United Nations (1997) *Kyoto Protocol to the United Nations Framework Convention on Climate Change*, FCCC/CP/1997/L 7/Add 1 (December), United Nations, New York

United Nations Department for Policy Coordination and Sustainable Development (UN/DPCSD) (1996) *CSD Panel on Finance 1996*, United Nations, New York

UN-FCCC (1996) *Activities Implemented Jointly: Annual Review*, United Nations Framework Convention on Climate Change, New York

US Council on Environmental Quality (1992) *United States of America National Report* UN Conference on Environment and Development, Washington, DC

US Department of Energy, Federal Energy Management Program (FEMP) 'The Federal Procurement Challenge', http://www.eren.doe.gov/femp/procurement/challenge.html

Vincent, J R (1993), 'Reducing Effluent While Raising Affluence: Water Pollution Abatement in Malaysia,' Harvard Institute for International Development, March

Vincent, J R (1994) 'Sustainable Development, Financial Issues, and Multilateral Policy Reform', Harvard Institute for International Development, Harvard University Press, Cambridge, MA, p 1

Vincent, J R and R Mohamed Ali (1997) *Environment and Development in a Resource-Rich Economy: Malaysia Under the New Economic Policy*, Harvard Institute for International Development, Harvard University Press, Cambridge, MA

Vincent, J R, T Panayotou, and J M Hartwick (1997) 'Resource Depletion and Sustainability in Small Open Economies', *Journal of Environmental Economics and Management* 33: 274–86

Watson, P L and E P Holland (1978) 'Relieving Traffic Congestion: The Singapore Area License Scheme', *World Bank Staff Working Paper No 281*, World Bank, Washington, DC

World Bank (1988) *Economic Policy Reform for Natural Resource Conservation*, World Bank, Washington, DC

World Bank (1989) *Philippines Forestry, Fisheries and Agricultural Resources Management Study*, World Bank, Washington, DC

World Bank (1994b) *Indonesia Resource Mobilization: Challenges and Opportunities*, Country Operations Division, East Asia and Pacific Region, World Bank, Washington, DC

World Bank (1995) 'Mainstreaming the Environment', *World Bank Group and the Environment since the Rio Earth Summit*, World Bank, Washington, DC

World Bank (1996a) 'The Privatization Dividend, Finance and Private Sector Development', *Department Note No 68*, World Bank, Washington, DC

World Bank (1997a) 'Five Years After Rio: Innovation in Environmental Policy', *Environmentally Sustainable Development Studies and Monograph Series No 18*, World Bank, Washington, DC

World Bank (1997b) *Pollution Prevention and Abatement Handbook*, World Bank, Washington, DC

World Business Council for Sustainable Development (WBCSD) (1996), Progress Report on International Business Action on Climate Change (IBACC), World Business Council for Sustainable Development, Geneva, Switzerland, July 18

World Resources Institute and International Institute for Environment and Development (1987) *World Resources 1987*, Basic Books, New York

Yang, W (1996) 'Ecolabeling Appendix II: A Compendium of Global Ecolabeling Programs/Schemes', paper presented to the China Council for International Cooperation on Environment and Development: Working Group on Trade and the Environment, Beijing, September

Zhong, M, Zou Ji, Zhang Shiqiu and Ma Xiaoying (1994) *Study IV – Development of an environmental regulatory reform plan: A review of existing environmental regulation framework in Chongqing Municipality*, Institute of Environmental Economics, Renmin University, Beijing

Zollinger, P and R C Dower (1996) *Private Financing for Global Environmental Issues: Can the Climate Convention's 'Joint Implementation' Pave the Way?*, World Resources Institute, Washington, DC

Bibliography

Ackerman, F (1992) 'Waste Management: Taxing the Trash Away',
  Environment 34(5):2–7
Agency for International Development (AID) (1988) *Environmental and
  Natural Resource Management in Central America: Strategy for AID
  Assistance*, Agency for International Development, Washington, DC
AID (1989a) 'The Economics of Man-Made Natural Disasters', *Safeguarding
  the Future: Restoration and Sustainable Development in South Thailand*,
  USAID Team Report, Bangkok: AID, May 1989
AID (1989b) 'The Economics of Man-Made Natural Disasters: The Case of
  the 1988 Landslides in South Thailand', Agency for International
  Development, Washington, DC August 1989
Alm, A L (1992) 'Tools to Protect the Environment: A Need for New
  Approaches', *EPA Journal* 18:6–11
Anderson, D (1991) 'Energy and the Environment', Special Briefing Paper
  No 1, The Wealth of Nations Foundation, Edinburgh
Asian Development Bank (1997) Emerging Asia: Changes and Challenges,
  Asian Development Bank, Manila
Barbier, E B (1989) *Economics, Natural Resource Scarcity & Development*,
  Earthscan, London
Barde, J-P (1994) 'Douze Criteres pour choisir un intrument de politique
  environmentale', *Ecodecision* (January):32–35
Barde, J-P and J B Opschoor (1994) 'From Stick to Carrot in the
  Environment', *OECD Observer* 186:23–27
Barde, J-P and J Owens (1993) 'The Greening of Taxation', *OECD Observer*
  182:27–30
Barlow, H (1996), 'World's Best Fishing Law Finds Critics,' *The Wellington
  Dominion*, August 3, p 2
Bates, R, S Gupta, and B Fiedor (1994) 'Economywide Policies and the
  Environment: A Case Study of Poland', *Environment Working Paper No
  63*, World Bank, Washington, DC
Bernstein, J D (1991) 'Alternative Approaches to Pollution Control and
  Waste Management: Regulatory and Economic Instruments', UNEP
  Urban Management Program Discussion Paper, UNDP-World Bank,
  Washington, DC
Bernstein, J D (1993) 'Alternative Approaches to Pollution Control and
  Waste Management, Regulatory and Economic Instruments', *Report No
  11711*, World Bank, Washington, DC
Bertram, I G 'Tradable Emission Quotas, Technical Progress and Climate
  Change', *Environment and Development Economics* 1(4)
Bhatia, R, P Rogers, J Briscoe, B Sinha, and R Cestti (1994) 'Water
  Conservation and Pollution Control in Industries: How to User Water

Tariffs, Pollution and Fiscal Incentives?' *Currents*, UNDP-World Bank, Water and Sanitation Program, Washington, DC

Bingham, T E (1994) *Application of Residuals Charges for Achieving Environmental Quality Objectives in the Czech Republic*, Harvard Institute for International Development, Cambridge, MA

Binswanger, H P (1991) 'Brazilian Policies that Encourage Deforestation in the Amazon', *World Development* 19(7):821–9

Blum, E (1993) 'Conservation Profitable: A Case Study of the Merck/Inbio Agreement', *Environment* 35(4):17 f

Bohm, P and C S Russell (1985) 'Comparative Analysis of Alternative Policy Instruments' in A V Kneese and J L Sweeney (eds) *Handbook of Natural Resource and Energy Economics*, Vol 1, North Holland, Amsterdam, pp 395–460

Bongaerts, J C and R A Kramer (1989) 'Permits and Effluent Charges in the Water Pollution Control Policies of France, West Germany, and the Netherlands', *Environmental Monitoring and Assessment* 127(12):128–37

Bressers, H T A and J Schuddeboom (1993) 'A Survey of Effluent Charges and Other Economic Instruments in Dutch Environmental Policy', Informal Workshop on the Use of Economic Instruments in Environmental Policies, OECD, Paris

Broadway, R and F Flatters (1993) 'The Taxation of Natural Resources', *Policy Research Working Papers, WPS 1210*, World Bank, Washington, DC

Burtraw, D (1993) 'The Promise and Prospect for SO_2 Emission Trading in Europe', *Resources for the Future Discussion Paper QE93–22*, Washington, DC

Capros, P T et al (1996) 'Results from the General Equilibrium Model GEM-E3', Commission of European Committees, DGX11, Brussels

Castro, R and F Tattenbach (1997), 'The Costa Rican Experience with Market Instruments to Mitigate Climate Change and Conserve Biodiversity,' paper presented at the Global Conference on Knowledge for Development in the Information Age, Toronto, Canada, Workshop on Global Climate Change and Biodiversity, June 24 Harvard Institute for International Development, Cambridge, MA

Cestti, R (1993) 'Policies for Water Demand Management and Pollution Control in the Industrial and Household Sectors in the Jabotabek Region, Indonesia', World Bank, Washington, DC, unpublished draft

Connery, F and S Rooney (1996) 'Making Markets Work for the Economy and the Environment: Lessons from Experience in Greece, Ireland, Portugal, and Spain', in *Environmental Taxes and Charges: National Experiences and Plans, Papers from the Dublin Workshop*, European Foundation for the Improvement of Living and Working Conditions, Dublin, Ireland

Council on Sustainable Development (1995) 'Financial Resources and Mechanisms', E/CN 17/1995/8 Economic and Social Council for Environmental Subsidies, United Nations, New York

Cramer, J, J Schot, F Van Den Akker, and G Maas Geesteranus (1990) 'Stimulating Cleaner Technologies through Economic Instruments: Possibilities and Constraints', *UNEP Industry and Environment*, (April/May/June):46–53

Dasgupta, P (1996) 'The Economics of the Environment', *Environment and Development Economics* 1:387–428

Davis, G (1989) 'Indonesia Forest, Land and Water: Issues in Sustainable Development', World Bank, Washington, DC

Dixon, J A and Maynard M Hufschmidt (eds) (1986) *Economic Valuation Techniques for the Environment*, Johns Hopkins University Press, Baltimore

Dixon, J A, L Fallon Scura, and T van Hof (1993) 'Meeting Ecological and Economic Goals: Marine Parks in the Caribbean', *Ambio* 22(2–3):117–25

Duncan, L (1995) 'Closed Competition: Fish Quotas in New Zealand', *The Ecologist* (March–June):97–104

Dworkin, D (1980) *The Potable Water Project in Rural Thailand*, United States Agency for International Development, Washington, DC

The Economist (1987) 'The Extended Family: A Survey of Indonesia', 15 August p 42

The Economist (1989a) 'City Lights', 18 February p 34

The Economist (1989b) 'The Environment Survey ' 2 September p 53

The Economist (1989c) 'Traffic Jams: The City, the Commuter and the Car', 18 February, pp 19–22

The Economist (1995) 'No Plaice Like Home (1995)', April 22, p 17

The Economist (1997) 'The Island that Became Too Popular', 19 July p 36

Engineering Science, Inc, Thai DCI Co and Systems Engineering Co (Submitted 1989) 'National Hazardous Waste Management ' Main Report, Vol 2, National Environmental Board, Bangkok

Erlanger, S (1989) 'Indonesia Takes Steps to Protect Rain Forests', *New York Times*, 26 September III, 4:1

Eröcal, D (ed) (1991) *Environmental Management in Developing Countries*, OECD Development Center, Paris

Eskeland, G S (1991) 'Curbing Pollution in Developing Countries', *Finance & Development* 28(1):15–19

Eskeland, G S and S Devarajan (1996) 'Taxing Bads by Taxing Goods: Pollution Control with Presumptive Charges', World Bank, Washington, DC

Eskeland, G S and E Jimenez (1991) 'Choosing Policy Instruments for Pollution Control', *Policy Research Working Papers, WPS 624*, World Bank, Washington, DC

Farrow, S J Margolis, G Trivedi (1995) 'Feasibility assessment: Developing an areawide emissions trading bubble for the city of Almaty, Republic of Kazakhstan', Harvard Institute for International Development, Cambridge, MA, June

Feder, G, T Onchan, Y Chalamwong, and C Hongladarom (1988) *Land Policies and Farm Productivity in Thailand*, Johns Hopkins University Press, Baltimore

Feitelson, E (1992) 'An Alternative Role for Economic Instruments: Sustainable Finance for Environmental Management', *Environmental Management* 16(3):299–307

Field, B G (1992) 'Road Pricing in Practice', *Transportation Journal* (Fall):5–14

Food and Agricultural Organization (FAO) (1988) *Integrated Pest Management in Rice in Indonesia*, FAO, Jakarta

Fujita, R (1996) 'Creating Incentives to Curb Overfishing', *Forum for Applied Research and Public Policy*, 11:29

Fultang, B (1991) 'The Efficiency of the Forestry Taxation System in Cameroon', in K Cleaver, M Munasinghe, M Dyson, N Egli, A Peuker and F Wencélius (eds) *Conservation of West and Central African Rainforests,* World Bank Development Paper No 1, World Bank, Washington, DC

Ghate, P (1987) *Determining Irrigation Charges: A Framework,* Asian Developmental Bank, Manila

Gibson, J E and W J Schrenk (1991) 'The Enterprise for the Americas Initiative: A Second Generation of Debt-for-Nature Exchanges – with an Overview of other Recent Exchange Initiatives', *The George Washington Journal of International Law and Economics* 25:1–70

Gillis, M (1988) 'West Africa: Resource Management Policies and the Tropical Forest', in R Repetto and M Gillis, (eds) *Public Policies and the Misuse of Forest Resources,* Cambridge University Press, New York

Goodland, R and G Ledec (1987) 'Environmental Management in Sustainable Economic Development', *International Association of Impact Assessment,* Spring

Grafton, R Q (1994) 'A Note on Uncertainty and Rent Capture in ITQ Fishery', *Journal of Environmental Economics and Management* 27:286–95

Grafton, R Q (1995) 'Rent Capture in a Rights-Based Fishery', *Journal of Environmental Economics and Management* 28:48–68

Grafton, R Q (1996) 'Experiences with Individual Transferable Quotas: Overview', *Canadian Journal of Economics* 29:s135–40

Hahn, R W (1991) 'Reshaping Environmental Policy: The Test Case of Hazardous Waste', *The American Enterprise* 2(3):72–80

Hahn, R W (1993) 'Getting More Environmental Protection for Less Money: A Practitioner's Guide', *Oxford Review of Economic Policy* 9(4):112–23

Hahn, R W and V Foster (1994) 'ET in LA: Looking Back to the Future', Paper P–94–01, Center for Science & International Affairs, Kennedy School of Government, Harvard University, Cambridge, MA

Hahn, R W and R N Stavins (1992) 'Economic Incentives for Environmental Protection: Integrating Theory and Practice', *American Economic Review* (May):464–69

Hamrin, R D (1990) 'Policy Control Options for Comparative Air Pollution Study in Urban Areas', *Environment Working Paper No 28*, World Bank, Washington, DC

Hanley, N (1993) 'Controlling Water Pollution Using Market Mechanisms: Results from Empirical Studies', in R K Turner (ed) *Environmental Economics and Management,* Belhaven Press, London

Harrison, D (1992) 'Economic Fundaments of Road Pricing', *Policy Research Working Papers, WPS 1070,* World Bank, Washington, DC

Harrison, D (1993) 'Who Wins and Who Loses from Economic Instruments?' *OECD Observer* 180:29–31

Harvard Institute for International Development (1989) 'Natural Resources and the Environment in the Economies of Asia and the Near East: Growth, Structural Change and Policy Reform', HIID, Cambridge, MA

Hiebert, M (1992) 'Second time lucky? Foreign oil firms bullish about Vietnam's prospects', *Far Eastern Economic Review* 7, May

Hill, L (1992) 'Pricing initiatives and development of the Korean power sector; Policy lessons for developing countries', *Energy Policy,* April

Holst, J, P Kondal, and J Vincent (eds) (1997) *Finance for Sustainable Development: The Road Ahead*, United Nations, New York

Homan, S, R Frances, and J E Wilen (1997) 'A Model of Regulated Open Access Resource Use', *Journal of Environmental Economics and Management* 32:1–21

Huppes, G, E van der Voest, W van der Naald, P Maxson, and G Vonkeman (1992) 'New Market-Oriented Instruments for Environmental Policies', European Communities Environmental Policy Series, Brussels

International Union for Conservation of Nature and Natural Resources (IUCN) (1988) *Economics and Biological Diversity: Developing and Using Economic Incentives to Conserve Biological Resources*, IUCN, Gland, Switzerland

Jaffe, A B, S R Peterson, P R Portney, and R N Stavins (1994) 'Environmental Regulation and International Competitiveness: What Does the Evidence Tell Us?' *Resources for the Future Discussion Paper 94–08*, Washington, DC

Jenkins, G (1992) 'Market-Based Incentive Instruments for Pollution Control', *Bulletin for International Fiscal Documentation* 46:523–38

Johnson, S H, III (1984) *Physical and Economic Impacts of Sedimentation of Fishing Activities: Nam Fong, Northeast Thailand*, University of Illinois, Urbana-Champaign

Kate, A T (1993) 'Industrial Development and the Environment in Mexico', *Policy Research Working Paper, WPS 1125*, World Bank, Washington, DC

Kete, N (1994) 'Environmental Policy Instruments for Market and Mixed Market Economies', *Utilities Policy* (January):5–18

Koomney, J and A H Rosenfeld (1990) 'Revenue-Neutral Incentives for Efficiency and Environmental Quality', *Contemporary Policy Issues* 8:142–56

Kritiporn P, T Panayotou, and K Charnprateep (1990) *The Greening of Thai Industry: Producing More and Polluting Less*, Thailand Development Research Institute, Bangkok

Krupnick, A J (1991) 'Urban Air Pollution in Developing Countries: Problems and Policies', *Resources for the Future Discussion Paper QE91–14*, Washington, DC

Krupnick, A J (1992) 'Measuring the Effects of Urban Transportation Policies on the Environment', *Policy Research Working Papers, WPS 1030*, World Bank, Washington, DC

Laird, S A (1993) 'Contracts for Biodiversity Prospecting', in W V Reid, S A Laird, C A Negers (eds) *Biodiversity Prospecting: Using Genetic Resources for Sustainable Development*, World Resources Institute, Washington, DC

Larsen, B (1994) 'World Fossil Fuel Subsidies and Global Carbon Emissions in a Model with Interfuel Substitution', *Policy Research Working Paper, WPS 1256*, World Bank, Washington, DC

Ledec, G and R Goodland (1988) *Wildlands: Their Protection and Management in Economic Development*, World Bank, Washington, DC

Leonard, H J (1987) *Natural Resources and Economic Development in Central America*, Transaction Books, New Brunswick

Lewis, S R Jr, (1984) *Taxation for Development: Principles and Applications*, Oxford Press, New York

Lindberg, K (1991) *Policies for Maximizing Nature Tourism's Ecological and Economic Benefits*, World Resources Institute, Washington, DC

Lopez, R (1992) 'The Environment as a Factor of Production: The Economic Growth and Trade Policy Linkages', in Patrick Low (ed) *International Trade and the Environment*, World Bank, Washington, DC

Lovei, M (1995b) 'Financing pollution abatement: Theory and practice', *World Bank Environment Department Paper No 28*, Environmental Economics Series, World Bank: Washington, DC

Lutz, E and H Daly (1990) 'Incentives, Regulations, and Sustainable Land Use in Costa Rica', *Environment Working Paper No 34*, World Bank, Washington, DC

Lutz, E and M Young (1990) 'Integration of Environmental Concerns into Agricultural Policies of Industrial and Developing Countries', *World Development* 20(2):241f

Mahar, D J (1989) *Government Policies and Deforestation in Brazil's Amazon Region*, World Bank, Washington, DC

Markandya, A (1997a) 'Economic Instruments: Accelerating the Move from Concepts to Practical Application', in J Holst, P Kondal, and J Vincent, (eds) *Finance for Sustainable Development: The Road Ahead*, United Nations, New York

Markandya, A (1997b) 'What Have We Learned about Market-Based Instruments', in C Jeanrenaud (ed) *Between Market and Regulation*, Birker, Basle

Matulich, S (1996) 'Toward a More Complete Model of Individual Transferable Fishing Quotas', *Journal of Environmental Economics and Management*, 31:112–128

McKay, S, M Pearson, and S Smith (1990) 'Fiscal Instruments in Environmental Policy', *Fiscal Studies* 11(4):1–20

McNeely, J A (1987) 'How Dams and Wildlife Can Coexist: Natural Habitats, Agriculture, and Major Water Resource Development Projects in Tropical Asia', *Journal of Conservation Biology (JCB)* 1(3) 3 October

McNeely, J A (1989) 'Protected Areas and Human Ecology: How National Parks Can Contribute to Sustaining Societies of the Twenty-First Century', in D Western and M C Pearl (eds) *Conservation for the Twenty-first Century*, Oxford University Press, Oxford

McNeely, J A (1993) 'Economic Incentives for Conserving Biodiversity: Lessons for Africa', *Ambio* 22(2–3):144–50

Menck, K W (1993) 'Umweltsteuern und Finanzierung von öffentlichen und privaten Umweltschutzinvestitionen in Entwicklungslädern', *Schriften des Vereins für Socialpolitik* 226, December

Michaelis, P (1992) 'Environmental Policies in OECD Countries: Lessons for ASEAN', *ASEAN Economic Bulletin* 9:169–86

Mirante, E (1989) 'A 'Teak War' Breaks Out in Burma', *Earth Island Journal*, Summer

Morgenstern, R D (1992) 'The Market-Based Approach at EPA', *EPA Journal*, (May/June):27f

Munasinghe, M (1990) 'Managing Water Resources to Avoid Environmental Degradation: Policy Analysis and Application', *Environment Working Paper No 41*, World Bank, Washington, DC

Munro, G (1996) 'Approaches to the Economics of the Management of High Seas Fishery', *Canadian Journal of Economics* 29:5157–8

Nunnenkamp, P (1992) 'International Financing of Environmental Protection', *Working Paper No 512*, Kiel Institute of World Economics, Kiel, Germany

Oates, W E (1993) 'Pollution Charges as a Source of Public Revenues', in Giersch, H (ed) *Economic Progress and Environmental Concerns*, Springer, Berlin

Oates, W E (1996) *The Economics of Environmental Regulation*, Edward Elgar, Brookfield, VT

Occhiolini, M (1990) 'Debt-for-Nature Swaps', *Working Paper No WPS 393*, Research and External Affairs Complex, World Bank, Washington, DC

Opschoor, J B and R K Turner (eds) (1994) *Economic Incentives and Environmental Policies: Principles and Practice*, Kluwer Academic, Dordrecht

OECD (1981) *Economic Instruments in Solid Waste Management*, Organization for Economic Cooperation and Development (OECD), Paris

OECD (1992) *Market and Government Failures in Environmental Management: Wetlands and Forests*, OECD, Paris

OECD (1993a) *Economic Instruments for Environmental Management in Developing Countries: Proceedings of a Workshop Held at OECD Headquarters, Paris, 8 October 1992*, OECD, Paris

OECD (1993b) *Taxation and Environment: Complimentary Policies*, OECD, Paris

OECD (1994a) 'Investing in Biological Diversity' proceedings of The Cairns Conference OECD, *Integrating Environment and Economics: The Role of Economic Instruments*, OECD, Paris

OECD (1994b) *Task Force for the Implementation of the Environmental Action Programme for Central and Eastern Europe*, OECD, Paris

OECD (1996a) *Agricultural Policies, Markets, and Trade in OECD Countries*, OECD, Paris

OECD (1996c) *Reconciling Trade, Environment, and Development Policies: The Role of Development Cooperation*, OECD, Paris

Ong, A S H, A Maheswaran and A N Ma (1987) 'Malaysia', in L S Chia (ed) *Environmental Management in Southeast Asia*, Faculty of Science, National University of Singapore

Opschoor, J B and H B Vos (1989) *Economic Instruments for Environmental Protection*, OECD, Paris

Opschoor, J B, A F de Savornin Lohman, and H B Vos (1994) *Managing the Environment: The Role of Economic Instruments*, OECD, Paris

Owens, G M (ed) (1994) 'Financing Environmentally Sound Development', Asian Development Bank, Manila

Panayotou, T (1987) 'Economics, Environment and Development', *Development Discussion Paper No 259*, Harvard Institute for International Development, Cambridge, MA

Panayotou, T (1988) 'Natural Resource Management: Strategies for Sustainable Asian Agriculture in the 1990s', Harvard Institute for International Development, Cambridge, MA

Panayotou, T (1989) 'An Econometric Study of the Causes of Tropical Deforestation: The Case of Northeast Thailand', *Development Discussion Paper No 284*, Harvard Institute for International Development, Cambridge, MA

Panayotou, T, T Schatzki, and Q Limvorapitak (1997) 'Differential Industry Response to Formal and Informal Regulations in Newly Industrializing Economies: The Case of Thailand', A Case Study for the Harvard Institute for International Development 1997 Asia Environmental Economics Policy Seminar, Harvard University, Cambridge, MA

Paris, R, I Ruzicka and H Speechley (1993) 'Performance guaranteed bonds for commercial management of natural forests – Early experience from the Philippines', (draft) Commonwealth Forestry Review 73(2):106–112

Passeld, P (1995) 'One Answer to Overfishing: Privatize the Fisheries', *New York Times*, 11 May, pp pc2(n) pd2(L) col 1

Pearce, D W, D Whittington, and S Georgiou (1994) *Project and Policy Appraisal: Integrating Economics and Environment*, OECD, Paris

Pelekasi, K and M S Skourtos (1991) 'Air Pollution in Greece: An Overview', *Ekistics* (May–August):348–49, 135–55

Perrings, C, J A Opschoor, A Gilbert, and D Pearce (1988) *Economics for Sustainable Development – Botswana: A Case Study*, Ministry of Finance and Development Planning, Gabarone

Phantumvanit, D and T Panayotou (1990) 'Industrialization and Environmental Quantity: Paying the Price', Thailand Development Research Institute, Bangkok

Portney, P (1990) 'Economics and the Clean Air Act', *Journal of Economic Perspectives* 4(4):173–82

Rebelo, J (1996) *Essentials for Sustainable Urban Transport in Brazil's Large Metropolitan Areas, Policy Research Working Paper No 1633*, World Bank, Washington, DC

Rehbinder, E (1993) 'Environmental Regulation Through Fiscal and Economic Incentives in a Federalist System', *Ecology Law Quarterly* 20(57):57–83

Reich, M R (1992) 'Environmental Policy in India: Strategies for Better', *Policy Studies Journal* 20(4):643–62

Reid, W (1992) 'Conserving Life's Diversity: Can the Extinction Crisis Be Avoided?' *Environmental Science and Technology* 26(6) 1090–95, Renewable Natural Resources, OECD, Paris

Reid, W V, S A Laird and C A Meyer (1993) *Biodiversity Prospecting: Using Genetic Resources for Sustainable Development*, World Resources Institute, Washington, DC

Repetto, R (1986) *Skimming the Water: Rent-Seeking and the Performance of Public Irrigation Systems*, World Resources Institute, Washington, DC

Repetto, R (1996) *Has Environmental Protection Really Reduced Productivity Growth?* World Resources Institute, Washington, DC

Report of First Global Forum on Environmental Funds (1994) Santa Cruz, Bolivia 30 May–2 June, 1994, Washington, DC: IUCN, Washington, DC

Rosegrant, M W and H P Binswanger (1993) 'Markets in Tradable Water Rights: Potential for Efficiency Gains in Developing-Country Irrigation', Mimeo

Schramm, G and J J Warford (eds) (1989) *Environmental Management and Economic Development*, World Bank, Washington, DC

Sedjo, R A (1992) 'A Global Forestry Initiative', *Resources* 109:16–19

Shankar, K (1992) 'Water Market in Eastern UP', *Economic and Political Weekly* 2

Simpson, R David, R Sedjo and J Reid (1993) 'The Commercialization of Indigenous Genetic Resources: Values, Institutions, and Instruments', *Resources for the Future Discussion Paper*, Washington, DC

Sorsa, P (1994) 'Competitive and Environmental Standards', *World Bank Working Paper 1249*, International Economics Department, World Bank, Washington, DC

Southgate, D and D Pearce (1988) 'Agricultural Colonization and Environmental Degradation in Frontier Developing Economies', *Environment Department Working Paper No 9*, World Bank, Washington, DC

Squires, D (1996) 'Individual Transferable Quotas in a Multiproduct...', *Canadian Journal of Economics* 29:318–325

Srivardhana, Ruandoj (1982) *The Nam Pong Case Study: Some Lessons to be Learned*, Environment and Policy Institute, East–West Center, Honolulu

Stavins, R N (1989) 'Clean Profits: Using Economic Incentives to Protect the Environment', *Policy Review* (Spring):58–63

Stavins, R N (1993a) 'Market Forces Can Help Lower Waste Volumes', *Forum for Applied Research and Public Policy* (Spring):6–15

Stavins, R N (1993b) 'Transaction Costs and the Performance of Markets for Pollution Control', *Resources for the Future Discussion Paper QE93–16*, Washington, DC

Stavins, R N (1995) 'Transactions Costs and Tradable Permits', *Journal of Environmental Economics and Management*, 29:2

Steele, P and E Ozdemiroglu (1994) 'Examples of existing market-based instruments and the potential for their expansion in the Asian and Pacific region', in *Financing Environmentally Sound Development*, Asian Development Bank, Manila

Szulc, T (1986) 'Brazil's Amazonian Frontier: Bordering on Trouble', in A Maguire and J Welsh Brown (eds) *Resources & Politics in Latin America*, Adler and Adler, Bethesda, MD

Tahunaho, A (1997) 'Conservation and Management', *Ocean Development and International Law* 28:1–58

Tang, D T (1990) *On the Feasibility of Economic Incentives in Taiwan's Environmental Regulations: Lessons from the American Experience*, Institute of American Culture Academia, Sinica, Nankang, Taipei

Tanzi, V (1990) 'Quantitative Characteristics of the Tax Systems in Developing Countries', in R M Bird and O Oldman (eds) *Taxation in Developing Countries*, Baltimore and London, 5f, Johns Hopkins University Press, Baltimore

Terrebonne, R (1995) 'Property Rights and Entrepreneurial Income in Commercial Fisheries', *Journal of Environmental Economics and Management* 28:68(15)

Thailand Development Research Institute (TDRI) (1987) *National Resources Profile*, TDRI, Bangkok

Thomas, V (1981) 'Pollution Control in Sao Paulo, Brazil: Costs, Benefits and Effects on Industrial Location', *World Bank Staff Working Paper No 501*, World Bank, Washington, DC

Tietenberg, T H (1990a) 'Using Economic Incentives to Maintain Our Environment', *Challenge* (March/April):42–46

Tietenberg, T H (1991) 'The Role of Economic Incentives Policy', in J S Tulchin and A I Rudman (eds) *Economic Development and Environmental Protection in Latin America*, Lynne Rienner, Boulder, CO

Torman, M, J Cofala and R Bates (1993) 'Alternative Standards and Instruments for Air Pollution Control in Poland', *Resources for the Future, Discussion Paper ENR 93–16*, Washington, DC

Turner, R K (1992) *Policy Failures in Managing Wetlands*, OECD, Paris

United Nations Department for Policy Coordination and Sustainable Development (1996) 'Sustainable Development Finance: Opportunities and Obstacles', *Proceedings of the Third Expert Group Meeting on Financial Issues of Agenda 21, 6–8 February, 1996, Manila, Philippines*, United Nations Department for Policy Coordination and Sustainable Development, Division for SD, New York

Vincent, J R, R Mohamed Ali, et al (1995) *Natural Resources, Environment, and Development in Malaysia: An Economic Perspective*, HIID publication, Cambridge, MA

Vincent, J R and T Panayotou (1997) 'Consumption: Challenge to Sustainable Development', *Science* 276:53–55

Viscusi, W K, J M Vernon and J E Harrington (1995) *Economics of Regulation and Antitrust*, 2nd edn, MIT Press, Cambridge, MA

Warhurst, A (1992) 'Environmental Management in Mining and Mineral Processing in Developing Countries', *Natural Resources Forum* 16(1):39–49

Wesney, D (1989) 'Applied Fishery Management Plans: Individual Transferable Quotas and Input Controls', in P Neher, R Arnason and N Mollet (eds) *Rights-Based Fishing* Kluwer Academic, Dordrecht

Westin, R A and S E Gaines (1991) 'Environmental Taxes in the United States', in *Taxation for Environmental Protection: A Multinational Legal Study*, Quorum Books, New York

Willey, Z (1992) 'Behind Schedule and Over Budget: The Case of Markets, Water, and Environment', *Harvard Journal of Law & Public Policy* 15(2):391–425

Winpenny, J (1995) *The Economic Appraisal of Environmental Projects and Policies, A Practical Guide*, OECD, Paris

World Bank (1994a) 'Adjustment in Africa: Reforms, Results and the Road Ahead', *A World Bank Policy Research Report*, Oxford University Press, Oxford

World Bank (1996b) 'Toward Environmentally Sustainable Development in Subsaharan Africa: A World Bank Agenda', Development in Practice Series, World Bank, Washington, DC pp 111–113

World Resources Institute (1988) *The Forest for the Trees? Government Policies and Misuse of Forest Resources*, World Resources Institute, Washington, DC

World Resources Institute (1989) *Natural Endowments: Financing Resource Conservation for Development*, World Resources Institute, Washington, DC

Index

Page numbers in **bold** refer to boxes, figures and tables